Clashing Myths in German Literature

Clashing Myths in German Literature
FROM HEINE TO RILKE

by Henry Hatfield

HARVARD UNIVERSITY PRESS, CAMBRIDGE, MASSACHUSETTS, 1974

For Stachu and Dorrit

Acknowledgments

For help and encouragement of various kinds I am indebted to
W. M. Frohock, Walter Grossmann, Barbara Hatfield, Joan
King, Harry Levin, Gisela Lincoln, Ruth Oppenheim, Christa
Saas, the late Ernest J. Simmons, and Eugene Weber. Jack
Stein gallantly aided me in my work on Wagner, although he
was well aware that my view of that figure was and is radically different from his own. I must thank too the staffs of the
libraries at Harvard University, Dartmouth College, and the
Free University of Berlin; and also the editor of *Mosaic*
(Winnipeg) for permission to use, in expanded form, my essay
on Nietzsche as a chapter in this book. I am deeply grateful
to the American Council of Learned Societies for a grant that
did much to help me complete this book. Above all, I wish to
express my gratitude to Jane Hatfield, who typed the entire
first draft and made many helpful suggestions; to Maria Tatar,
to whose criticisms of large parts of the manuscript I am much
indebted; and to Theodore Ziolkowski, for his criticism of the
work as a whole. Not for the first time, he commented on a
manuscript of mine incisively, including always a stimulating
admixture of encouragement.

H. H.
Cambridge, Massachusetts
October 1973

Contents

Clashing Myths in German Literature

I Introduction

German literature of the nineteenth and early twentieth centuries is more complicated and varied than that of the eighteenth. No group gained the leading position that the Weimar writers maintained for over half a century. In the later period the myth of Greece no longer held the clear hegemony it possessed in the eighteenth century, though thanks largely to Nietzsche it remained probably the most fascinating. Even in the Age of Goethe, only Hölderlin seems to have accepted the myth completely, with an almost childlike faith. Germanic lore, especially the tales of the Nibelungen, gained greatly in prestige and popular appeal.

Since the sheer bulk of literary material in German seems to have increased greatly in the years after 1800, it has proved necessary to be highly selective in this survey. Few, presumably, will object to the inclusion of Heine, Burckhardt, Wagner, Nietzsche, George, and Rilke in a study of this sort, but some of the exclusions may seem unfortunate. Hofmannsthal, for example, may well have the stature of George and Rilke, but despite *Elektra*, he was not basically a mythical poet though often mythological; he created no Maximin, no Orpheus. Whereas Bachofen is of course highly important in the interpretation and reinterpretation of myth, he does not seem to have had as direct an impact on literature as did Burckhardt and Nietzsche. Although most of the minor treatments of the Nibelungen theme are insignificant, it might have been appropriate to discuss Hebbel's *Die Nibelungen*, with its confrontation of Northern paganism and Christianity. Yet Wagner's *Ring* was and remains an enormous success; Hebbel's drama is virtually forgotten. For all his fascination with myths, Thomas Mann's use of them, except

1

in *Death in Venice* and *Doctor Faustus*, is essentially playful.

Basically, only two traditional myths figure here: the myth of Greece and that of the Germanic past. Yet since the authors discussed were generally antichristian or at least highly critical of Christianity, that religion plays the role of the other, the opponent. (Naturally, Judaism appears in a similar light.) Above all, the figure of Jesus exerts a unique fascination, even on avowed neopagans, as it had on Hölderlin. When Heine wrote, in *On Ludwig Börne*, that the old pagan gods were dead, he was basically correct, though even today an occasional eccentric may erect an altar to Apollo. When the poet added that Jesus would soon follow them to the shades, he was, to put it mildly, premature.

It is necessary to distinguish as sharply as possible between the authentic myth, which is believed in, and mythology, which is made up of motifs and tales, and expresses a poetic or symbolic truth at best. Sometimes the boundary is very difficult to draw. Presumably, Wagner did not believe that the stories of the Nibelungen were literally true, but that in his own version they express profound truths. Is this a matter of myth, mythology, or both? A sophisticated Christian might reject numerous "facts" related in the New Testament, but believe quite viscerally that the story of Jesus is essentially and profoundly true. Nietzsche's Zarathustra is unacceptable either as myth or mythology; his Dionysus is not to be written off so easily.

For this complex situation, in which one has neither total acceptance of a myth, nor playful or academic exploitation of a mythology, the Germans normally use the term *Mythos*. Thus the "myth of the state" is not literally true in detail but it is supposed to embody the essential truth, as is the "myth of Napoleon."[1] In fact, *Mythos* is taken to express a life-giving force. Rosenberg's "Mythos of the Twentieth Century" is a case in point. Even here, there is no terminological exactness; Ernst Bertram's *Nietzsche: An Attempt at a Mythology* might better have been subtitled "An Attempt at a *Mythos*"—unless Bertram was deliberately questioning the validity of his own book. This seems most unlikely. In any case, *Mythos* is a "good" word in German; in English "myth" is pejorative or neutral, except in the usage of some literary critics, of Jungians, and a few others. Mere references to a myth—like the allusions to Hermes in *The Magic Mountain* —are of no real significance from the point of view of this book.

Often it is helpful to distinguish between public myths (or mythological tales) like the story of Achilles or Amphitryon, and private ones—often the invention of the author—like George's boy-god, Maximin. Rilke's Orpheus is public in ancestry but largely private in interpretation—as is Goethe's Iphigenia, for that matter. Since it is based on intuition and imagination, we may speak of Rilke's view of love as a myth, but cannot so characterize Freud's inductively arrived-at theories, even if they should prove wrong. If a myth gets too far from accepted reality or from the experience of a given group, it fades away and may eventually perish. Thus Arminius, a hero of generations of nationalistic Germans, has been under an opaque cloud for some time.

In the nineteenth century, myth is often drawn closer to the "real" world, in line with the growing industrialization of the Germanys, the increasing population, the rise of great cities, and not least the increasing realistic tendencies in literature after about 1850. Thus while Schiller could frankly "flee into the ideal" and Goethe lamented that he had to write his *Iphigenia* as if there were no starving workers in a nearby village, Heine, generally no champion of the proletariat, often brought sordid reality directly into his mythological poems.

Similarly, Burckhardt confronted "the glory that was Greece" with the harshest facts of Athenian life; the social conflict is dimly apparent behind the struggle between wretched dwarves and gold-hungry masters in the *Ring*. Even Nietzsche used his mythical Greek and Persian figures to express his views of contemporary problems. The approach to myths becomes a multiple one: they may be used traditionally or radically revised, they may be rejected or parodied, or essentially new myths may be created. This last avenue was often chosen by Nietzsche, George, and Rilke, and to some extent by Wagner.

In the German eighteenth century, neopagan opposition to Christianity and emphasis on the enjoyment of this world was often aesthetically based: one should live in beauty, like the Ancients. To be sure, Ludwig Feuerbach and Gottfried Keller also urged a century later: live fully on this earth, for there is no other; but since there are no rewards or punishments to come, live ethically. Injuring another person is unforgivable because irreparable. Heine and other writers influenced by the Saint-Simonian cult demanded the good life for all. Characteristically, Heine wanted not mere basic subsistence but roses and wine. He seems to be the first nineteenth century German author of importance consistently to treat the Greek gods with skepticism, though usually without hostility. It has been well pointed out that he is roughly contemporary with David Friedrich Strauss,[2] whose epoch-making *Life of Jesus* (1835) questioned the historicity of much of the New Testament and stressed the notion that Jesus was seen in the Gospels as the fulfiller of many Old Testament prophecies. As the old myths became trite, incredible, or both, the tendency for the poet to devise new ones of his own, or to seek for exotic material outside the biblical, Greek, or Germanic sphere, naturally increased. On the other hand, Nietzsche maintains a rigorously aesthetic attitude, unconcerned with the "herd"; Burckhardt's main worry is the threat of a "revolt of the masses." No amoralist, he was an archconservative. Around 1890 the swing back begins to an "art period" of the sort that seemed to have ended some sixty years before. While Goethe's devotion to art was balanced by his moral and social concerns, writers like Swinburne, d'Annunzio, Huysmans, and the early George were much more single-minded in their aestheticism. The young Rilke did not ignore poverty but glorified it as beautiful: the absolute nadir (or zenith) of *l'art pour l'art.*

Heine, the first writer treated here, was a child of the eighteenth century who was shaped by romantic influences he later largely outgrew. His work forms a bridge between the age of Goethe and the era of Nietzsche. Toward the Greek gods his attitude was one of skepticism tempered by sympathy. On the one hand they appear powerless, indeed unreal; mighty once, they are now fictions or ghosts; but as exiles, they command his compassion. Novalis was the first significant writer of the age of Goethe to question the primacy of the Greek gods; Heine the first to treat them ironically. Partially a romantic, Heine desired something warmer and more colorful than cold marble.

In other moods he allies the Greeks, divinities and men, with Saint-Simonian doctrines of enjoyment and the rehabilitation of the flesh. Out of the contrast between Greeks and Jews or Christians he forms the famous typology of Hellenes versus Nazarenes, adopted by Matthew Arnold in his opposition of Hellenism to Hebraism. Essentially it is a matter of beauty and joy versus morality and social justice. The two ideals fought it out in Heine's works for years. Toward the end of his life he came to feel that great Hebrew figures like Moses were far more impressive than any Greek hero. He admitted, rather wryly, that justice was more important than beauty. After his Saint-Simonian period was over, he never claimed that the two ideals could be combined in a synthesis.

Since the Greeks were not Jacob Burckhardt's first love, he was able to view Greek culture with considerable detachment. Athens was not the unique pinnacle of human achievement to him, as it had been to so many of his predecessors, but shared its eminence with Florence. Burckhardt's conservative bent made him skeptical of Greek democracy, even of such figures as Pericles and Socrates. Nor did he feel that there was any special affinity between Germans and Greeks. If allowance is made for the pessimism that pervades Burckhardt's writings, his image of Greece was probably the most nearly objective formed in the nineteenth century. Controlling the tools of political and social history, well versed in Greek literature as well as art, he was uniquely qualified to render such an account.

For Greek mythology he had great flair and empathy. (To him the myth of Faust was exemplary, for it provided an image that everyone finds relevant to his own nature.) Yet he steadfastly refused to make a myth of the historical Greeks, on whose government, morals, mores he cast a very cold eye. They were almost uniquely gifted but had numerous vices and faults: lying, cruelty, jealousy, for example.

Similarly, he held that the Greek gods were doomed to perish because they were morally evil; history has an element of morality, though that is not predominant. Furthermore, the truly great man—there are no supermen in Burckhardt—must have a dash of goodness. In Heine's terms, the Hellene in Burckhardt was attracted to the aesthetic, the Nazarene upheld ethical standards. Neither side dominated the other.

Like Rilke, Wagner borrowed from many myths and revised them freely. While he was attracted by Greek mythology early in his career, nothing much came from this
intellectual flirtation, though there are a few, mainly minor,
analogies between Greek tragedy and the *Ring of the Nibelungen*. Naturally enough, Wagner turned to native material:
German medieval legend and the myths centering on Siegfried.

Precisely because of his towering musical genius and mastery of theatrical effects, Wagner was able to endow his
"music dramas" with dynamic power. Nor did he hesitate
to incorporate contemporary problems into medieval or prehistoric actions. Again like Rilke (in his early "religious"
verses) Wagner was capable of exploiting a theme or a view
of life without having the slightest belief in it: *Parsifal* is the
classic example. This may be seen to be the height of artistry,
of cynicism, or of both.

"The show must go on"—and of course it did. In their
power, their theatricality, their grandiloquence, Wagner's
operas do seem to anticipate the tone of the reign of Wilhelm
II, who came to the throne in 1888, five years after the composer's death. Later they were to fascinate a truly sinister
ruler.

At first Wagner's most brilliant disciple, Nietzsche rather
soon became his sternest critic. Yet he sensed in Wagner's
music a dynamic, even intoxicating quality which helped him
to discover, or rather rediscover, the Dionysiac, which was
to become his most challenging concept. Roughly, the Dionysiac symbolizes the transcendence of individuality in
mythical unity, the excitation of sexual and other frenzy, the
acceptance of life although, or rather because, it is tragic.
These elements do seem to have been characteristic of the
authentic cult of Dionysus, as it appears in Euripides'

Bacchae. Since Attic tragedy arose from this cult, Nietzsche argued in *The Birth of Tragedy,* why should not the return of the Dionysian spirit lead to the rebirth of the drama, especially since Greek tragedy, like Wagner's, depended heavily upon music? Soon Nietzsche came to feel that Wagner's music was far from Dionysiac, but the concept persisted in his thought, and later in works as different as Hofmannsthal's *Elektra,* Thomas Mann's *Death in Venice,* Gerhart Hauptmann's *The Heretic of Soana,* and much of Carl Orff's music. Nietzsche's influence on the interpretation of Greece by German writers was enormous; scholars on the whole were skeptical. He completely reversed Winckelmann's neoclassic dogma of a Greece marked by "noble simplicity and quiet grandeur" with a romantic vision of an ecstatic, Dionysian culture. Winckelmann was fascinated by sculpture, Nietzsche by music; and while the former's knowledge of Greek art was necessarily very imperfect, the latter's grasp of Greek music was virtually nil.

In creating myths of his own, Nietzsche was less fortunate. It is hard today to use the word "superman" without irony; and as will appear below, the doctrine of the "eternal return" has been shown to be mathematically impossible. Further, the two notions largely cancel each other out; the superman is an optimistic concept, that of eternal return basically nihilistic. Even in *Thus Spoke Zarathustra* Nietzsche's dread appears; the specter haunting Europe is not communism but nihilism. Indeed, mythical figures like Zarathustra and the superman may be regarded as Apollonian figments which divert man from the flux of nothingness. Nietzsche's famous statement "God is dead," undoubtedly inspired by lines of Heine, is relevant here.

Very broadly speaking, the psychological insights of Nietzsche's works seem more valuable, more likely to endure, than his symbolic mythical figures. That these have nevertheless had a great impact may be due to the fact that his whole way of writing and thinking, his *Denkform,* was more mythical than logical, as the briefest comparison of his works with those of Kant or Spinoza will show. Nietzsche's books began to become well known in Central Europe around 1890, precisely when taste was swinging sharply from naturalism to symbolism and neoromanticism generally, and the writers of the nineties generally accepted his view that the world was to be approached as an aesthetic phenomenon. Nietzsche often protested, no doubt sincerely, against romanticism, but his most famous works, especially *Zarathustra,* are archromantic.

Whereas Stefan George owed a great deal to Nietzsche, especially in his rejection of any "other" world and his tough, aristocratic ethics, he is basically independent of that philosopher. In fact he regarded him rather as a self-isolated martyr to be pitied than as a hero to be emulated. Further, he was at heart conservative in his view of Hellas, closer to Winckelmann than to Nietzsche or Bachofen. Aware of dark, irrational forces in Greek culture, he subordinated them to the Apolline ideal: clarity, form, discipline, reason.

In his poetic career, George moved gradually from "art for art's sake" to cultural, quasi-religious, and even political involvement. For each stage he found an appropriate mythical figure, but these were nearly always based on actual historical or contemporary persons. Thus Algabal in the cycle of that name is based on the Roman boy-emperor Heliogabalus; in George's verse he embodies complete aestheticism, amorality, and a certain charisma. Algabal is associated with a black flower, a flower of evil; the now trite blue flower of German romanticism has been discarded. Similarly, Maximin is a stylized portrait of Maximilian Kronberger. Undoubtedly,

George was passionately in love with this handsome youth, but in the poems devoted to him as in George's cultural politics Kronberger served as a radiant, divine symbol who helped to hold his followers, the "George Circle," together. The much later poem "To a Young Officer [Führer] in the First World War" is a tribute to a member of the Circle but at the same time a militant statement about international politics.

In George's most characteristic poems the myths center on one dominant figure. The Circle or "League" is grouped around a star, a god in human form, a prophet or poet. This pattern beautifully expresses George's absolute demand for dominance, whether over words or people. He had no need to learn the cult of power from anyone, and in fact lived what Nietzsche only preached. The theme of masters and devoted servants occurs again and again in George's poems. Given the rigid hierarchical structure of the Circle, it is hardly accidental that women are banished to its periphery. When George declared that the ensouled body was God, he obviously had the youthful male body in mind. The poems make it overwhelmingly probable that the whole Georgean establishment was basically though by no means exclusively homosexual, though they do so in a dignified and restrained way. Presumably the Georgeans felt, not without some reason, that their sexual orientation linked them even more closely to the Greeks.

Essentially, Rilke—by his own choice—was not linked with anyone: he walked by himself. His employment of myths was completely eclectic, ranging from Buddha to Apollo to inventions of his own, like the angels of the *Duino Elegies* or the dogma of "intransitive" (unrequited) love. Of all the writers discussed in this book he was the most radical in revising or parodying traditional stories and reinterpreting famous figures. This is most evident in his treatment of biblical materials; his anti-Christianity was more bitter than even Nietzsche's. When he used myths more positively, as in the case of Orpheus or the angels in his later poetry, they served as objective correlatives of inwardness: the figures evoked became symbols of states of the soul.

In the chapters that follow, I shall try to demonstrate what these few introductory pages have merely asserted.

II Heine and the Gods

O dieser Streit wird enden nimmermehr,
Stets wird die Wahrheit hadern mit dem Schönen.

Oh, this quarrel will never end,
Always truth will wrangle with the beautiful.
—Heine

Greece was only one, though the most beautiful, of a series of myths that Heine exploited, generally without believing in them literally. He drew on Jewish and Christian lore, on Germanic tales of elemental spirits, on Moorish and Arabian sources, and on the "myth" of Napoleon, who had become a legendary figure long before he died. Inevitably Heine tended to the syncretic mingling of many myths in a single work, as in "The North Sea" or "Doctor Faust." Repeatedly he turned to parody when dealing with the gods; he describes an ancient Bacchic dance as "the cancan of antiquity"[1] and introduces the braying of an ass into his confrontation of Hellenes and barbarians in his most serious philosophical poem, "For the Mouche." Like many other writers, Heine tended to parody figures and forces toward which he felt ambivalently attracted. Yet parody was not his usual reaction to the Greek tales: he found that they formed the most lovely, poetically useful, and symbolically suggestive of all mythologies.

Heine was first attracted to Greek mythology while a student at the lyceum in Düsseldorf.[2] Apparently he learned very little of the Greek language there,[3] but he took it up again as a student in Berlin in 1821–23, impressed by the lectures of Friedrich August Wolf. Soon thereafter he read Homer

and Aristophanes (he had heard Wolf lecture on the latter)
in the original.[4] One must bear in mind that Greek was only
one among Heine's many cultural enthusiasms: he was fascinated by Spanish culture, by Shakespeare, by the Germanic
past. Not for nothing had he been the pupil of August Wilhelm Schlegel, the most catholic of the major German romantics.

In fact, his brief essay "Romanticism" (1820) shows Heine
as a faithful disciple of Schlegel: he glorifies the Middle Ages
and praises Christianity above antique religion, yet warns
that the romantic poet must use as clear and definite images
as the classicist (VII, 149–151). There is no reason to doubt
his admiration and sympathy for Christianity at this time.[5]
Heine, a true son of the Enlightenment, was not completely
convinced that Christianity would prevail; but his well-
known poem "The Pilgrimage to Kevlaar" shows how deeply
he felt the attraction—by no means merely the aesthetic attraction—of Catholicism. As, however, the day of his conversion drew near—it took place in 1825—Heine compen-
sated for his sense of guilt (he did not really "believe") by
ever sharper sarcasms directed against Christians and Christianity. No one has the right to condemn Heine for undergoing conversion without conviction, any more than to attack
Winckelmann's comparable actions.[6] If the poet wished to
become either a lawyer or a professor—and he had ambitions
along both those lines—conversion was literally the "ticket
for admission to European culture" (VII, 407). "Berlin is
worth a sermon," as he characteristically put it (VI, 57). Yet
how guilty Heine must have felt for deserting the religion of
his fathers! A letter of April 1823 runs in part: "God, Christ
& Co. . . . This firm won't last long . . . it will go bankrupt
in Europe. Every day I am more convinced that this final
crash of Christianity is clearly coming."[7] Two years later he

wrote to his admirable friend Moses Moser that he would
like to become a Japanese. "They hate nothing so much as
the cross." [8] In June of that year he had become a Lutheran;
the pastor who baptized him praised his seriousness, religious
knowledge, and conviction.[9] What makes the whole affair
bitterly ironic is that Heine gained little or no practical advantage from his conversion; in fact he thought it had injured
him. A few months after his baptism he wrote to Moses
Moser that he was "now hated by both Christian and Jew," [10]
which sounds like a classic case of "projection." Nor can one
easily imagine that the Parisians, among whom he was to
spend most of the rest of his life, cared much about Heine's
religious allegiance.

As a student in Berlin Heine heard Hegel lecture and knew
him socially. Just what Heine learned from him is hard to
discover. Heine himself stated that he found the philosopher
very difficult to understand (VI, 46). In any case, a gulf
separates a mind like Heine's, which operates best with
images and metaphors, from Hegel's formidably abstract
brain. Perhaps Heine learned from Hegel an approach, primarily: to examine the roots of the various ideologies criti-
cally.[11] No transcendental religion was valid for Hegel—nor
normally for Heine. Man was the motor of history.[12] One
thinks of Heine's skeptical attitude toward myths and gods:
they may be lovely, even helpful, but they are constructs.
(It is hardly accidental that Heine is not even mentioned in
the index of Rehm's *Griechentum und Goethezeit*, the standard account of German Hellenism as seen by German professors.) Heine eventually came to feel that Hegelianism, in
its deification of man and of the idea, was a form of atheism
(VI, 48). More, he became convinced that the "trade secret"
of German idealistic philosophy as such is aggressive atheism,
hidden behind clouds of mysticism. Heine anticipated San-

tayana's formidable if tendentious polemic *Egotism in German Philosophy* (1916) by over sixty years.

To turn to Heine's early works: his unsuccessful tragedy *Almansor* (1823) centers on the problem of conversion in the milieu of the conflict between Spaniard and Moor. The Spanish fanatics proceed from burning books to burning people; Almansor feels that Catholicism is a religion of blood in every sense (II, 259, 296, 285). He believes that the earth is a "church of love"; to his beloved, Zuleima, a convert to Christianity, it is "a great Golgatha" (II, 286f).

The drama was not Heine's strong point but the prose sketch, often mingling the serious with the comic, was one of the subgenres in which he most excelled. Early in his *Journey through the Harz Mountains* (1826, the best known of these sketches), Heine relates a dream set in the library of Göttingen and writes of the holy place there—"where the sacred statues of the Apollo Belvedere and the Venus de Medici stand side by side, and I cast myself down at the feet of the goddess of beauty; viewing here I forgot all the wild doings I had escaped from, my enraptured eyes drank in the harmony and eternal loveliness of her most blessed body, Greek calm permeated my soul, and over my head Phoebus Apollo poured out the sweetest sounds of his lyre like blessings from Heaven" (III, 23). It was still very much the mode to evoke the Olympian gods in this exalted manner. What is unusual about the passage is the subtle, indeed sly way in which Heine half-seriously uses Christian language to describe the body of Venus and the music of Apollo.

With their mingling of disparate myths and imagery, the free-verse poems of the double cycle "The North Sea" (1826–1827; I, 161–194) are parts of a literary experiment that did not quite come off. Yet as mirrors of Heine's attitude toward myth, toward the Greek myth in particular, they are enlight-

ening. Here, as he does so often later on, Heine shows the
gods as shabby and déclassé. They can neither live nor die:

> Und die armen Götter, oben am Himmel
> Wandeln sie, qualvoll,
> Trostlos unendliche Bahnen,
> Und können nicht sterben,
> Und schleppen mit sich
> Ihr strahlendes Elend.   (I, 166)

(And the poor gods, up in the sky/They trace, tormented/
Drearily endless courses,/And cannot die,/And drag with
them/Their radiant misery.) "Poseidon" contrasts the glorious past of the gods—

> Und der leuchtende Menschenfrühling,
> Und der blühende Himmel von Hellas.   (I, 168)

(And the gleaming youth of mankind,/And the blossoming
sky of Hellas)—with their grubby present:

> Amphitrite, das plumpe Fischweib,
> Und die dummen Töchter des Nereus.   (I, 169)

(Amphitrite, the ungainly fishwife,/And the stupid daughters
of Nereus). Heine has a very nonmythic way of coming out
with the blunt truth. He reminds us that Poseidon helped
Odysseus to lie successfully; Zeus was a parricide and a vo-
luptuary who enjoyed burnt offerings, and boys as well as
nymphs. (Heine seems to have been the first German poet
to write quite openly about Greek homosexuality.)[13]

One poem calls for discussion at some length. In "The
Gods of Greece"—Heine of course used Schiller's title as a
deliberate challenge to orthodox classicism—the gods appear
out of great white clouds in a brief epiphany or pseudo
epiphany. Juno is no longer the queen of heaven, Aphrodite
no longer golden but silver; she is now the Venus of death.
The "inextinguishable" laughter of the Olympians has been
extinguished—a typically Heinesque turn.

The poet condemns them to their faces: "Ich hab' euch niemals geliebt, ihr Götter!" (I, 188; I have never loved you, you gods!). Like Jacob Burckhardt after him, he finds the Greek gods morally repellent. Yet he feels compassion for those forsaken gods and prefers them to the "cowardly and shallow" modern deities who overcame them. Here the point of view of the poem comes close to Schiller's after all.[14] At the end of the poem the cloudy figures dissolve; the "eternal stars" appear. One need not take the stars here in the sense of Kant and Schiller as the symbols of eternal law. These stars represent reality: they stand for facts against cloudiness. That is all we need to know.

"The North Sea" is most effective in its bare statement of the plight of the gods—and in its wit. Thus Heine addresses the sea as "grandmother of love" and has one of the eternal gods demand tea with rum, to prevent a cold. It is most grandiose and least convincing when it evokes Christ as a hero of gigantic size, whose heart is the sun.[15] Written around the time of Heine's conversion, the poems remind us how far from converted the poet really was. Nor is a given mythology of central importance in itself. Besides the Greeks and Jesus, Heine includes allusions to the *Edda* and the Old Testament (I, 168); similarly, he mixes Latin with Greek names for the classical deities quite promiscuously. All these mythologies are set off against the very prosy reality of seacoast life. As Barker Fairley put it, the mythology in the North Sea poems disturbs rather than enriches them.[16] "The Gods of Greece," clearly focused on the contrast between a dead tradition and an unworthy present, is by far the most successful of these poems.

As the 1820s neared their end, Heine's prose writings indicated a gradual change in his attitude. In his review of Wolfgang Menzel's *Die deutsche Literatur* (1828), Heine interpreted Menzel's approach as a sign that the Goethean "art period" was over. Criticism must no longer be aesthetically based but universal and scientific; the man of culture is not to play a neutral role but to take his stand, as a good liberal, with the educated middle class. In general Heine accepts and even welcomes Menzel's tendency, but characteristically he objects to Menzel's fierce attacks on Goethe. The dominion of aestheticism had indeed come to an end (as Goethe had himself realized for some years, one may add) but that was no reason for underrating or attacking the poet. Heine's Nazarene side insisted that no one be enslaved or go hungry; his Hellenic side maintained that beauty and joy were irreplaceable values. Another shift from the orientation of the art period is Heine's new emphasis on political freedom. From the late 1820s on, it became a sort of religion to him;[17] the theme occurs frequently, and appropriately, in the section "English Fragments" of his *Travel Pictures* (1825–1831).

Other passages in *Travel Pictures* confirm one's impression that Heine was moving away from the academy (the myths learned in the lyceum, the constructions of Schlegel), and toward an acceptance of the reality of his own time. A very important criterion of the Hellenists was wholeness: a man, a poet, a poem should be an integrated whole.[18] Heine, his historical eyesight presumably sharpened by Hegel, realizes that aesthetic and even moral norms can be changed by time: "Once the world was whole, in antiquity and in the Middle Ages, despite external struggles there was still a continuously united world, and there were whole poets. Let us honor these poets and rejoice in them; but every imitation of their wholeness is a lie, a lie which every healthy eye sees through, and which then cannot escape mockery" (III, 304). There can be no more naive poets in Schiller's sense of the term—no Homers, Shakespeares, or Goethes. To be torn like Byron, to be oppressed by *Weltschmerz*, is to be modern—and to be honest.

A well-known passage in the fourth volume of *Travel Pictures* (III, 394f) takes up a theme first stated in Novalis' fifth "Hymn to Night": the confrontation of feasting Greeks with the pale figure of death, ensuing in the defeat of the pagans. In Heine the encounter is between Jesus—"a pale Jew dripping blood, with a crown of thorns on his head and a great wooden cross on his shoulder"—and the Olympian gods themselves. First we see the gods feasting, as described by Homer. Again antiquity is routed: when Jesus throws his cross on the gods' table, they turn pale and finally dissolve into clouds. (In "The North Sea," we recall, they also became literally nebulous.) Heine's vision was to evoke Max Klinger's famous painting "Christ on Olympus" some sixty years later.

After the fall of the old gods, the world "became gray and dark." One thinks of Hölderlin, but how ineffably different Heine's tone is. Mount Olympus became a hospital "where gods who had been skinned, roasted, and fixed on a spit slunk around boringly, bound up their wounds, and sang gloomy songs" (III, 395). Goethe had expressed his fear that a world dominated by an excessive humanitarianism would be "one great hospital";[19] using a still more drastic idiom, Nietzsche exclaimed that this world had been a madhouse too long.[20] As so often, Heine supplies the link between German classicism and the modern period. One notes that his gods—saints at best—seem more grotesque than tragic: skinned, roasted, and spitted like game. And they have not even escaped boredom, the malady of the age.

The German eighteenth century saw Greek religion as joyous; Heine perceives that Christianity afforded "not joy but solace"; it was a religion for delinquents. Perhaps that is

precisely what a downtrodden humanity needs, and only a
god who has suffered himself can understand the oppressed.
Again Heine appears as the precursor of Nietzsche: his insights illuminate the view of life which that philosopher was
to label, too harshly, slave morality. Heine's whole stance is
far more humane. He calls compassion the ultimate con-
secration of love, and even goes so far as to equate it "perhaps" with love itself. Since he appealed to compassion,
Christ was loved more than other gods. But Heine was still
half a Hellene, and indeed even capable of what might today
be called male chauvinism. Christ, he said, is the most beloved of gods: "especially by women" (III, 395). Heine was
anything but an antifeminist, but he manages here to impute
a certain softness and sentimentality to Christianity in the
same passage that demonstrates its continuing vitaliy and
appeal.

Broadly speaking, Heine was moving in those years toward
"beauty and the reinstatement of the senses" [21]—the "Hellenic" strain—and at the same time toward championing the
poor and the oppressed, the "Nazarene" attitude, as he was
to call it. When he heard, in early 1831, of the new Saint-
Simonian sect based in Paris, which called for a synthesis of
spirit and flesh in a "third Kingdom," he was inevitably attracted; it seems in fact to have been a decisive factor in his
removal to Paris.[22]

Essentially pantheistic, Saint-Simonianism was a "both–
and" rather than an "either–or" creed. Its tendency to em-
brace opposites corresponded to Heine's own dual nature as
well as to the antithetic/synthetic style of thinking he had
learned from Hegel. Thus Saint-Simonianism recognized the
virtues of Christianity as a cure for decadent Rome, but held
the ascetic virtues obsolete in the nineteenth century.[23] The
new faith was generous and humane in its social intentions,

but it was anything but egalitarian.[24] Neither was Heine, who often spoke of himself as a royalist and wrote of the "crude dominion" of the American rabble (VII, 44; cf. V, 37). In the Saint-Simonian system there was room for Germanic as well as Greek gods, though all deities of the past were relativized.[25] It was an optimistic creed: there was no "Fall"; as in Novalis, the Golden Age is yet to come.

While Heine was an enthusiastic admirer of the sect, he was an eclectic one.[26] Thus he wrote from Paris, where he had moved in May 1831, to Varnhagen von Ense: "As for me, I am really interested only in the religious ideas which have only to be stated to be realized sooner or later. Germany will fight most vigorously for its spiritualism [philosophical idealism]; mais l'avenir est à nous."[27] It has been observed that Heine's vision of an ideal society suggests Paris rather than Athens.[28] Precisely so; but Paris was open to him and he went there. Generally, the German Hellenists, before Schliemann, did not go to Greece; Schiller and Hölderlin never even reached Rome. Heine's ideal was less lofty than that of his predecessors, but he did what he could to realize it.

Heine's own personal version of Saint-Simonianism is expressed in the following verses as well as anywhere:

> Auf diesem Felsen bauen wir
> Die Kirche von dem dritten,
> Dem dritten, neuen Testament;
> Das Leid ist ausgelitten.
>
> Vernichtet ist das Zweierlei,
> Das uns so lang bethöret;
> Die dumme Leiberquälerei
> Hat endlich aufgehöret.   (I, 228)

(Upon this rock we build/The church of the third,/The third, new Testament;/Suffering has been suffered to the end./Destroyed is now that dualism/Which made fools of us for so

long;/The stupid tormenting of the body/Has finally ended.)
This "third gospel" is not Lessing's Third Kingdom, where
man does the good for its own sake. It is a pantheistic realm
in which the distinction between flesh and spirit has been
abolished; God is in lovers' kisses, as everywhere else. Similarly the poet proclaims in *Germany, A Winter's Tale* that all
men shall be given not only bread but "roses and myrtles,
beauty and joy"—and, Heine whimsically adds, sweet peas
(II, 432). Happiness is to be found on earth if anywhere, and
by men; neither God nor the gods is to be trusted. Thus Eden
was not an authentic paradise: "there were forbidden trees
there" (I, 302). The aesthetic element is no longer primary,
but in theory at least it has been reconciled with the social.
Heine's prose works of the thirties and forties characteristically aim at showing the interaction of two primary factors,
related to but not identical with the opposition of social to
aesthetic: in *On the History of Religion and Philosophy in
Germany* (1834) they are called sensualism and spiritualism;
in *Ludwig Börne* (1840), the Hellenic and the Nazarene.

In *Religion and Philosophy*, Heine, as he often did, offered
the public the insights of a popularizer in the best sense of
the term. What he provides is primarily an account of the
interplay of Christianity and pantheism. In the opening pages
he discusses the advantages and disadvantages conferred by
the former, admitting that during 1800 years of human
misery, the Christian religion afforded real consolation; its
symbols, especially in art and architecture, had unique power
(IV, 171). The antithesis to this thesis is equally impressive.
In the Middle Ages everything sweet and lovely was thought
diabolic (IV, 173f); above all, the Classic and Teutonic gods
were regarded as devils, especially in northern Europe. German pantheism has degenerated into pandemonism. Heine
suggests a happy synthesis of other- and this-worldliness:

now that the Middle Ages have at last ended, the time has come to establish paradise on earth. Future generations, he prophesies, "who will flourish in a religion of joy, will regard with a melancholy smile their poor ancestors, who gloomily abstained from all joys of this fair earth and have almost turned into pale, cold shades by suppressing the warm, colorful life of the senses" (IV, 170). With striking honesty Heine admits here that all dreams of heaven, on this earth or elsewhere, may be vain. Yet he pointed up the paradisiacal nature of the pantheists' goals by contrasting them with the simple material demands of "sans-culottes" and "frugal citizens": "We are founding a democracy of equally splendid, equally holy, equally blissful gods. You demand simple dress, temperate mores, and unspiced pleasures; we on the other hand demand nectar and ambrosia, crimson cloaks, costly perfumes, voluptuousness and splendor, laughing nymphs dancing, music and comedies" (IV, 223). Heine quotes Sir Toby Belch to defend this utopia against the censure of puritanical republicans—or rather he misquotes him: "Dost thou think, because thou art virtuous, there shall be no more fancy pastries and sweet [sic] champagne?" (IV, 224). Cakes and ale no longer suffice.

Roman Catholicism, with its indulgences, arranged a compromise between Christianity and sensualism, "a concordat between God and the devil" (IV, 183) that Heine finds very sensible. A still better solution would be "lovely and splendid" sensualism based on pantheism not materialism (IV, 209). In any event Christianity—like absolute monarchy—no longer represents a viable solution. Mankind must recover; the holy vampires of the Middle Ages have sucked too much of its vital blood. Not only the flesh but all matter needs to be rehabilitated; Christianity tried to destroy it but could only stain it (IV, 221). Again, we seem to hear Nietzsche talking. When Heine turns to the death of Jehovah, slain by Kant (IV, 245), the Nietzschean note is still clearer, but the poet speaks with a relaxed good humor far different from Nietzsche's shrillness. Heine described Jehovah as born in Egypt—one can see why many of Heine's worst enemies were Jews—"brought up among divine calves, crocodiles, holy onions, ibises, and cats" (IV, 245). From there he proceeded to Palestine, was later civilized by Assyrian and Babylonian influences, and finally went to Rome. With the development of a more humane theology—*contradictio in adiecto?*—Jehovah became a loving father, a friend of the world and of man. But His accommodation was made too late. "Do you hear the little bell ringing? They are carrying the sacraments to a dying God" (IV, 246).

As he moves through the history of German thought, Heine is repeatedly attracted by figures who illustrate his major antithesis of sensualist versus spiritualist. Thus in Goethe he divines a Christian strain beside or rather behind the pagan: "Goethe's paganism is wondrously modern. His robust pagan nature is manifest in his clear, sharp rendering of all external phenomena, all colors and forms; but Christianity has simultaneously endowed him with a more profound understanding; despite his reluctance and resistance Christianity has initiated him into the secrets of the world of spirits, he has tasted the blood of Christ, and thus he understood the most hidden voices of nature, like Siegfried the Nibelung, who suddenly understood the language of birds when a drop of the slain dragon's blood wet his lips. It is remarkable how Goethe's heathen nature was permeated by our most up-to-date mode of sentiment, how the antique marble throbbed with so modern a life, and how he sympathized just as strongly with the sorrows of a young Werther as with the joys of an old Greek god" (IV, 272). Goethe's pantheism is thus modern not Greek; he is "the Spinoza of poetry." The last may be wit for wit's sake, but Heine is serious in presenting Goethe as a synthesis of ancient and modern. Indeed, without his modern endowment he would lack "profound understanding" and be far less challenging as a writer. We recall Schiller's characterization of *Werther* as a sentimental subject presented naively.[29] Like Schiller, Heine refuses to subordinate the modern to the ancient. His ideal is totality in poetry, a panpoetry, corresponding to pantheism in life and thought. Miss E. M. Butler has stressed and perhaps overstressed that Heine often associated marble with Goethe's alleged coldness;[30] here there is no such association.

Diverse and undulant though Heine's mind was, it still comes as a surprise that *Religion and Philosophy* ends with a warning against the Germanic pantheism of which he had just sympathetically written. The day will come when Christianity will no longer be able to hold the Teutonic love of battle in check; the old stone gods will arise; the Gothic cathedrals will be smashed. The French, Heine's immediate audience, are warned to keep their guard up (IV, 293f). This famous passage is often read as a prophecy of Hitlerism and the Second World War. It is hardly that, but it does show an amazing awareness of the uncanny explosive power latent in the Biedermeier Germany of Heine's day.

In writing on religion and philosophy, Heine obviously appeared as an outsider, a dazzling amateur. His book *The Romantic School* (1836),[31] however, is the work of a romanticist of European rank, comparable in stature to Byron and Pushkin. To be sure, as has been charged, Heine "overcame" or "betrayed" romanticism. Who would think more of a Goethe who had not "overcome" *Werther*, a Mann who had School is tendentious, but it is honest about its own tendency: not "betrayed" *Buddenbrooks*? Obviously, *The Romantic* it is one of the most provocative books ever written about German literature. Its aim is both to praise the romantic school and to bury it.

Heine's perspective was a dual one. Until rather recently he had been primarily a romanticist himself. For some members of the school he felt personal sympathy, and there were many whose talents he respected. At the same time he was convinced that romanticism, at least to the extent that it is based on Christianity and the Middle Ages, was mistaken, indeed death-oriented. German romanticism, Heine wrote, "was nothing but the revival of the poetry of the Middle Ages, as it had made itself manifest in songs, works of painting and sculpture, in art and life. This poetry however had grown out of Christianity, it was a passion flower, sprung from the blood of Christ . . . It is that strange, discolored flower, in whose calyx can be seen the instruments of torture that were used at the Crucifixion . . . a flower by no means ugly but only uncanny, the sight of which, indeed, stirs up a cruel pleasure in our soul, like the morbidly sweet sensations that arise from pain itself. In this regard the flower would appear to be the most fitting symbol for Christianity itself, whose most gruesome attraction consists precisely in the ecstasy of pain" (V, 217).

Like a good Hegelian, Heine assures us that Catholicism (which is expressly equated with Christianity in this book), was valuable in its own time, as a healthy reaction against the materialism of the Roman Empire. That time, however, is past (V, 218f). And such "Jewish spiritualism," as Heine calls Christianity, proved to be a poison for the Romans though healthy for Northern barbarians. In the passage just quoted, he has allied romanticism not only with the past but with a sado-masochistic glorying in pain. (One recalls the linkage between Christianity and blood in Heine's *Almansor*.)

In his essay "Winckelmann" Goethe had similarly linked Catholicism, decay, divorce, and apostasy, also with the intention of annoying the romanticists.[32]

Having rejected Catholicism, Heine defined Protestantism in such a way as to make it acceptable to Saint-Simonians and neopagans generally. In *Religion and Philosophy* he had pointed out that Luther was a spiritualist who upset the sensible Catholic "concordat" between body and soul. Now, taking Protestantism in the widest possible sense, Heine enrolls Leo X, Michelangelo, Ariosto, and others among the protesters: "The blossoming flesh in Titian's paintings, all that is Protestantism. The loins of his Venus are far more solid theses than those the German monk pasted on the Church door at Wittenberg" (V, 227). The argument is more amusing than convincing, and in any case was hardly intended to be deathly serious. The flesh was to be vindicated: that was the central point for Heine in the thirties. For the upholder of the real, the tangible, the up-to-date, neither romanticism nor the "marble" classicism of Goethe could suffice. Yet, as Heine wrote in the foreword of the first edition of the work, he was not a materialist: "rather I give bodies back their spirit, I fill them with spirit, I sanctify them" (V, 528).

Heine's *On Ludwig Börne* (1840), a polemic arising from a protracted hostility between two writers of different temperament, far transcends in interest the gloomy occasion of its writing. With some oversimplification, one may view this conflict as a clash between the doctrinaire Börne, consistent but narrow, and the aesthete Heine, unstable but dazzling. In the most interesting parts of the book, Heine himself moves away from personalities to a typology. (He could be very nasty but he was not petty; he called Börne "a good writer and a great patriot"; VII, 107). He rightly sensed that Börne's failure to appreciate Goethe was significant: "he was like the child who, having no glimmer of the glowing meaning of a Greek statue, simply feels its marble contours and complains about coldness" (VII, 18).[33] (The passage shows, incidentally, that when Heine compared Goethe's works to Greek statues, he was not necessarily complaining.)

From the specific Heine rapidly proceeds to the typical: the ascetic, overmoral Nazarene is contrasted to the life-accepting Hellene. Again we think of Nietzsche and again recall that Heine had the better style. Börne is to Goethe as Nazarene is to Greek, Heine argues: "the little Nazarene hated the great Greek, who, on top of everything else, was a Greek god" (VII, 23). "Nazarene" may seem virtually synonymous with "Jew," but it is not a matter of race or nation: "In this connection I should like to remark: all men are either Jews or Hellenes, men with ascetic drives yearning for spiritualization and hostile to representation in art, or men of a nature that serenely accepts life, prides itself in development, and is realistic. So there were Hellenes in the families of German pastors and Jews who were born in Athens and are perhaps descended from Theseus" (VII, 24). In his classic essay "On Naive and Sentimentive Poetry" Schiller had divided mankind into realists and idealists. Matthew Arnold, borrowing directly from Heine, used the polar terms Hebraism and Hellenism.

Writing in his most pantheistic decade, Heine might be expected to come down on the side of the Hellenes, all the more since he has so clearly labeled Börne a Nazarene. He does in fact state that all Nazarenes are incapable of true joy (*Freude*) though they may experience flashes of gaiety or wit, and he declares himself "a secret Hellene" and argues, in the mood of *The Romantic School,* that the one-sided striving for spiritualization has made the world sick (VII, 24f, 46, 47). Yet Heine, at his most characteristic, is unpredictable. He devotes several eloquent pages to the Bible, just as Goethe, the "Great Pagan Number One," as Heine called him, had done in *Poetry and Truth*. Heine's contrast between the Jews, who are characterized in Hegel's phrase as "the people of the spirit," and the other nations of the eastern Mediterranean (VII, 47) is by no means hostile to Jewish culture, though it ends in the warning just cited against excessive spiritualization. (Only Shakespeare achieved a true synthesis of spiritualism and art, he believed; VII, 47.) The most amazing of all is Heine's tribute to Christ: "What a sweet figure this God-man! In comparison to him, how limited the hero of the Old Testament! Moses loves his people with a touching inwardness; he worries like a mother about the future of this people. Christ loves humanity, that flaming sun moved around the whole earth with the warming rays of his love. What a soothing balm for all the wounds of this world his words are! What a fount of salvation for all sufferers was the blood that flowed on Golgatha! . . . The white marble Greek gods were spattered by this blood and grew sick from inner horror and could never again recover" (VII, 47). Heine has repeated and varied the motif of Christ overcoming the Olympians that he had already used in *Travel Sketches*. Normally he writes of Christ with affection and respect. The former, at least, appears in his apostrophe of Jesus as his "poor cousin":

> Mit Wehmut erfüllt mich jedesmal
> Dein Anblick, mein armer Vetter,
> Der du die Welt erlösen gewollt,
> Du Narr, du Menschheitsretter!   (II, 457)

(Every time it makes me sad/To see you, my poor cousin,/ You who wished to redeem the world,/You fool, you mankind-saver!)

It is striking that while the Hellenic gods generally appear in Heine as old, exiled, sick, the Hellene as a type is marked by energy, health, and beauty. One might say that Heine has secularized the Olympian ideal. He notes that only poets keep the gods alive, as an *ecclesia pressa* (VII, 55). Throughout this part of *Börne* he uses the ominous words "Great Pan is dead" as a leitmotif. The old gods, presumably Germanic as well as Greek, are banished to their "cloud home" under the earth, but He who sent them "into the realm of eternal night" will soon join them here (VII, 59).[34] Obviously, Christ is meant.

Heine seems to lament neither the incarceration of the pagan gods nor the imminent fall of Christ as such; rather it is the coming departure of poetry and beauty from a utilitarian world. Poets, he believes, will depart with the kings. Another of his symbolic evocations of Greece, this time presented as a dream, closes the book. He encounters pretty, naked nymphs, but they are cold, thin, with an expression of bitterness. Heine speaks to the most interesting but most emaciated of them; her bosom is "touchingly cold, Greek in its meagerness" (VII, 145f). At the very end the shouts of a mob and the "giggling" of the bell at mass are heard. The nymphs turn into clouds—the same symbol of unreality that is central in Heine's "The Gods of Greece."

In 1848 Heine was struck down by syphilitic paralysis; the disease had harassed him for some time but only now overcame him physically. He never capitulated psychologically, but the days of triumphant paganism and pantheism were over. Repentant now for the days of "tending swine with the Hegelians," he wrote in the "Afterword to *Romanzero*," 1851, that he had destroyed those of his new poems that were even halfway blasphemous (VII, 485). He now believed in "the old superstition, a personal God," but not in the dogmas of any church (VII, 487). In fact he did not forswear

even the pagan gods completely but took an affectionate fare-
well from these "lovely idols": "It was hard to drag myself
to the Louvre, and I almost collapsed when I entered the
lofty hall where the blessed goddess of beauty, Our Lady of
Milo, stands on her pedestal . . . And the goddess looked
down at me with pity, and yet so disconsolately, as if she
were trying to say: can't you see that I have no arms and so
can't help?" (VII, 487).[35] The ancient gods, it would appear,
could help only those who needed no help. At any rate, Heine
soon renounced the role of "great pagan Number 2."[36]

Yet in "The Goddess Diana," written two years before
Heine's last illness struck him down but not published until
1854, the Greek gods do help, decisively. This scenario for a
ballet shows the conflict between Christianity and paganism
and the absolute triumph of the latter. Heine used a variant
of the *Tannhäuser* story, in which not Venus but Diana is
the central figure. The latter, having been Saint-Simonized
as it were, is no longer the representative of chastity but appears as a second goddess of love. In *Atta Troll* Diana also
appears as a woman whose sexuality awakened late but vio-
lently:

> Spät zwar, aber desto stärker
> Ist erwacht in ihr die Wollust.   (II, 395)

Similarly, the "Diana" of the three poems grouped under this
title (I, 235f) is a prostitute of enormous stature. To return
to the ballet: a medieval knight, madly in love with Diana,
forsakes his wife to follow the goddess into the Venusberg,
where the pagan gods are leading an underground existence.
He is warned and then slain by Faithful Eckart, a figure often
representing conscience and common sense in German leg-
ends. In the final tableaus (in the Venusberg) Apollo and
then Bacchus manage between them to resuscitate the
knight. The role of Bacchus—"the god of the joy of life"—

is central; Venus can do nothing. At the end the entire company dances "the festival of resurrection."

The ballet clearly shows the direct conflict between spiritualism (medieval Christianity) and sensualism (Greek paganism). Only Heine, perhaps, could have assigned a philosophical clash to the dance without seeming absurd. Far from being abstract, the action is "simple, sensuous, and passionate." Instead of allegorical persons Heine has introduced a series of figures, real or imaginary, into his final tableau in the Venusberg. They range from Helen of Troy to Goethe; all have "a sensualistic reputation" (VI, 109).

Since Bacchus and his train appear in every tableau, usually playing a central role, it is tempting to see in him, as E. M. Butler does,[37] the Dionysus who was to appear to Nietzsche a quarter of a century later. Indeed Heine's Bacchus—he is *not* called Dionysus—is vastly more vital, more exuberant, more sexual than the god of wine invoked in eighteenth century German poetry. He has however nothing to do with the tragic acceptance of life; one cannot imagine him saying, with Nietzsche: "I believe in eternal life." It is of course suggestive that the knight—*not* Bacchus—undergoes resurrection at the end of the ballet. Yet what we have there is not the celebration of a risen god but the secularizing or sensualizing of the resurrection, a perfectly logical procedure for a Saint-Simonian or former Saint-Simonian.

Heine's other ballet, "Doctor Faust," written in 1847, also involves the weltanschauung, even the philosophy, of his own time—not only the general "battle between religion and science, between authority and reason, between belief and thought," but the specifically Saint-Simonian "revolt of the realistic, sensualistic joy of life against old-Catholic, spiritualistic asceticism" (VI, 506). Yet though Heine feels that this is the central thrust of the story, he remains true to the pessimistic ending of the *Faust Book*, criticizing Goethe quite harshly for saving Faust from hell.

Since Marlowe, the idea of Greek beauty had become an integral part of the Faust story. Heine set one act of his ballet in the Greek archipelago. Emerald sea, turquoise sky, a temple of Aphrodite: nothing is lacking. The scene is as "classic" as Goethe at his most Winckelmannian: "Here everything breathes Greek serenity, ambrosial, divine peace, classic calm. Nothing is reminiscent of a cloudy Beyond, of mystic shivers of voluptuousness and anxiety, of the supernatural ecstasy of a spirit that has emancipated itself from the physical: here everything is real, solid happiness without retrospective melancholy, without empty, yearning foreboding" (VI, 490). Neither the entrance of Faust and Mephistophela—Heine has feminized Faust's familiar spirit—nor the Bacchic dance she initiates destroys the mood. Then suddenly the Duchess, a witch known to the spectator or reader as the chief spouse of Satan himself, bursts upon the scene. She reduces everything to ruins; Helen and her train now appear as corpses and ghosts. From the point of view of the legend, we infer, the isles of Greece are less real and hence less potent than grotesque medieval sorcery.[38] The outcome is a direct reversal of the ending of "The Goddess Diana."

In "The Gods in Exile" (1853) Heine returns to an old theme: the gods as déclassé. In fact they are seen as émigrés, forced by the (Christian) revolution to leave home, their sacred woods confiscated. They must take up some humble trade. Apollo served for a while as a shepherd; on being unmasked, he was put to death; "but they found the grave empty" (VI, 79), as Heine puts it with a flash of parody.

A major part of Heine's sketch is concernd with an annual Bacchanal attended by hundreds of gods and lesser figures, in Tyrol. In a minor way, it recalls Goethe's "Classical *Wal-*

purgisnacht." These "phantoms" are white and cold as marble, but three of them—Bacchus, Silenus, and Priapus—have disguised themselves as monks, the better to survive life in exile. That precisely these gods—representing respectively wine, drunkenness, and phallus-worship—are installed in a monastery is a typically Heinean touch.

Heine's account of the Bacchanal, written with even more than his usual verve, moves on two different planes of time. On the one hand, it seems to be an authentic Greek orgy: for once he uses the name Dionysus; and Corybants join the train, wounding themselves, "seeking ecstasy in pain itself" (VI, 83). Yet he does not neglect to point out that he is still very much a Parisian. Bacchus is "the savior of sensual pleasure," the dance is "the cancan of antiquity, quite without hypocritical veils, quite without the intervention of the *Sergeants-de-Ville* [policemen] of a spiritualistc morality" (VI, 83). The orgy that literally takes place in the Tyrol symbolically occurs in Greece and Paris; three cultures, each radically different from the others, play their parts in this brief episode.

Heine once planned to devote a whole book to the theme of exiled and humiliated gods (VI, 98); in a sense he was one himself. The sketch for the book as we have it does not seem to be carefully articulated. In the grotesque story of the whales who rub their bodies against a wall of ice to decrease the itching caused by rats feeding on their fat, no symbolic meaning is immediately obvious, but there is a connection between the tortured monsters and the notion that the old gods are indeed in decay. "Hidden rats are gnawing away at everything great on this earth, and the gods themselves must perish ignominiously in the end" (VI, 98). There seems to be a connection—not an identity—between these rats and "The Migrant Rats" in the poem of that name. The latter are the communistic proletariat:

> Sie tragen die Köpfe geschoren egal,
> Ganz radikal, ganz rattenkahl.   (II, 203)

(They wear their hair shorn equally,/All radically, all rattily.)
These redoubtable animals are atheistic, have their "women"
in common, and are out to divide up the world on new lines.
Heine has great respect for them—and great fear of them.

The last episode of the work concerns an enormously old
man who lives on Rabbit Island not far from the North Pole.
Accompanied only by an eagle and a goat, he ekes out a miserable living by selling rabbit skins. Yet he has a "tall, stately
figure," his features are "noble and severely carved," and he
has a mysterious dignity (VI, 85). An exile from Greece, he
hears from a countryman, a sailor, that the temple of Zeus
has been pressed into use as a pigsty. He is Zeus himself, we
discover, with his eagle, and with the goat that nourished him
when he was an infant, and is now doing so again in his
second childhood. At the same time he suggests one of those
miserably poor exiles, Polish, German, Austrian, or Italian,
whom Heine must have often encountered in Paris.

In "Diana" the Hellenic element, utterly real, triumphs; in
"Faust" it is unreal, hence easily defeated; in "Gods in Exile"
it is shabby but existent. It would be philistine indeed to try
to force a definite weltanschauung on Heine; consistency
meant little to him, and he was not out to construct a system.
It is nevertheless significant that Hellenism loses out in two
of these three encounters.

In the early fifties Heine distances himself further from
pantheism and any sort of paganism, but he remains Heine:
even at his most serious he does not become pious. In the
same Afterword to *Romanzero* in which he said a sad fare-
well to Our Lady of Milo, he has his fun with the doctrine

of immortality. Life after death may reverse the course of earthly life. Thus chaste Susannah's pride of virtue led to her downfall in heaven, whereas Lot's daughters became extremely virtuous there; however, "the old man, alas, stuck with his wine bottle" (I, 488f). This is hardly a tone of a man crushed by a sense of sin. Yet both the "return to God"[39] and the mockery of dogma are authentic. The preface (1852) to the second edition of *Religion and Philosophy in Germany* is somewhat more serious but not without its quips and wanton wiles. Heine did not withdraw from publication what he had written about "the great God-question," but here he declares it false. God lives, he states; deism (by which he seems to mean theism) is very much alive, for Hegelian dialectics cannot kill a cat, let alone a god (IV, 156). Keeping his hand in, he describes the sophistical snake in Eden as a blue-stocking without feet (IV, 158).

Heine's brief *Confessions* (1854) move in the same general direction. Here he comes out firmly for the Nazarenes, especially the Jews, and against the Greeks. Now "like Uncle Tom," he cites the Bible, not Homer (VI, 56). While he does not reject the artist as a type, the Hellene, he now finds Moses, who shaped nations, a far greater artist than the Greeks. Admitting that he had formerly been predominantly a Hellene, he now judges the world very differently: "Now I see, the Greeks were only handsome youths, the Jews however were always men, mighty, indomitable men, not only in the old days but down to the present, despite eighteen centuries of persecution and misery" (VI, 55). "Goodness is better than beauty" (VI, 60)—a death sentence to any cult of aestheticism. He sees Judea as a bit of the Occident that got lost in the Orient—like Israel today—and stresses the severe, chaste character of the Jews in contrast to the neighboring peoples who indulged in the most luxuriantly sensual of na-

ture cults and "frittered away their lives in wild, bacchanalian, sensual exultation" (VI, 60f). Shades of the Great Pagan
Number 2, of Saint-Simonian revels in Paris! Now Heine
confesses that he had, like Goethe, overrated the Greeks: "at
bottom they were heartless." [40] Actually, he had often pointed
this out about the gods; now he extends it to an entire culture.

Obviously, illness and worry have greatly changed Heine,
but the tone in which he writes about "bacchanalian, senusal
exultation" makes it extremely unlikely that he really anticipated Nietzsche's concept of Dionysus. One may even doubt
that he would have thought the Dionysiac ideal particularly
intelligent, if he *had* encountered it. A cultural critic who
described the Protestant sectarians of Northern Europe and
North America as Jews who eat pork (VI, 60), Heine was not
the man to swallow any god whole—with the understandable
and partial exception of Jehovah. (As the Boston joke puts
it: "We Unitarians believe in one God—at most.") Heine's
statement that the Jews and the Teutons are "the two people
of morality" (VI, 62) reads strangely today; the ending of
The History of Religion and Philosophy in Germany seems
far more relevant (see above, p. 25).

Several of the late poems are pertinent to our theme; I
shall comment on only a few of them. "The Apollo-God" has
the tripartite form often used by Heine, but it does not move
from thesis to antithesis to synthesis; rather, there are three
disparate points of view.

In the first part we see, from a cloister high above the
Rhine, a ship bedecked with laurel and flowers. In it a handsome youth, dressed in antique style, plays the lyre and sings;
nine women "marble-fair" lie at his feet; a poor nun, who
has been observing the ship and its crew, falls hopelessly in
love with the youth, who, she thinks, is Apollo.

In the second section "Apollo" sings of his love for

"Grācia" and his longing to return there. But Greece and
Paris have merged into one:

> Mein Tempel hat in Grācia
> Auf Mont-Parnass gestanden.   (I, 349)

(My temple in Graecia/Stood on Mont-Parnasse.) At this
point, as Professor Prawer puts it, we seem to see "the face of
the exiled Heine . . . peep through his *personae*." [41] There is
something tawdry about "Apollo's" language with its "la-la,
la-la!" and the use of the corruption "Artemisia" for Artemis.
He speaks of "Gloria"—rhymed with "Ambrosia" (I, 350)—
but it is hard to believe that he was ever either divine or
Greek. His music, we infer, is closer to Offenbach than to
Gluck. (In "Hebrew Melodies" the "real" Apollo is referred
to as "the divine Schlemihl"; I, 460.)

In the third part the poor nun, who has been asking everyone where Apollo is, encounters an old peddler, who tells her
the truth, or better, his aspect of it. "Apollo" is an ex-cantor,
Faibisch, who lost his position because of freethinking, gam-
bling, and playacting. His "muses" are nine wenches from
the Amsterdam theater; one of them, fat, is known as the
"green sow." "Sow" is the last word of the poem.

We have then three views: those of the sentimental nun,
the dubious but not despicable pseudo-god, and the realistic,
all too realistic peddler. We have another variation on the
theme of gods in exile, as well as a wry comment on appearance and reality. I cannot agree with Prawer that the poem
presents "undeniable beauty" [42] but find poignancy in the
fate of the nun and of "Apollo," and above all great skill in
the presentation of the various aspects of the latter. Is Faibisch a corruption of Phoebus, or did the poor cantor adopt
the god's name in desperation?

Heine's long verse fragment "Bimini" reminds us that Hellenic goals can be sought in the New World, and that the
name of a real island can serve to denote a utopia. Bimini

stands not only for the pathetic and perhaps rather vulgar
search for physical rejuvenation, but equally for the aim of
the poet's search, like the country of Atlantis in Hoffmann's
The Golden Pot. At the end it takes on a darker meaning.

As a narrative the poem is a partial account of the aging
Ponce de Leon's search for the fountain of youth. This ac-
count is given with great charm, but as we would expect,
Heine is after bigger game. Sketching the background of
Ponce de Leon's time, Heine notes that God has written two
books for man: the "book of beauty" from Byzantium—as in
Yeats, a cipher for art—and the "book of truth" from Egypt.
Greece and Judea are not mentioned, but it is clearly the old
Hellenic-Nazarene polarity.

"Bimini" is partly a serious, partly a playful work. The
numerous "i" sounds, commonly used as diminutives, warn
us not to break a butterfly upon a wheel, as do other childlike
touches:

> Kleiner Vogel Kolibri,
> Kleines Fischchen Brididi
> Fliegt und schwimmt voraus, und zeiget
> Uns den Weg nach Bimini!   (II, 145)

(Little bird Colibri [hummingbird],/Little fishlet Brididi,/Fly
and swim ahead, and show/Us the way to Bimini!) Yet the
basic statement of the poem is a serious one. For Ponce and
the poet—the two are often identified—there are two ways
to Bimini. One is through poetry itself: the magic ship is
made up of trochees, metaphors, and hyperbole, and steered
by imagination (II, 130). The other and ultimate way to
escape sickness and old age is death,

> —denn dieses Land
> Ist das wahre Bimini.   (II, 146)

(for this land/Is the true Bimini). Similarly, the much
grimmer poem "Morphine" views death as the only satisfactory resolution of man's troubles.

Heine's last poem, "For the Mouche,"[43] returns to the old dichotomy of Hebrew versus Greek, presented in the form of a dream in which personal and cultural experiences are combined. In the moonlit landscape of the dream, Renaissance and classical ruins appear, with sculptures of Greek figures contrasted with biblical ones. The former are "lüderlich" (dissolute), the latter stupid. (In speaking of the Judeo-Christian scene, Heine rhymes "orthodox" with "ox," suggesting that his return to God was not an unconditional surrender.)

A dead man in a marble sarcophagus suddenly seems to be the poet himself; a passion flower by his grave appears to him as his last love, whom he called "la Mouche." Their communion, in the dream, goes far beyond words: "Das Schweigen ist der Liebe keusche Blüte" (II, 48; Silence is the chaste blossom of love). Suddenly a noisy quarrel between Hellenes and Nazarenes (here called barbarians) destroys the lovers' wordless happiness. The poet has no hope that it will cease:

> O, dieser Streit wird enden nimmermehr,
> Stets wird die Wahrheit hadern mit dem Schönen,
> Stets wird geschieden sein der Menschheit Heer
> In zwei Partein: Barbaren und Hellenen.   (II, 49)

(Oh, this quarrel will never end,/Always truth will squabble with beauty,/Always the host of mankind will be divided/Into two parties—barbarians and Greeks.) Balaam's ass brays for the barbarians, most noisily of all; the poet awakes.

We recall that Heine, in writing of German medieval poetry, used the passion flower as a symbol of Christianity itself, of the ecstasy of pain.[44] Thus the necessarily unfulfilled love of the sick poet appears sick itself, as Nazarene. Further, whereas Goethe had used the symbol of a cross entwined with roses to express the reconciliation of the classical and the Christian, Heine rejects the notion of any synthesis of the two great factions; in fact he finds the whole controversy boring (II,

49). In the last lines of his last poem, Moses, truth, barbarians, saints, and Balaam's ass are ranged against Pan,
beauty, Hellenes, and gods. Somewhat surprisingly, the Hellenes have the best of it.

Yet "this quarrel will never end," and Heine has dropped
a strong hint that the debate has sunk to the point of literal
asininity. Pagan or Nazarene, beauty or truth—who can decide? In *The Magic Mountain* Hans Castorp comes to feel
that such pairs of antitheses do not present men with true
alternatives.[45] Heine vacillated, as indeed the Great Pagan
Number 1 had done before him.[46] Thus in his will of June
10, 1848—an intimate document, certainly—he stated that
he been baptized a Lutheran, "but my thought has never sympathized with the beliefs of any religion." Having lived as
a good pagan, he wishes a nonreligious funeral (VII, 515).
In his legally valid will, however (November 13, 1851), he
declared that he would die "in the belief in a single God, the
eternal creator of the world, whose mercy I implore for my
eternal soul" (VII, 520). He regrets having written irrever-
ently, on occasion, about sacred matters, but puts most of the
blame on the *Zeitgeist*.

One of the last important documents Heine wrote is his
preface (1855) to the French translation of *Lutezia*, a work
based on journalistic reports written in the early forties. In
this preface he gives a reasoned, balanced account of his relation to communism. (For Heine, communism was the Nazarenism of the future—and that future might not be far off.)
First he gives the case against communism, employing his
favorite motif of the marble statue with great effect: "it is
with horror and fright that I think of the era when those
gloomy iconoclasts will come to power; with their calloused
hands they will mercilessly break all the marble statues of
beauty, so dear to my heart . . . they will cut down my laurel

groves and plant potatoes instead; the lilies which toiled not, neither did they spin, and which nevertheless were clothed as magnificently as Solomon in all his glory, they will be torn up from the soil of society . . . the roses, those idle fiancées of the nightingales, will meet the same fate; the nightingales, those useless singers, will be put to flight; and alas! my *Book of Songs [Buch der Lieder]* will serve the grocer for making little bags in which he will put coffee or snuff for the old women of the future" (VI, 572). Even if one rejects Heine the poet—which would be a mistake—Heine the wit remains, to say nothing of Heine the prophet. No one who has seen Prague or East Berlin since the war is likely to underrate the passage just quoted.

Nevertheless, Heine concedes, he cannot resist communism, hostile though it is to his interests and his tastes. Logic, which in this case coincides with justice, holds that food for all is more important than poetry. Moreover, communism is the only force that can crush contemporary German chauvinism, as a giant would crush a toad. Thus he feels "almost" enamored of the communists (VI, 572f). Again, Heine has sensed the emergence of forces that would not show their full significance until the twentieth century. A third force, politics, has entered the tug-of-war between Hellene and Nazarene and has inevitably allied itself with the latter. A very grim and godless sort of Nazarenism—communism—seemed likely to determine the future. To be sure, Heine's prophecies were fulfilled only in a very loose sense. Ludwig Marcuse noted in 1955: "For what rules—is not communism; what he [Heine] was horrified to see coming—did not come; what did come—he did not suspect." [47] This pours out the prophet with the bathwater. In any event, however we evaluate Heine's diagnosis, we can hardly deny that, broadly speaking, he had an amazingly keen sense of things to come.

III The Burgher and the Greeks: Burckhardt

But of all the peoples of high culture
the Greeks are the one which inflicted
the bitterest, most grievous sorrow
upon itself.
—Jacob Burckhardt

Jacob Burckhardt (1818–1897) was born in the Age of Goethe, and though he lived almost to the twentieth century, he remained at heart a man of that age. That was his strength and his weakness. He was born early enough to be a student of Jacob Grimm's at Berlin; he knew Bettina von Arnim, the sister of one famous romanticist and the wife of another. Industrialism, nationalism, and democracy all pained and frightened him.[1] Proud of being a burgher, he used the word plebeian as a term of extreme reproach.[2] On the death of Leopold von Ranke—another former teacher—Burckhardt was offered Ranke's chair in Berlin; at that time, it was probably the most prestigious position in history in the world. Burckhardt refused: partly no doubt because he was a good Swiss, partly because he did not like the direction of events in Prussia, but not least because of his devotion to the calm, cultured atmosphere—*ruhige Bildung* in Goethe's phrase—of Basel, where he had been born and where he taught. In his most memorable works, whether devoted to Italy or Greece, Florence or Athens, his focus tends to rest on the town of small or moderate size as the basic cultural unit. Only here, he apparently believed, did the proper ratio between the indi-

43

vidual and the group provide the right milieu. His tastes remained conservative, some might say old-fashioned: like the Weimar classicists he believed in the good, the true, and the beautiful; he rejected the "mockers" Voltaire and Heine and the grandiloquent Wagner. While admitting the importance of Dionysian forces in antiquity, he was not prepared to follow Nietzsche's god. Here he appears eminently sensible: like Heine, he was no myth-worshiper. Often he is indeed an archconservative, though hardly a reactionary.[3] While still a young man, he wrote to his sister Louise: "I had the courage to be conservative."[4] Yet in his own fields—art history and the history of culture—he was a pioneer and a guide. What interests us today is the quality of his mind, not his political opinions.

In his love of Italy, he was equally the heir of German classicism and romanticism: both Graeco-Roman and Christian monuments appealed to him, above all those of the Renaissance—to use a term whose present meaning was largely shaped by him. Rome and Paestum moved him greatly; Florence still more. (He rejected the term "Northern Renaissance" and was ambivalent about the Baroque.[5]) By the time he was twenty-one he had made three trips to Italy, once quoting Goethe's "Know'st thou the land" on the Gotthard Pass to persuade his friends to continue the journey southward.[6] This is the delightful enthusiasm of youth, but it did not evaporate. Years later, in a poem, he apostrophized the "ardently loved South" to receive him, stranger though he was.[7] Still later he prefaced his *Cicerone* (1855) with the line: "Haec est Italia diis sacra"—This is Italy, sacred to the gods. There can be little doubt that he knew more about Italy and Italian art than any other German scholar, poet, or artist of the eighteenth and nineteenth centuries. At times he almost made a myth of Italy, and of Florence in particular.

After his first visit he wrote of "eternal homesickness."[8] But his "burgherly" common sense and his increasing devotion to Basel kept him in the realm of the rational. His attitude may remind us of Mann's Tonio Kröger: he remained emotionally attached, in spite of all the magnetism of the romantic, to the solid virtues of his native place. For all its élan and fire, *The Culture of the Renaissance in Italy* does not let us forget that "renaissance men" were very fallible human beings; Burckhardt's account of Greek culture is more critical still. Obviously, the former work is more a labor of love.

In the apolitical tradition of Weimar, Burckhardt disliked the state and any active involvement in politics. He even shared Goethe's aversion to journalism, though ironically enough he had to edit a conservative Basel journal for eighteen months. Rather timid and withdrawn, he loathed the thought that the masses would come to power[9]—though it is hard to think of Swiss "masses" as terrifying. The old burgher families should rule so that barbarism would be averted. Toward the end of his life he foresaw a struggle between the mob and the *terribles simplificateurs* who would reestablish order and discipline by the strictest military means.[10] As between anarchy and tyranny Burckhardt—very reluctantly—opted for tyranny. Again, his position recalls Goethe's. While he enormously valued the Germany of 1800, he disliked Bismarck's state. His early letters reveal great enthusiasm for "the future of the splendid German fatherland" but by calling himself conservative he rejected the mixture of nationalism and democracy that made up German liberalism in the 1840s.[11] Like Nietzsche he held that culture was declining in Germany as the nation's power rose. He lamented the "dreadful completeness"[12] of Prussia's revenge on France and, four years later, complained of Bismarck's ruthless control of the press: "That's the way power acts in the nineteenth century." [13] Being theoretically in favor of keeping the "masses" down, Burckhardt might well have been delighted with Bismarck; but he was too humane, too tenderminded (some would say) for that. An able East German monograph argues that Burckhardt was a pre-Fascist.[14] The evidence it presents is carefully, all too carefully selected. Crusty, conservative old gentlemen have a way of rejecting demagogues of all stripes; Burckhardt rejected Bismarck, who was far more than a demagogue—though he was that too.

Like the great German interpreters of paganism from Winckelmann on, Burckhardt reacted to the magnetism of Greek beauty. He was a profoundly aesthetic man, not an aesthete in the pejorative sense, and was sensitive to music and even more so to literature.[15] A student of theology for two years, he nevertheless broke with Christianity quite early,[16] retaining however a genuine religiosity throughout his life. To be sure, as a young man he composed music for Goethe's ardently anti-Christian ballad "The Bride of Corinth"[17] and wrote, in 1849, a poem celebrating love and Dionysus:

> O, wann führst du wieder
> Deinen Zug vom Meer,
> Schöner Gott der Freude[18]

(Oh, when wilt thou again lead/Thy procession from the sea, /Lovely God of joy)—but the celebration is mild, not to say "burgherly." His Dionysus is still farther than is Heine's from Nietzsche's deity. There is a certain anti-Christian note in his *Constantine* (1855), yet it is never shrill or fanatic. As one would expect, his relatively extreme, highly enthusiastic utterances are the product of youth; in the *History of Greek Culture* he remains "most unusual calm." He notes there the "feeling" that a "sacred marriage" has existed, since Winckelmann, between the Hellenic and the German spirit, but quietly distances himself from it.[19] As Edgar Salin has remarked, Burckhardt's paganism—really an astute combination of Stoicism and Epicureanism—is pre- rather than anti-Christian.[20] His attitude on the tension between Christianity and aesthetic paganism reminds one of Herder's very sensible viewpoint: an ascetic Christianity cannot be combined with a humanistic love of art, but a "more joyful," enlightened Christianity knows no such difficulty.[21]

One of the most thoughtful of historians, Burckhardt was the declared enemy of any philosophy of history; he was resolutely anti-Hegelian. Nor did he make out a definite pattern of development: he distrusted all utopias[22] and wrote scathingly against the idea of progress. Yet he was not a historical nihilist: he believed that there are ideals in history—though they may perish—and that we must follow the course of culture through time.[23] He came also to realize the significance of the moral element; whereas he wrote as a young student that history knew no good and evil but only "thus or otherwise," he remarked in his *Reflections on World History* (translated into English as *Force and Freedom*, 1943) that no good could spring from evil antecedents.[24]

In method Burckhardt occupied a middle position between the precise, positivistic scholarship of his teacher Leopold von Ranke and such eighteenth century historians as Winckelmann and Voltaire, with their love of sweeping, often brilliant generalization. He was not interested in research for its own sake but in "that past which is clearly connected with present and future"[25]—or, to use an all too familiar term, relevance. No one can doubt either the depth or the range of his scholarship. It is amazing to observe that his monumental *History of Greek Culture* represents only a tertiary interest of Burckhardt's, clearly subordinate to his studies in the history of the Renaissance and of art history in general.

Like most of the great German Hellenists, Burckhardt never went to Greece, but his trips to Italy were many. With the inner security of the established scholar, he told his students at Basel that he "had no method at all, at least not that of the others" (V, 7), and in preparing his work on Greek culture, he largely ignored contemporary scholarship.[26] Anyone who doubts Burckhardt's own scholarship, however, need only read the work to realize its sovereign command of the Greek authors from Homer down. For all his (very modern) disbelief in historical patterns, he does follow, in his accounts of art, the scheme of rise, flowering, and decay that had been traditional in German histories of art since Winckelmann.

Despite his characteristic skepticism about the use of history as a philosophy, Burckhardt defended the historical sense as one of the very few good characteristics of the nineteenth century. The contrast to his semi-friend and colleague Nietzsche could not be greater. Barbarians have no feeling, Burckhardt wrote, for history; conversely, ahistorical persons are barbarians. Even educated Americans are deficient in the historical sense (IV, 6). A sense of the past, "reverence for the remnants of art and tireless reconstruction of the remnants of tradition form a part of the religion of today" (IV, 195). It has been charged that the religion of the European burgher was based on culture and property—*Bildung und Besitz*. Culture was indeed a part of Burckhardt's creed. As for property, he lived in two rooms above a baker's shop; his one "dissipation" was drinking wine in the evenings in unpretentious Basel pubs. Renowned even in his own time, he had none of the airs of the *Herr Professor*. In the best sense he was a saint: he was utterly devoted to what seemed to him the most authentic concern of his life. *Unum est necessarium*—one thing alone is necessary. History, he wrote to a friend, is the highest poetry, but it is not romantic poetry.[27]

As a historian, Burckhardt was of course much concerned with the role of the great man in history. If hastily read, his *Culture of the Renaissance in Italy* may give the impression that he was one of those who looked up to Renaissance princes and warriors as shining models beyond good and evil; but the impression would be wrong. Viewing the Renaissance as the age in which true individualism was reborn, he admired the "universal man" and was fascinated up to a point by condottieri and other colorful figures, but he painted the dark sides along with the bright ones.[28] Thus he wrote of Francesco Sforza, one of the Renaissance rulers he most admired: "Never was the triumph of genius and individual power more brilliantly displayed than in him; and those who would not recognize his merit were at least forced to wonder at him as the spoilt child of fortune. The Milanese claimed it openly as an honour to be governed by so distinguished a master; when he entered the city the thronging populace bore him on horseback into the cathedral, without giving him the chance to dismount" (III, 26).[29] He quoted a description of Sforza by Pope Pius II, further demonstrating the Duke's stature. At once, however, Burckhardt proceeded to show the corruption that overtook Sforza's children, the result of growing up in an atmosphere of "unlimited princely power" (III, 27). Similarly, after quoting Machiavelli—"acts that are great in themselves bring more glory than blame, of whatever nature they are and whatever their outcome may be"—Burckhardt used the word "demonic" and pointed out that this principle would clear the way for any sort of atrocity (III, 104). In writing of the great men of Greece he is equally far from hero-worship. He questioned the veracity and sincerity of Pericles in the great Funeral Oration (V, 209), and had some sharp things to say even about Socrates; Burckhardt accorded him the highest moral praise but implied that he suffered from hubris (VII, 348–354). As we have seen, he was more repelled than impressed by Bismarck. Generally speaking, he wrote with unmixed praise of only a few artists and poets. Raphael is the most striking example—the painter who was also a major hero to Winckelmann and Goethe.

In *Reflections on World History* Burckhardt gives his last word on great men; he does not call them heroes, let alone supermen. (A late letter makes it clear that he does not include men of violence and outlaws in the category; "rather I've thought of them as scourges of God." [30]) The truly great man must "have a grain of kindness." *The Reflections* put creative men, including discoverers, first. Yet certain political figures who "live on as ideals" have a high value for posterity; thus Napoleon, despite all his crimes. Perhaps the pressures of the nineteenth century would grind down a great man, he wrote, but we sense that the "right man" could come over night (IV, 151–180, esp. p. 180). This appreciation of the cardinal value of the outstanding leader is balanced, perhaps overbalanced, by the most famous of all Burckhardt's statements: power is evil in itself—"die Macht ist an sich böse" (IV, 25, 70). Over against this he often made it clear by implication that political or cultural impotence could be even worse.

In his middle and later years Burckhardt's pessimism about the "power drunk" nineteenth century and its successor became increasingly clear. Schopenhauer was "his" philosopher. Optimistic illusions must disappear.[31] It was ironic that he predicted "an era of wars" in 1870,[32] just as Bismarck was winding up the martial part of his program, but in the long view he was only too correct. As early as 1846 he felt that barbarism was approaching and decided to steep himself in culture while the times permitted; he would be glad to die "for the culture of Old Europe."[33] Later, as has been noted above, he foresaw an authoritarian state in which the (militaristic) masters would brutally keep the masses down.[34] Summing up in the *Reflections*, he stated that we must get rid of the notion of happiness in history but keep that of unhappiness. Evil is part of the structure of world history (IV, 188, 190).

Burckhardt's great specialty, if one may use that word for so broad a concept, was cultural history—*Kulturgeschichte*. Culture, to him, was with the state and religion one of the three great forces in the world. He defined it very broadly; it is: "the essence of all the forces that have arisen *spontaneously* to further the material side of life and express its intellectual and moral aspect—all social life, technique, arts, works of high literature, and fields of knowledge [*Wissenschaften*]. It is the sphere of the versatile, the free, not necessarily of the universal, of the element that does not claim any absolute validity [*Zwangsgeltung*]" (IV, 20). It is interesting but quite uncharacteristic that Burckhardt speaks first of the material aspects of culture; it would be misleading to translate his word *Kultur* by "civilization," as has been done in the case of his great book on the Renaissance. He declared in the *Reflections* that the arts are the most noteworthy achievements of man, providing the "only lasting elements on earth, a second, ideal creation" (IV, 45). More important: any reader of his major works will see that while he neglects no aspect of Greek or Renaissance life, he puts the accent squarely on art and literature. When he says *Kultur* he means culture—and not in the anthropological sense. His common sense, taste, and solid standards are sorely needed in the United States today.

Culture then being defined, what is cultural history? Burckhardt's own brief description in the introduction to his *History of Greek Culture* (V, 3–12) spells out the answer. The
aim of the discipline is to recount the history of the modes of
thinking and the views of a given people and to try to make
out the constructive and destructive forces at work within its
culture. Intellectual and psychological tendencies are more
important than isolated events. (Moreover, the Greek addic-
tion to lying "makes it hard to trust their account of any
given fact"!) Events or situations that recur are more important than unique happenings. Cultural history is an attempt to discover what a particular people *"was, willed,
thought, saw* and *could accomplish."* Through it one gets to
know the *"eternal* Greek" (V, 5). (Such sweeping claims are
most uncharacteristic of the historian.) By "eternal Greek"
he is not setting up an ethical-aesthetic norm for all mankind,
as Stefan George attempted to do; the book as a whole makes
that abundantly clear; rather he wishes to find the characteristic pattern of the (ancient) Greek personality, with its many
virtues and many vices. Since cultural history aims at the
general, all literature may serve it as a source. Burckhardt
draws his examples from virtually all areas of life and art, at
times noting similarities in the spirit of various of these manifestations, but his view is not distorted by any rigid *Zeitgeist*
theory. He is aware that various arts, for example, may well
develop at different rates.[35] Above all, myth, the great "spiritual ocean" encompassing Greek life and thought, is a major
resource of the historian.

Burckhardt ends his introduction with a few lapidary statements containing his central theses about the Hellenes (V,
11f). First he quotes in part a famous sentence from his
former teacher August Boeckh; as it sums up his own views
admirably, I cite it in full here: "In the splendor of art and

the flowering of freedom the Hellenes were unhappier than most people think; they bore the germ of their downfall within them, and the tree had to be felled when it had become rotten." [36] It has been noted that Burckhardt devotes more space to the decline of Greece than to its flowering.[37] Yet most of the following statements are more cheerful. Thus: "What they did and suffered, they did and suffered as *free men* and differently from all other peoples." (Similarly, he found the freedom of the Renaissance individual one of his highest characteristics.) As "*the* people of genius," the Greeks appear original, spontaneous, and self-aware at a time when all the others are more or less the dull, unthinking slaves of compulsion. In the characteristic fashion of the true humanist, Burckhardt shows the unique value and indeed necessity of Greek studies, reaching a climax with the line: "We see with the eyes of the Greeks and speak with their expressions." Throughout the *History* he returns again and again to his basic antithetical motifs: the Greeks were uniquely gifted but by no means especially good; their attainments were of the highest brilliance (matched only by the Renaissance), but their frailties and errors were equally outstanding.

In the chapter "An Overall Balance [*Gesamtbilanz*] of Greek Life" (VI, 319–395)—the title has a mercantile ring—Burckhardt gives abundant evidence of Greek frailties. (There is a great deal more evidence in the discussion of Athens and of the city-state as such.) In the Homeric sphere he found a purity, kindness, and moral delicacy that the mature Greek world did not possess. True to his title, Burckhardt does aim at a balanced account, though at the end he devotes some fifteen pages to suicide among the Greeks and the reasons therefor. On the one hand, he pictures Greek life as an aesthetic unit, in which "endowment, will and the strokes of fate form an indivisible whole" (VI, 341). That they held the ideal of moderation honors the Greeks, even if they did not actually practice it, and it speaks for them that they always thought highly of the arts. But how many vices plagued them! Vengefulness, disloyalty, ambition, and envy are listed. The Greeks had no sense of the need of repentance and atonement; as Burckhardt puts it, à la Voltaire, it would have been up to the Greek gods—who excelled in vices as well as in virtues—to act as models. In opposition to many German Hellenists, including Nietzsche, he maintains that life as such was not the highest Greek value. Like Heine, Burckhardt wrote, at the end of the "Overall Balance," that paganism died none too soon; it was time that a new society, with "a new, lofty purpose in life" (VI, 395), replaced it. One is reminded of Heine's comments on the decadence of Roman culture and its supersedure by Christianity.

Burckhardt attached enormous importance to the role of myth in Greek life; the pages he devoted to it (V, 15–50) are among the brightest in his often rather dark work. In this section he does not define myth explicitly; a passage from his letters may be useful. "*Faust* is a genuine and true myth, that is, a great, ancient image in which everyone must sense his own nature and fate in his own way." [38] Myth was "the great, general basis of the nation's life" (V, 27); for the Greeks, uncritical about historical matters, really relived the events of their legendary past; they "saw" them, unaware that what appeared to their inner eyes was the creation of their own imagination. On the whole, mythical persons were more real to them than historical ones, so it is not surprising that many epiphanies, particularly of Dionysus, were recorded. And of course numerous heroes and kings claimed direct descent from the gods, who after all were not necessarily men's superiors except in power and stature. The gulf between human and divine was relatively small: in part a result of the myths, presumably, but in itself a source of new tales. Reversing the usual labels, Burckhardt remarked that the mythic aspect of Greek culture was "colossally romantic" (V, 36). In any event, myths were a source of strength as well as of joy: the flowering of Greece ended at about the time at which people began to turn away from myths. Here one rather expects one of Burckhardt's frequent comparisons between the Greek past and his own time. He was quite as aware as Matthew Arnold that the sea of faith was receding, but at this point he casts no glance at the nineteenth century, perhaps finding the parallel too obvious to draw. The discussion concludes with an extremely eloquent tribute to the Greeks as the great transmitters of culture, who preserved the continuity of world history. Then, in the last sentence, the historian typically shifts to the minor key: "But of all the peoples of high culture the Greeks are the one that inflicted the bitterest, most grievous sorrow upon itself" (V, 50).

One of the most striking features of *History of Greek Culture* is its repeated stress on the element of the agonistic (competitive; Burckhardt calls it *das Agonale*) in Greek life. On the whole, it is an aspect of which he approves, though it does not have the poetic appeal that myth exerted on him. Further, the high evaluation of the agonistic is one of the main links between his view of the world and Nietzsche's; what is the competitive spirit if not will to power? He may well have influenced Nietzsche in this matter, though not necessarily; just as the philosopher's interpretation of the god Dionysus contributed to Burckhardt's but did not necessarily shape it. Walter Kaufmann's remark that the question of "who influenced whom" is not too important in this case [39] is eminently sound.

The agonistic society was made up of people, virtually un-

interested in material rewards, who could devote themselves
(rather like the British aristocracy before the First World
War) to sports and contests of many kinds. In the Greek
case, however, the contests prominently included drama,
music, and philosophical debates. To the Greeks, as Socrates
put it, leisure was the sister of freedom (VIII, 138). Burckhardt compares their life with that of the patricians in medieval towns, especially the Italians (VIII, 82). In a sense the
agonistic life is nonpurposive, like art in Kant's definition: it
is not directed at practical gain. (Burckhardt notes that in his
own century, open competitiveness was limited to business
matters—VI, 330). From another point of view, nothing
could be more purposeful than a life of competition; but
among the Greeks, he tells us, both ambition and envy were
shown without hypocrisy (VI, 331). In fact, the agonistic
element permeated Greek life; its influence is everywhere,
like that of the myth and the city-state. In art, architecture,
literature, music, the symposia, law, and above all in athletics,
and indeed down to cockfights, its spirit rules (VIII, 89). Not
however in business; that was "banausic"—basely practical,
unworthy of the free Greek man. Above all, such great
athletic contests (*agones*) as the Olympic games contributed
to the Greek sense of national unity (VIII, 93).

Yet Burckhardt would not be Burckhardt if he failed to
point out the darker sides of the agonistic existence. With
great empathy he describes the life of the athlete, living—as
in the twentieth century—under constant strain, and in some
sports always liable to serious injury or death. The historian
is aware that the glorification of the male body led to, or was
already, homosexuality, and notes that, with the exception of
one event, women were not allowed even to watch the great
games. But the really great danger, he states with an implied
reference to both the Greek future and that of modern

Europe, lay in the circumstance that politicians would strive agonistically for the favor of the masses (VIII, 117).

It was in the agonistic period, Burckhardt believes, that the cult of Dionysus expanded; its festivals put all the others in the shade. In Athens this in turn led to the development of the drama (VIII, 156). Here the Dionysiac urge was disciplined by a formal principle; with a bow to Nietzsche, the historian accepts the name Apollonian for it (VIII, 156). While he did not make Dionysus a symbol of his own beliefs, as Nietzsche did, nor write of "the Dionysiac" as an eternal force in life, he was nevertheless fascinated by this half-Greek, half-barbarous divinity and devoted a great deal of attention to him.

Like the cult of Pan, that of Dionysus may be rooted in the Greek feeling that wild, uninhabited places like forests and ravines are the homes of gods and as such sacred but frightening. A god's epiphany similarly releases opposing feelings, but to a much higher degree. For whatever reason, Burckhardt writes, the epiphanies of Dionysus were felt to be far more real than those of the other divinities (V, 44). (Was it perhaps because Dionysus appealed, as the god who overcame the sense of individuation, by unleashing the sexual powers?) Burckhardt sees the essence of the cult rather in epidemics of mass madness which swept over Greece. Once they were established, the epidemics were induced at regular intervals. It was a feminine cult: the maenads roamed over the countryside, tore (or thought to tear) a bull into small pieces in mythic repetition of the dismembering of Dionysus by the Titans, and continued to swarm through the woods until they found the reassembled deity as a child (VI, 162). (The maenads were separated from men during the biennial outbursts; in fact we infer from the *Bacchae* that any males who got in the way were likely to be torn to bits.) Doubtless sexual deprivation made the Bacchantes more likely to see visions and generally carry on like the wilder sort of *femmes libérées*. Perhaps, given the notoriously low position of Greek women, such outlets were psychologically natural, even therapeutic. Burckhardt does not go into this point; rather, he describes the rites of Dionysus calmly and objectively. He courteously cites the theories of his younger colleague without betraying a special predilection for the god of intoxication, let alone Nietzsche's fiery devotion. Had Burckhardt realized that Nietzsche was well on the way to becoming a sort of male maenad ranging the dark forest of German ideology, he would doubtless have distanced himself still further from the Dionysiac view.

To the enthusiastic admirer of Greek culture, Burckhardt's treatment of the city-state and particularly of Athens comes as a shock. Burckhardt takes his motto from the *Inferno: Per me si va nella città dolente*—Through me is the road to the city of sorrow. Recalling all that Athens brought forth, one wonders if the Greek cities were really *that* doleful. The historian concedes the lofty aim of the city-state but stresses the "bitter sorrows" of its inhabitants, which he feels were almost unique in history (V, 62f). Antiquity knew no human rights as such; free citizens had rights, but that is something radically different (V, 72). He ventures a mild pun: when men move to the polis, they become politicians (V, 67f). Burckhardt gives a sort of typology of conceivable city-states: tyrannical, aristocratic, democratic. In his description, Sparta appears as the ancient analogue of eighteenth century Prussia: easy to respect but virtually impossible to like. To Burckhardt's credit, it is the inhumanity of Greek city politics that most repelled him. The notorious Athenian atrocity against the people of Melos he attributes to "the most highly developed philosophy of the right of the stronger" (V, 276)—

distinguishing his own position clearly from Bismarck's practice and the theories of Nietzsche and Hegel. Knowing from Thucydides that Greek political cruelty was all too frequent and that Athens' crimes may well have been the blackest—*corruptio optimi pessima*—we may yet wonder if Burckhardt has been completely just. What were things like in the non-Greek cities around the Eastern Mediterranean? Possibly Burckhardt transferred to the Greek setting some of his own worries about political changes in Basel and the "realization" of Swiss life (II, 377–458).

While admitting that Athens was the "Greece of Greece," the outstanding city, like Florence in the Renaissance, Burckhardt makes it the subject of a brief but cutting satire. Citing Pericles' Funeral Address, he contrasts rhetoric with actuality. Pericles stressed the equality of the Athenian citizens, standing next to the reckless and unprincipled Cleon, who was outstripping him in power. He praised the free, relaxed life of Athens, while he himself, like Aspasia, was involved in lawsuits. Athens, he said, loved beauty without extravagance; why not, Burckhardt asks, since the allies had to pay for the magnificent buildings. And so forth (VIII, 175–177). His method, it should be noted, could be devastatingly applied to the glorification of Switzerland in Schiller's *William Tell*. Apparently he was angered by Pericles' "optimism," which he mentions twice. The Swiss historian goes very far in his debunking but must admit that we can get to know the Athenians through Pericles' speech after all; ideals and aims are also part of man's nature (VIII, 176). As a conservative aristocrat Burckhardt appears skeptical about the replacement of the *kalokagathia* of the agonistic age by the goal of "making people better" and the mixture of various "racial" stocks in democratic Athens (VIII, 206). Waste of men and treasure was part of the democratic life style (VIII, 180–183).

Although, "as every schoolboy knows," Burckhardt praised
the Renaissance as the period that brought forth true individuals, his attitude toward the rise of individualism in
Athens is rather sour. He connects the development of the
individual with the rise of medicine: Athenian politics, with
its acts of "satanic" malice, made people "necessarily sick and
nervous" (VIII, 208). In fact, he seems to prefer the agonistic
athletes to the more sophisticated artists and intellectuals of
the fifth century (VIII, 208–211). As Athens represented the
best and the worst of Greece, Alcibiades, in Burckhardt's
view, "personified Athens to the highest degree" (VIII, 183;
215). There is a case to be made for this view (and Burckhardt of course makes it ably) but the selection could hardly
be more damning. It is rather like choosing Benedict Arnold
as the typical American or Klaus Fuchs as England personified. Knowing Burckhardt's prejudices, we are not surprised
to read that the permissiveness of Athenian democracy led
to completely compulsive behavior *(alles . . . müssen*—to be
impelled to do *anything;* V, 211), and that the Greeks, by
definition, were "ready for unlimited (or absolute) actions"
(V, 212), in other words, they would stop at nothing. This
would be high praise if it came from Nietzsche; certainly
Burckhardt does not mean it as such. At least, he concedes,
the intellect (*Geist*) was honored in Athens, even in a poor
man (VIII, 197). Yet he ends his discussion of the fifth century, surely one of the great ages in all history, with the
speculation that many a man of that time must have expected
the final catastrophe and said to himself: "If only the earth
would devour me in good time" (VIII, 268). Burckhardt's
apocalyptic Greeks seem no more convincing than the joyous
Hellenes envisioned by the eighteenth century.

In the "Overall Balance of Greek Life" Burckhardt force-
fully rejects the German humanist ideal of Greek life, as presented in Schiller's "The Gods of Greece." Rather, Greece

was a society in which the diabolic played a perhaps unex-
ampled role (VI, 348, 341). Pessimism informs the whole
Greek myth (VIII, 41), and the judgments of fate and of the
gods reflect inevitability far more often than justice (VIII,
351, 355). To be sure, the Greek temperament was optimistic;
all the more striking that pessimism, based on experience,
prevailed (VIII, 363–365). Yet somehow Hellenic life was
nobler: the historian tells how the whole family of Prince
Nikokles committed suicide out of a sense of decorum, adding
the remark that today they would have all applied for pen-
sions (VIII, 389f).

As Rudolf Marx puts it in the afterword to his edition of
the *History of Greek Culture*, themes of decay and aging
wind through the entire work like leitmotivs.[40] Burckhardt's
account of the fourth century stresses "petulance" (which he
ascribes to democracy), badly brought up sons, corruption,
and degeneration (VIII, 278–282). He calculates that there
"must" have been a higher proportion of dangerous criminals
in Athens than in any nineteenth century metropolis (VIII,
324). At the same time, a new, far rougher type of ruler was
emerging: the portrait of Philip of Macedonia is similar to
the impression of Bismarck given by Burckhardt's letters.
Yet, even in the fourth century, he believed, Greek culture
and the Greek language remained a "ferment of culture,"
and art—alone of all the manifestations of life—did not decay
(VIII, 481, 373). No doubt Burckhardt's synthetic view of
Greek culture is truer in many important ways than are the
panoramas of Greek life, from Winckelmann through Nietzsche, that preceded it. Yet how strongly we see reflected in
it his own personality—conservative, pessimistic, skeptical
about life though not about art. To quote Friedrich Schlegel:
"Everyone has found in the Greeks what he wanted in them,
especially himself." [41]

IV Aestheticism and Myth in Wagner

My baton will yet become the scepter of the future.

—Wagner

Er huldigt dem Genie, das sich
Nicht von der Natur entfernt hat,
Sich nicht mit Gelehrsamkeit brüsten will
Und wirklich auch nichts gelernt hat.

He pays homage to genius, which
Has not departed from nature
Does not wish to boast of learning
And really hasn't learned anything, anyway.

—Heine

Richard Wagner's impact on his own century, and on ours, was enormous and continues to be at least considerable. Not only did his operas conquer the world, as Thomas Mann put it,[1] and help to shape the future of music; he influenced the development of stagecraft and even, via Baudelaire, of symbolist poetry. To anyone who has read *Mein Kampf*, it is painfully clear that "the Master" also contributed a great deal to the education of "der Führer." To mention the many skeletons in the Bayreuth closets is unnecessary; Harry Levin's reminder that Wagner "forged in the smithy of his soul the uncreated conscience of the Third Reich" must suffice.[2]

But the case against Wagner is not primarily a political one: other great artists have espoused disastrous causes, though few, aside from Ezra Pound, so embarrassingly. It was a more than political factor that made the keenest minds of the German-Austrian tradition mistrust him, while in part acknowledging his power: Heine, Nietzsche, Robert Musil, Thomas Mann, Heinrich Mann. In each case the mistrust has to do with a false or at best pretentious element in Wagner's character and work. Nietzsche repeatedly called him an actor.[3] Sham is almost everywhere in Wagner's writings: in the theories of the total work of art, in the pretense of vast knowledge about cultures past and present, in the gaseous verbiage of essays like "Judaism in Music" or "Paganism and Christianity." In turn, Wagner's followers were infected: thus, as Jacques Barzun remarks, "few are the living Wagnerians who could face a performance of the librettos as plays."[4] The most formidable of Wagner's critics was Leo Tolstoy, who was moralistic in his artistic judgment but at the least a gifted amateur in musical matters.[5] No one is likely to call *him* a sham, and his artistic stature reduces the Fasolts and Fafners to their proper size, dwarfs them: "Above all, from the very beginning to the very end, and in each note, the author's purpose is so audible and visible that one sees and hears neither Siegfried nor the birds, but only a limited, self-opinionated German, of bad taste and bad style, who has a most false conception of poetry."[6] As a total judgment on the *Ring* this is manifestly unfair, but note the key words: "a limited, self-opinionated German, of bad taste and bad style, who has a most false conception of poetry." This is no Philistine speaking.

In a way it is an honor to be attacked by a Tolstoy or a Nietzsche. Wagner was less fortunate with his intellectual champions—aside from Bernard Shaw—than with his opponents. It is no coincidence that Kaiser Wilhelm II (whom Stefan George called a stage king) had himself painted as Lohengrin, savoring as he did the pomp and circumstance of Wagnerism. Other emulators were still less attractive: the pseudo intellectualism of Wagner's essays anticipates works like Houston Stewart Chamberlain's *Foundations of the Nineteenth Century*, Adolf Hitler's *Mein Kampf*, and Alfred Rosenberg's *Myth of the Twentieth Century*. All of these are the works of false prophets, word-intoxicated men with universal pretensions: all share in the Wagnerian habits of false assertion, reckless generalization, chauvinistic praise of one's own culture. Wagner's ideas, generally those of late German romanticism, were largely dated by 1850, to say nothing of 1880, but his musical genius and personal magnetism gave his essays an appeal they otherwise could hardly have exerted. As much as anyone he represented that sub-intellectual German underground [7] made up of faddists, amateur geopoliticians, and anti-Semites, which finally vanquished, for a while, the spirit of Weimar. In fact Wagner's prestige in his later years, his alliance with figures like Chamberlain and Gobineau, and his control of the *Bayreuther Blätter* must have aided the radical, pseudo intellectual Right enormously.

Nietzsche referred to Wagner as the "old magician," [8] and so we prick up our ears when Thomas Mann entitles a story of the will, freedom, and fascism, "Mario and the Magician." Here the magician, Cipolla, is endowed with the strongest hypnotic and generally magic powers; hardly anyone can resist him. (Incidentally, *cipolla* means onion: many layers, no core.) It would be crude to say that Cipolla "is" Wagner, but a relationship clearly exists between the two.

In his use of the myth for artistic purposes, Wagner was highly eclectic, drawing on Germanic, Celtic, and Christian material, and to some extent, in an indirect way, on Greek. Totally unconcerned with the question of anachronism, he introduced "free love" into *Tannhäuser*, and later had Wotan voice assorted doctrines of Schopenhauer and Feuerbach. More or less everything is possible to the genius. When however Wagner, a solipsist and/or an atheist, blandly exploited the appeal of Christianity in *Parsifal*, not only Nietzsche was shocked. "The world beheld with awe the Catholic mysticism of this Protestant Freemason turned atheist."[9] On the one hand, Christianity is reduced to a fad, one myth among many; on the other, each drama, as the egos of Richard and Cosima Wagner demand, must be taken with utter seriousness.

To use the word myth in a lower sense: Wagner also embraced as myths several contemporary tendencies: vegetarianism, redemption through "Art," anti-Semitism, the supremacy of the "Aryan" race. Again one thinks of the onion: this conglomeration of notions has no center. At bottom, I think, he truly believed in one myth only: "Richard Wagner, Lord of the Arts, Supreme Musician, Redeemer, World Thinker." Artists are not notoriously modest, but the closest parallel to Wagner's egregious self-esteem is that of the Emperor Nero: "Qualis artifex pereo"—What an artist dies in me. Nero also felt himself too gifted to be confined to one art. In both, the primacy of aestheticism; in the one the actual conflagration, in the other, the self-fulfilling prophecy of *Götterdämmerung*.

Inevitably, the case of Wagner raises the old, perhaps boring question: is there a relation between the artist's morality and the quality of his work? Naturally, I am not speaking of Wagner's peccadilloes or his debts, but of the morality that appears, often shifting, in his operas and essays. If a man presents, for decades, a medley of sweeping assertions, dubious details, and meretricious logic as deep thoughts, does not this absence of intellectual integrity or capacity cast a shadow on his art? If *Figaro* and *Fidelio* had taken a stand against the Enlightenment, our estimate of Mozart and Beethoven would be a different one. No doubt any number of artists have done evil things, but in Wagner the evil is intrinsic to the work. If one reads the books of writers as radically different as T. S. Eliot and Günter Grass, one senses in both integrity and genuine intelligence. Precisely these qualities Wagner lacked, for all his shrewdness, for all his genius.

Apparently no great artist, in any medium, was produced by the Third Reich, except perhaps Leni Riefensthal. Whether Wagner, the greatest and most influential of proto-Nazis, attained the highest rank despite the ideology which weighed him down, is perhaps an arguable question. No sensible person is likely to question the brilliance, scope, and impressiveness of Wagner's musical productions. Whether they are both pure and broad enough, however, to remain "possessions forever" like the achievements of Monteverdi, Mozart, and Beethoven seems dubious.

As a schoolboy Richard Wagner shared in that enthusiasm for the Greek past that was central in German education for over a century. In his autobiography he tells us that he greatly admired the Greek heroes, but that he tended to neglect the grammar and the language generally.[10] In fact we know that he had little flair for languages, ancient or modern.[11] Thus when he claims to have translated as a boy twelve books of the *Odyssey* in a few months, in his spare time, one has a right to be skeptical, all the more so since he wrote vaguely in *My Life* of translating Homer.[12] Of course the manuscript of the problematic translation could easily have been lost, but if so, why did Wagner not mention so untoward an event, the vanishing of a document that would have marked him as a child prodigy, perhaps as a budding poet? Whether the translation, if it existed, covered more than a few pages, no one knows.

The matter is one of importance, for if Wagner's music dramas do derive largely from Greek literature, as he maintained, he is, at least in intention, a part of the Western dramatic tradition. Even the *Ring* would then have a classical aspect in some sense. Per se the subject matter is not important—thus Kleist's *Penthesilea* obviously treats a classical myth but is the height of brilliant barbarism. Two questions arise: How much did Wagner know about Greek literature and culture? Was he at least subjectively honest in making his solemn pronouncements about Greek tragedy, Apollo, Athens, and so forth?

As to the matter of knowledge, the most damning witness about Wagner is Wagner. Some two years after the alleged translation of Homer, Wagner was fortunate enough to be tutored in Sophocles by "a scholar" not further identified. What a marvelous opportunity for anyone devoted to Greek literature and particularly interested in classical tragedy—as Wagner, thanks to his uncle Adolf, a translator of *Oedipus Rex* into German, already was. Alas, nothing happened: the smell of a nearby tannery drove Wagner away.[13] A culinary —or rather nasal—approach to literature! Abandoning the claim to linguistic knowledge of Greek, Wagner henceforth restricted himself to secondary works and translations. He claims to have read, along with J. G. Droysen and Barthold Niebuhr, Edward Gibbon, of all people.[14] One thinks of some Vandal or Ostrogoth, wandering through the ruins of Rome, and wondering, gutturally, what it had all been about. "Das Ende! Das Ende!" to quote one of the composer's better lines.

Apparently, the most incisive critic of Wagner the classicist is William Wallace,[15] who seems to have enjoyed a sound British classical education. His stringent criticism reminds us of Goethe's dictum: there is no greater arrogance than claiming to understand the spirit before one has mastered the letter. (This insight casts a clear light on Wagner's intellectual pretensions.) Wallace points out that Wagner, though completely ignorant of Greek accentuation, liked to talk of Greek prosody; that he was grossly misinformed about dramatic productions in Athens; and that it proves nothing to find superficial parallels between Wagner's dramas and the Greek.[16] On one point Wallace performs the neat trick of making Wagner seem even more ignorant of the Greeks than he actually was; Ernest Newman, with his usual soundness, has put things straight.[17]

Again however the most relevant witness is Richard Wagner. In his essay "Art and Revolution" (1849), Wagner tells his audience that the god Apollo "was the Greek folk."[18] Whatever happened to Zeus and Athena, one wonders? But the really demagogic stroke was bringing in the highly charged word "folk." He mentions Dionysus as the inspirer of tragic poets but develops the theme no further. Unsurprisingly, he states that the Greek drama was a *Gesamtkunstwerk*—total work of art—including, implausibly enough, sculpture and painting (III, 29). At the end of the essay, Wagner takes up the topos of the Third Kingdom, hoping to raise the "altar of the future" to Jesus and Apollo (III, 41). This would sound nicer if we did not know that, even then, Wagner had become an anti-Semite. Two years later, in the second part of "Opera and Drama," Wagner clearly called for a drama based on myth, noting predictably that such was the case with Greek tragedy (IV, 33). In later years, influenced by Count Gobineau, his accent became unambiguously racist: thus the story of the labors of Hercules symbolized the mighty feats of the "noblest Aryan tribes" (X, 277f).

Wagner planned an "Achilleus" as early as 1849,[19] and it seems sensible to infer that his Achilles is to some extent a forerunner of his Siegfried. Both are strong, handsome, and fearless—authentic heroes of divine ancestry. To be sure, the differences are equally striking: the Greek, however wrathful, is a man and a great gentleman; the German is an attractive youth, an eternal sophomore, not quite housebroken, who grows up too late if at all. Becoming versus being, to cite a favorite cliché.

Various other parallels between aspects of Greek literature and of Wagner's operas have been pointed out; not all of them are convincing. It seems rather clear that J. G. Droysen's translations and explanations of Aeschylus (1832) were useful to the composer.[20] Wotan obviously does owe something to Zeus; whereas Petsch's analogy between the good fire-god Hephaestus and the nasty Loge is not persuasive.[21] It is worth noting that the Greek impact on the *Ring* recedes as a "Hellenistic-optimistic" view of the world yields to that of Schopenhauer, and possibly of Feuerbach.[22] Nevertheless, Wolfgang Schadewaldt has recently returned to the finding of parallels, thus: "Brünnhilde is Prometheus."[23] *Quantum mutata ab illo*—How different from him she has become! Similarly, Wieland Wagner has balanced Lohengrin and Elsa against Zeus and Semele.[24] Richard Wagner himself descried Odysseus behind both the Flying Dutchman and Tannhäuser;[25] in the latter case both heroes have unconventional sex lives. Any parallel, however silly, seems acceptable. Indeed, if certain battles had turned out differently in 1944, Bayreuth would no doubt have established the equation: Pericles equals Wotan equals Wagner equals Hitler. Wagner himself liked to establish such identities: in "Die Wibelungen" (1849) he wrote that "the Hoard was also the Grail, and Friedrich was Siegfried, and Siegfried was Baldur, and Baldur was Christ."[26] Fair is foul, and foul is fair. Anyone can play this type of psychoanalytical and mythological game. Since Wotan has only one eye, for instance, he is a sort of Oedipus; at the same time Siegfried, who sleeps with his ersatz mother, Tante Brünnhilde, "must" be Oedipus too.

That Wagner was removed from the Greeks by light-years is indicated by his belief that the end of *Die Meistersinger* reflected that of the *Oresteia*.[27] To such bathos the dream of Winckelmann and Goethe had been reduced.

In his major operas, Wagner often makes appropriate and extremely effective use of myth and mythic "logic." Thus no one is likely to be shocked when Siegmund and Sieglinde commit incest: it all takes place in a realm in which the ordinary norms do not apply.[28] It is a different matter when the mythic way of thinking (*Denkform*) is employed in what is purportedly the world of rational discourse—in Wagner's political and general essays. Here begins a broad primrose path leading down to the Third Reich. (As J. M. Stein has shown, however, in his *Richard Wagner and the Synthesis of the Arts*,[29] the essays dealing with musical topics are on a very different level.)

Like his "Aristophanic" comedy "A Capitulation," the tract "Judaism in Music" (1850) ranks as one of Wagner's most abysmal performances. There is no point in recounting its contents. Rather, it is the perversion of the myth—the method in the madness—that is important here: the bland telling of half-truths and whole lies as if they were inspired insights. Thus: no dramatic character played by a Jew could escape ridicule (V, 69f), Wagner maintained (Shylock? Nathan the Wise?); the Jews do not speak good German (V, 70f); and so on. The latter point was perhaps true to some extent in 1850; but coming from Wagner, who spoke the ugliest of German dialects, the charge is absurd. For any even partially educated German, Herder had established the grandeur of Hebrew literature—it had been an open secret at least since Luther. Accordingly, when Wagner said that the Jew never had his own art (V, 76), he was either grossly ignorant or blatantly mendacious. Either or both would be quite in character. Yet his propagandistic genius rarely deserted him. When he wrote of Heine, whose integrity was by no means beyond reproach, that he "lied himself into being [thought?] a poet" (V, 85), he had the shadow of a case. A very thin one, if one compares Heine's *Last Poems*—both successful as art and deeply felt—with the libretto of *Parsifal* which, aside from the superb phrase "durch Mitleid wissend," knowing through compassion, contains little Christianity and less poetry. If unsurprising, it is nevertheless sickening to read today Wagner's advice to the Jews, laboring under their curse: accept the redemption of the Wandering Jew—*cease to be*. Although the last words of this essay, *der Untergang* (V, 85)—annihilation, the end—could be taken to mean that all Jews should physically perish, it would be anachronistic, obviously, to believe that Wagner was thinking in 1850 of the "final solution." Yet *Untergang* is the final word of his tract, and anyone who can miss the hostility is dull indeed. Unfriendly critics, as much as friendly ones, have the right to speculate about Wagner's unconscious or partly conscious motives.[30]

One final note: with a sad lack of courage, Wagner published this, his major anti-Semitic opus, under a pseudonym —he signed himself Karl Freethinker!—but later blamed unsympathetic reviews of his operas on Jewish resentment against this screed.[31] Here is the authentic Goebbels technique, seventy-five years ahead of time. Similarly, in the preface to "A Capitulation" Wagner wrote that it was not his intention to make fun of the starving Parisians, and then proceeded to do just that, in the grossest way. In an exact if perhaps unconscious parallel to Wagner's concept of *Veritas*, Goebbels announced in 1933 that not one single Jew had been hurt in the least. Wagner's anti-Semitic tract was no mere youthful folly; he remained consistently anti-Semitic to the last, as did his second wife, Cosima, and other leading figures of the Bayreuth group. Only on the carcass of a culture, he claimed, could members of an alien race feed—like worms (V, 84). When it appeared that the best available conductor for *Parsifal* was Hermann Levi, who was the son of a rabbi, Wagner had the gall to try to persuade Levi to convert, though the composer was by no means a Christian himself; it was a matter of sheer *Realpolitik*.[32] Like many other German anti-Semites, he was also deeply suspicious of the Jesuits.[33]

Equally typical of Wagner's style of thinking is his use of dreadfully inflated diction: *Wonne, Heil, ewig, herrlich, himmlisch, hehr, siegen, strahlen, leuchten, jauchzen, prangen* —ecstasy, salvation, eternal, splendid, heavenly, lofty, conquer, radiate, shine forth, rejoice, shine in splendor—to quote a few typical words more or less at random. It will be noted that they generally connote one or more of the following: extreme emotion, radiance, victory, or some lofty, often superhuman quality, like *herrlich, himmlisch, hehr*. They suggest a world dominated by heroes and hero worship, and infused with a truly adolescent fervor, a flair for the spectacular. Wagner's diction, too, was to leave his mark on writers who followed him in the discussion of cultural or political matters. Perhaps the use of such emotion-loaded words offset the otherwise deadening effect of so much Wagnerian prose: "the thought stumbling and spluttering its way through the involved syntax like a hippopotamus through a mud-flat,"[34] as his most distinguished biographer put it.

To turn to the "music dramas"—though they do not seem notably more dramatic than *Don Giovanni*—*Tannhäuser* (1845) is generally considered his first important, truly mythic opera. It is indeed richly mythical, and it displays, I believe, an essential trait of Wagner: his basic neutrality in many situations, his "negative capability." He does not take sides in the conflict between "the emancipation of the flesh" as advocated by the Young Germans of the day and "holy," Christian love as championed for example by the Catholic poet Joseph von Eichendorff. Wagner attempts no synthesis nor does he seem to strive toward objectivity; rather, as a born *Theatermensch*, he exploits each theme and scene to the utmost. To put it bluntly, the opera is about sex, as its working title "The Mount of Venus" ("Der Venusberg") made abundantly clear.[35] As Kurt Hildebrandt has noted, the erotic music here expresses barbaric not Athenian Dionysianism.[36] German literature—Helena versus Gretchen, Venus versus the Virgin—offered Wagner a convenient pattern for the theme's development; both profane and holy love are upheld. In the first part, the scenes in the *Venusberg* recall Heinse's novel *Ardinghello* and the amorous songs in *Faust*:

> naht euch dem Lande,
> wo in den Armen
> glühender Liebe
> selig Erwarmen
> still' eure Triebe!   (II, 5)

(approach the land,/where in the arms/of glowing love/may blissful warmth/satiate your urges!). Ballet and, of course, extremely erotic music support the mood. Later, when Tann-häuser sings of love as a matter of human, physical enjoyment, shocking his fellow minstrels, he makes a deep impression on the naive maiden Elisabeth.

Venus seems to be well on her way to victory, but that would have been rather simplistic. Probably there were also the censors to be thought about. Further, Tannhäuser has become satiated with love and longs for redemption; the weary amorist yearns for the "other world." Both in its eroticism and its religiosity the early opera points toward *Parsifal*.

Eventually, Elisabeth "in death"—an almost inevitable cliché —vanquishes Venus, and all the magic world of paganism disappears, as it had in *Faust* and in Eichendorff's story "The Marble Statue." When we read that Wagner planned a ballet combining a maximum of classical and Northern mythology, we think of Heine's "Dance Poem of Dr. Faust" and his projected ballet "The Goddess Diana," but there is no question of influence here.

Wagner's own religious and moral sentiments are probably better represented in his scenario and notes for a five-act drama "Jesus of Nazareth" (1848) than by *Tannhäuser*. Later he was to become conservative, even chauvinistic, but here he is very much the free-thinking Young German, ranging from liberal to radical in his opinions. His Jesus is against oaths, like Wotan, and abolishes the law, except for love. Love and the flesh are not enemies; Jesus feels no shame that he was born before his parents were married. "Love is free," he proclaims.[37]

The *Ring of the Nibelung* (text completed 1852) is Wagner's most staggering achievement as a mythic work and also as a work for the theater. Not everyone is entranced by plump "maidens" singing subaqueously, or militantly Teutonic types rushing about on horseback and "raising barbaric yawps,"[38] but there is more than enough to offset these infelicities.

To what extent does the *Ring* derive from Greek drama? Around 1847 Wagner's enthusiasm for Aeschylus reached its height, aided by the "truly Winckelmannian enthusiasm" he found in Droysen's translations and commentary.[39] He was deeply impressed by *Prometheus Bound*, but even more so by the *Oresteia*: "My ideas about the significance of the drama and especially of the theater were decisively shaped from these impressions."[40] His encounter with Aeschylus was intense but relatively brief.[41] Schadewaldt uses the term "breakthrough" to the Greeks, which of course devalues that problematic schoolboy translation of Homer.[42]

The theory, then, that the *Ring* is founded on the rock of the *Oresteia* rests on rather scanty evidence, though Wagner's lofty crags do seem Aeschylean. Subjectively, I would submit, Wagner was inspired by Aeschylus and strove to walk in his mighty footsteps; objectively the differences are enormous. One who knows nothing about Greek music—and around 1850 there was virtually nothing to know—cannot usefully discuss Greek "music drama," still less model himself on it. When Wagner writes that "the tragedy of Aeschylus and Sophocles was the work of Athens," he shows that he shares in the romantic belief in collective productivity but knows little about Aeschylus and Sophocles (III, 22). Perhaps his rhetoric ran away with him, as it so often did.

The most obvious difference between the two vast works is that in the *Oresteia* the myth is still virtually intact, unitary, basically authentic, however much the Athenian dramatist may have modified it for patriotic reasons. Apollo, Athena, and the Eumenides are to a high degree real. In treating Wotan, Wagner was dealing with a god who had been dead in Germany for over 1,000 years; he can be very convincing as an unhappy old man and he is an effective stage figure, but even the Nazis could not make him real as a god. There is nothing less mythic than a god manqué: thus Fricka is a scolding, jealous bourgeoise, possibly patterned on Wagner's first wife, Minna. If Wagner had gone back only a few centuries, say to the time of Luther, for his mythical data, he would have had more manageable, more credible material.

In style, Aeschylus' poetry is often grand and melancholy, like Marlowe's at his best, often soaring like Milton's. According to some of Wagner's formulations of the theory of the *Gesamtkunstwerk,* the text of a "music drama" should be sublime poetry; it is supposed to be even more important than the music. In a way, Wagner's hybrid alliterative verse form, which is not sublime and only rarely poetry, but tries to be Old and New High German at the same time, mirrors the mishmash of ideas and motifs drawn from medieval literature, Bakunin, Schopenhauer, and so forth, and combined into the *Ring.* It used to be maintained by some of the faithful that Wagner was a great poet, but this theory is hiding out in Argentina, so to speak. Two lines from one of his best libretti, *Tristan und Isolde,* are illuminating here:

> Vergessens gütiger Trank!
> Dich trink ich sonder Wank.   (VII, 26)

(Forgetfulness' gracious drink,/I drink without waver or wink.)[43]

Whereas the basic meaning, the poetic statement of the *Oresteia* is remarkably clear—it celebrates the victory of the male principle over the matriarchal, of Apollo and Athena over the Furies—the import of the *Ring* is fascinatingly evasive. No doubt the Rhine treasure and Alberich's curse point up the evil impact of materialism—and perhaps of capitalism. When Fafner is guarding the treasure in the guise of a dragon, he sings "Here I lie and possess; let me sleep!" It is perhaps less obvious that Wotan is torn between his divine duty to enforce the law or the treaties (codified in the runes on his spear) and his restless dynamism: why be bound by the past? He compromises and loses stature. On the one hand we see, through a Germanic glass darkly, the New Testament distinction between love and the law, referred to by Wagner himself in his "Jesus."[44] There are also the very different traditions of German resistance to the Roman law as too universal, and the Storm and Stress sense of charge and irresistible becoming as expressed, for example, in *Faust*:

> Rast nicht die Welt in allen Strömen fort,
> Und mich soll ein Versprechen halten? [45]

(Does not the world rage on in all its streams,/And I am supposed to be bound by a promise?) Probably also there are references to social oppression in the fate of the Nibelungen, but Siegfried, who presumably was indeed modeled on Bakunin as well as on Achilles,[46] cannot in terms of the myth do anything about these slave laborers. Perhaps Alberich and Mime are meant as anti-Semitic caricatures; this has been asserted by highly respected authorities, but I have seen no hard evidence.

Another aspect of the tetralogy is the conflict between generations; it is not a total clash because lines of affection run back and forth, especially between Wotan and his favorite daughter, Brünnhilde. Yet he is weak and indeed hypocritical: he is no longer really able to govern the world. While he does not break pacts overtly, he depends on the tricks and wiles of Loge. When Brünnhilde defies Wotan, in *Die Walküre*, his own will turns against him. In the third drama, *Siegfried*, he is a broken god and only too glad to abdicate in favor of Siegfried, the young and unselfconscious hero who has made his career without any help from above. Siegfried, we are led to expect, might well "redeem" this whole semi-mythical society; but things turn out differently. A henpecked All-Father, Wotan betrays his son Siegmund because he cannot stand up to his formidable wife Fricka. Being an indefatigable lecher Wotan is at a disadvantage vis-à-vis his spouse, who is aware of his straying; things become sordid, and we are a long way from Aeschylus. Wotan can break Siegmund's sword; Siegfried however breaks Wotan's spear, runes and all. Doubtless there is some unconscious phallic symbolism here.

In connection with the interpretation of the *Ring*, one asks: which is more important, the redemptive ending—Wagner is the master of facile redemption—or the tone set by the tough valor of Siegfried and the "Hojotoho" of the Wagner Maidens as they rush around the stage in *Die Walküre?* The composer apparently wished to synthesize Feuerbach, Schopenhauer, and Nordic paganism. Impossible intellectually, but it works on stage. *Qualis artifex.*

One of the more attractive figures of opera, Siegfried, not the declining Wotan, is the hero of the *Ring* though one cannot call him a tragic hero in the full sense. To be sure, we gather that a hero free of the law and the gods' protection—in the *Ring* such autonomy is symbolized by Siegfried's incestuous birth—may save the situation and indeed redeem the world. In the realm of myth, incestuous love seems to be especially powerful, even magic. That he is absolutely fearless, except for his adolescent fear of women, also speaks strongly for Siegfried as a potential savior. He is closer however to the "noble savage": his most characteristic words on stage are "Hoiho! Hoiho!" and he converses with birds. Normally good-humored, he is downright nasty in his confrontation with Wotan. (Obviously Wagner, still very much the anarchist when writing the text, sympathized when Siegfried-Bakunin broke the spear of Authority.) Normally rather bright, Siegfried is stupid when warned by the Rhine Maidens (VI, 238 f). In fact the entire tetralogy loses stature in the *Götterdämmerung;* even Siegfried is declassé, when, drugged, he loses his memory and is caught in a sordid intrigue. Anni Carlsson is not being frivolous when she asserts that Siegfried has much in common with Tarzan.[47]

The drama proceeds to its enigmatic ending. Despite Brünnhilde's self-immolation, Valhalla is not saved; the ring goes back to the Rhine. Will the cycle start over again?

Ernest Newman speaks of "a dénouement in which the world should go down in outer ruin yet somehow be taken up into the arms of a redeeming love." [48] This is persuasive, being in line with Wagner's usual compositional procedure: something for everyone, and plenty of redemption at the end. It would appear, however, that in the *Ring* at least, the role of redemption is to supply a semi-metaphysical figleaf for a basically Nordic-pagan action.

The *Ring* does indeed mirror the clash between "two worlds, one dead/The other powerless to be born." The old order, represented with impressive dignity by Wotan, must fall; it is built on compromises, in part on injustice and lust for gold. Wotan no longer believes in what he must uphold: the typical situation of the decadent. On the other hand, the "radiant hero" Siegfried stands for nothing except his own courage and strength. To Wotan's "pacts" he can oppose, quite literally, only anarchy, and so this Germanic Bakunin must perish. He is a sort of one-man youth movement, full of unconscious arrogance but without a program. Thinking of the fall of Valhalla, we think of Spengler and of the German attachment, in the nineteenth century at least, to the unhappy ending, the catastrophic ending. In the special case of Wagner's *Ring* Schopenhauer proved stronger than Bakunin, the desire for the end of all things triumphed over the hope for a moral and political revolution. It was Nietzsche who pointed this out;[49] to him Wagner was *the* artist of decadence.

Wagner's weakest dramatic effort, "A Capitulation" (written 1870/71), has, like the *Ring*, a certain alleged connection with Greek drama, though the former—described by Wagner as a comedy in the antique manner—is even farther from Aristophanes than the *Ring* is from Aeschylus. Wagner himself calls it a farce (IX, 4). Far from addressing himself, as

Aristophanes did, to the stirring problems of the day, Wagner gloats over the French defeat, the inefficiency of democracy, and—incredibly—the starvation of the Parisians. Here a chorus of rats plays its part; presumably these rodents are meant as a counterpart to Aristophanes' birds and frogs, but essentially they remind us that the people of Paris had to eat rats. Not only his music pointed toward the future; his *Zukunftspolitik* was, at times, equally significant. His political ideas are unfashionable at the moment, but it would be rash to conclude that they will always be obscure. It has been well said that Stefan George was among the losers of the second World War; clearly Wagner was also among the defeated, but both are very much alive as artists. One can understand a Wagnerite today who would try to suppress all the evil, the anti-intellectual aspects of the composer's works and thought; but the effort to make him appear a genuine intellectual or even an admirable human being would be worse than futile, for it is precisely as the "old magician," the unlikely synthesis of genius, charlatan, and proto-fascist that he fascinates us.

In sharp contrast to Nietzsche, Wagner is vastly more successful as a practitioner than a theorist. His education, aside from music, was mediocre at best, yet he repeatedly pontificated on a range of subjects that might have strained the knowledge of a Hegel, even of an Aristotle. Fortunately for him, his practice in writing operas was far from his prescription. After all, in the actual Wagnerian total work of art (*Gesamtkunstwerk*) music obviously dominates; according to some of Wagner's directives, however, "the word" was primary. In his case, were the word primary, absolute disaster would have ensued. (It cannot be shown that the libretti of say Da Ponte or Hofmannsthal are inferior to Wagner's, just because the former do not go in for amateur philosophizing.

On the contrary: in Wagner's thought and verse we have a close analogy to the style of Wilhelm II's Reich in architecture and in politics.) Here Wagner is close to the least attractive side of Nietzsche, which appears for instance in his blood-and-thunder vulgarization of the Renaissance, so vastly different from Burckhardt's interpetation. Had the *Gesamtkunstwerk* ideal prevailed, one would expect that the thrust of Wagner's ideas—what Aristotle called "thought"—would be clear. Aside from Shaw, however, the most intelligent Wagnerites do not pretend to define the central intention of the *Ring,* and generally speaking, the Master's ventures into the realm of the intellect bring back either the false or the obvious. With a few brilliant exceptions—like Abraham Lincoln or Friedrich Schiller—the worst pedants are not the professors but the autodidacts. How pleasant though to read that Wagner, in his successful old age, turned away from the semi-intellectual theories of his *Kampf.* Swept away by Shakespeare, on whom he had once, with characteristic modesty, looked down (III, 109), Wagner tacitly abandoned the total work of art and clearly implied that a work that stayed within its own genre was, other things being equal, the best. That is at least the opinion of Thomas Mann,[50] with Bernard Shaw perhaps the only Wagnerian of our century who is both morally and intellectually worthy of our respect. And even Mann had very grave reservations about the composer.

V Nietzsche and the Myth

It should have *sung*, this "new soul" not spoken.

—Nietzsche on *The Birth of Tragedy*

It is hardly fair to a writer like Nietzsche, so
poetical, fragmentary, and immature, to judge him
as a philosopher.

—Santayana

Perhaps the best way of "placing" Nietzsche is to compare
his intellectual profile with those of his sometime friend,
Richard Wagner, and his most respected colleague and mentor, Jacob Burckhardt. Inevitably, such comparisons involve
simplifications, but they have their uses.

Essentially, we may regard Nietzsche as the deeply committed thinker, Wagner as the artist, the *Theatermensch* who
in the long run built a broad public. (Poor Nietzsche's fate
was the opposite: his books were crushingly unpopular until
after his collapse.) At once we must modify this contrast:
Nietzsche's prose, aside from a few miscarriages, is clearly
"art," far more so than any of Wagner's literary efforts.
Wagner was that frequent phenomenon, the "intellectual"
who is not really very intelligent, least of all when he is being
"intellectual," as his championing of anti-Semitism, chauvinism, soothsaying,[1] and so forth demonstrates. To mis-
quote T. S. Eliot: Wagner had a mind so gross that any idea
could violate it. This factor, however, is largely offset by his
shrewdness. As we have seen, he wrote *Parsifal* while himself a decided unbeliever, being far too astute to base an opera

on an anti-Semitic or vegetarian theme. This "Christian" pose horrified Nietzsche. It is true that some of Nietzsche's notions, like the "blond beast," are as absurd as any of Wagner's, but one does sense behind them, despite the famous "masks" he liked to wear, a genuine religious search, whereas in Wagner it is a matter of a—perfectly legitimate—search for recognition and audience. Possibly he really believed the Wagnerite propaganda about Redemption and Truth that emanated from Bayreuth, but for all his egotism, I doubt it. Equally egotistic, Nietzsche had a fanatic sense of truthfulness: he ends his polemic *The Wagner Case* with the "demands" that the theater shall not lord it over the other arts; that the actor (= Wagner) shall not seduce honest folk; and that "music shall not become an art of lying."[2]

These are in part paradoxical demands for the author of *The Birth of Tragedy* to make, and the whole relationship is largely paradoxical. In Nietzsche one has a genuine ascetic who preached the bold, full life; in Wagner, a Schopenhauerian renouncer of the world who managed to live in luxury much of the time, whether he had any money of his own or not. Both were extremely ambitious, competitive, agonistic, to use that favorite word of Jacob Burckhardt's. Nietzsche was a sort of anti-Establishment preacher, Wagner primarily a great showman; but as Goethe pointed out in *Faust*, these two professions may very well coincide. Nietzsche's work was his life: when he tried to "live" like other men, as in his pathetic attempts at relations with women, the results were grotesque or worse. On the other hand, Wagner's life and work are distinct if interconnected areas. Naturally, poor Hans von Bülow thought that Wagner's life was as disgraceful as his work was great,[3] but from the composer's point of view both endeavors must have seemed extremely successful. Wagner's stance is very "Teutonic": anti-French, anti-Roman, anti-Semitic; Nietzsche's position is usually much the reverse. Alas, as will appear, he is not the complete Good European by any means, though certainly far above Bayreuth standards.

Yet the two men had a great deal in common. Not that they were contemporaries—Nietzsche was thirty-one years younger—but they were after all nineteenth century Germans, observers of the new Reich founded by Bismarck, and affected by certain aesthetic currents of the later nineteenth century. Hermann Hesse wrote that the music of both Wagner and his hated rival Brahms is overorchestrated.[4] Similarly, it has been remarked of Wagner that his music sweats. And what of the style of *Zarathustra*, with its strange mixture of passion, prophecy, and parody? Like the later works, it is marred by a crass superabundance of emphasized words and exclamation points. The effect is that of a person who screams for fear that people are not seriously listening; it is also extremely adolescent. If Nietzsche had lowered his voice, it has been suggested, perhaps more people would have really listened. But of course his impact on literature, philosophy, and scholarship was enormous, and sometimes disastrous; in Germany people did listen. Further, if one is propounding doctrines like "the superman" or "master morality" it is only natural to shout. There is a profound psychological similarity —I am not speaking of influence—between such flashy notions and Wilhelm II's phrases "place in the sun," "yellow peril," and so forth.

Nietzsche's relation to Jacob Burckhardt is easier to describe. On the one hand, the young philologist is very much the radical compared to the historian of art. Although not a believing Christian, Burckhardt did not scorn or denounce the church or ordinary middle-class morality. Even in history he found a moral element, and as we have seen, he thought that the truly great man must have "a grain of kindness."

One would search Burckhardt's works in vain for crude constructions like the superman. With all this, one might expect Nietzsche to look down on Burckhardt as stodgy and timid, but one would be wrong. While there are some hints that he found him at times a bit too cautious, Nietzsche writes of and to Burckhardt, consistently, with admiration and affection. He had lost his own father when he was five; here was a man whom he could genuinely revere.

Undoubtedly the agonistic element was Nietzsche's most characteristic trait: he carried competitiveness to a fault and beyond. Going beyond Goethe, who had asked: "Does one live, when others live?" he had inquired: "If there were a God, how could I bear not to be he?" (II, 344). Unlike Goethe, he appears more than half serious here. As Havelock Ellis wrote, Nietzsche had the intellectual pride of Marlowe's Faustus.[5] Crane Brinton notes his "sense of mission—mission to do something great";[6] the word "mission" neatly implies Nietzsche's evangelical aspect. Walter Kaufmann finds him agonistic in his very nature;[7] the notorious Nazi Alfred Rosenberg, speaking at Weimar a few months before his death, suggests rather intelligently that the central problem of Nietzsche's life was: "Is greatness possible—today?"[8] Hitler's minister gives the impression that fascist "greatness" has about run its course, but keeps a stiff upper lip. Only Santayana sees clearly the high cost of Nietzsche's agonistic attitude, contrasting Winckelmann's "real sympathy" with the Greeks to the patronizing attitude of later German scholars.[9] Perhaps only a non-German would have the perspective to make such an observation.

Nietzsche was jealous of every great German whose fame interfered with his own.[10] Possibly this observation may seem exaggerated, but it is borne out by the facts. Despite all his respect for Burckhardt, he considered him a rival.[11] From early on there was an agonistic element in his relationship with Wagner, quite apart from the matter of Nietzsche's at least partly unconscious love for Cosima, and when he shrewdly attributes Wagner's energy to desire for power, he is also saying something about himself.[12] As with the Greeks, jealousy and envy were the bad side of a strong, aristocratic sense of rank. His essay "Richard Wagner in Bayreuth" (1876), largely favorable to the composer, stresses Wagner's desire for power, his boundlessly tyrannical urges, fortunately held in check by a basically good disposition (I, 372).

Even as a student, Nietzsche was rather the keen competitor than the selfless scholar. He was afraid that his dynamic and unconventional teacher Friedrich Ritschl would sweep him into the study of Classics against his will; precisely that happened.[13] At twenty-four, Nietzsche found himself professor of Classics at the excellent university of Basel, victor in a contest he had not really desired to win. Even at this point, aesthetic, philosophical, even musical matters interested him more than philology or history. In an early Basel lecture, "Homer and Classical Philology," he came to the programmatic conclusions "philosophia facta est quae philologia fuit"—What used to be philology has been transformed into philosophy (III, 174). Earlier that year he had written his friend Erwin Rohde, who was himself to become a fine classical scholar, that fate was diabolically luring him, Nietzsche-Faust, with a professorship;[14] still earlier, he had equated the role of the philologist with Goethe's Wagner.[15]

It would be futile to stress the agonistic element further, were it not so intimately connected with most of Nietzsche's leading ideas and tendencies. It is closely linked with the will to power, which might be paraphrased "will to excel." The superman, of course, is he who has won the great contest; Zarathustra preaches an agonistic way of life, and so on.

Only in his middle, so-called rationalistic period did Nietzsche praise the hero who acted without thought of competition (I, 1003).

Further, those figures of the past and present with whom Nietzsche competes are generally figures whom he both hates and loves. It would be hard to think of another significant thinker who is, in the full sense of the word, so ambivalent. In some moods, he makes Socrates one of the major villains of all history, a "decadent," rationalistic type who slew the tragic culture of the Greeks; yet he admitted being particularly drawn to him (III, 333). His attitude toward Plato is comparable (II, 1028f; III, 652).[16] Despite his denunciations of Wagner, there is no reason to doubt his statement that the composer was the greatest benefactor of his life (II, 1092). Admiring Goethe enormously, he parodied and otherwise mocked him; he stood Schopenhauer's philosophy on its head, as radically as Marx had inverted Hegel's.

Nietzsche vied with gods as well as men. To what extent he competes with Dionysus, who seems at first to be Wagner cum vine leaves, but later resembles Nietzsche himself, is hard to say; and Apollo soon vanishes from the scene. In his last, semi-sane years he is the Antichrist but often identifies himself with the Crucified;[17] Dionysus is the antithesis but may himself be allied with Jesus. To the mythical mind, such contradictions do not contradict. Nietzsche claimed always to have written respectfully about Jesus, and this seems relatively accurate. In general, Nietzsche moves from emulation of these divine figures to identification with them—the very height of hubris. In *Twilight of the Idols* (1889), he described a walk along the Po as "the leisure of a god" (II, 1145); he was hardly joking. During his years of insanity, Nietzsche at times thought he was God—and at other times identified himself with two notorious murderers of women.[18]

Several of Nietzsche's "mad" letters refer to himself as the Crucified, others as Dionysus. It is the old neopagan dream of the great synthesis of Athens and Jerusalem, roses and the Cross, this time carried literally to the point of insanity. If Nietzsche could reconcile the two forces, would he not be the supreme victor in the great contest of history?

Nietzsche's first book, *The Birth of Tragedy* (1872), shows him competing not nearly as much with philologists as with philosophers, aestheticians, and psychologists. At the same time it introduces the reader to Nietzsche's most exciting, central, and debatable concept, the Dionysian. (Personally, Nietzsche was anything but Dionysian, any more than he was a superman or a blond beast; it was an extreme case of compensation. Often he was happily intoxicated with words; a glass of wine was however too much for him; beer too vulgar.) To publish this book, as a professor of Classics, was a brave, not to say rash act. It is not primarily that its theses were heretical, but the whole approach is "poetic," emotional, unduly romantic, as Nietzsche himself later admitted (I, 9–18). It is as if an Oxford professor of Elizabethan literature had come out with a lyrical book maintaining that Bacon wrote Shakespeare. (In fact, Nietzsche rather thought that Bacon had; III, 516). Even Nietzsche's eloquent style might have been forgiven him by his professorial rivals, but he showed little interest in objective truth, still less in logic. This jeopardized the very ethos of the profession, and Wilamowitz-Moellendorf was quite justified in attacking the book, though he later regretted the whole campaign.[19] Nietzsche's former teacher and mentor Friedrich Ritschl described the book as "brilliant dizziness."[20] Even today, opinions of excellent scholars vary radically, indeed diametrically. Thus the subtitle of Martin Vogel's superbly documented *Apollinisch und Dionysisch* is "Geschichte eines genialen Irrtums"—The

History of a Brilliant Error. He finds that Nietzsche is generally wrong about historical and philological matters and usually misleading about mythology. Perhaps Vogel throws out Dionysus with the wine, but when he writes, repeatedly, that a theory cannot be *tief*, deep, unless it is in accord with the facts, one is reminded of Lessing. On the other hand, Gerard Else writes of the "stunning impact" made by the book, and its "unforgettable power"; he feels that Nietzsche had an admirable insight into the nature of the Dionysian and, further, that remarks in the *Poetics* about the dithyramb and the satyr play support Nietzsche's statements.[21] Along with many errors and distortions, Nietzsche did provide dazzling, at times frightening insights into the human psyche and into a certain kind of tragedy.

To the Dionysiac elements—intoxication, dynamism, the transcendence of individuality in a mystic oneness—the Apollonian principles of clear visual form, dream, classic beauty are opposed. Nietzsche's images of these two gods often do not correspond with the Greek concepts, nor was that really his aim; his Dionysus is fairly authentic, but his Apollo was largely his own invention. In general, he is extremely fallible as a classicist.[22] He operates with one of those sets of bipolarities so dear to German intellectuals, like "naive/sentimental," "classic/romantic," "representation/will." Thus the Dionysiac, with the rejection of individuation and its stress on sex, seems to come straight from the "will" of Schopenhauer, though it was also of course a genuine Greek phenomenon. It is also linked to wine, to nature, to ecstatic music. (Nietzsche cites as Dionysian first Beethoven's setting of Schiller's hymn "To Joy," later the *Ring*.) When he stubbornly insists that the Dionysian is not romantic, one may be amazed; Nietzsche uses the term, however, in the narrow sense of many German critics to mean withdrawal from the world, the cult of death à la Novalis and others. In the broader, European sense Dionysus represents the height of romanticism. Realizing that life is tragic and cruel, the Dionysiac man nevertheless accepts and even glorifies it; this acceptance remains a cardinal principle of Nietzsche, long after he had distanced himself from the book. In every tragic hero Nietzsche saw (or *said* that he saw) the features of Dionysus behind the mask (I, 61). As we shall see, Dionysus, being linked with music here, was very close to the Dionysiac composer Richard Wagner.[23]

Through a sort of mystic marriage between the Dionysiac and the Apollonian, tragedy arises. Now the Apollonian is not really the equal of the Dionysiac, though it helps to tame and refine it. Rather, the Dionysian, in its tragic awareness, projects the vision of classic beauty and harmony on a chaotic, dissonant world (I, 21–40 *et passim*); this Apolline illusion, deriving from Winckelmann's ideal of Greece, Schopenhauer's "representation" (*Vorstellung*), and possibly from that too pretty statue, the Apollo Belvedere, is a beneficent fiction, which obviously would have no existence unless the raw, vital Dionysiac had engendered it. Here there is a quite striking analogy to Freud's "ego" and "id," but Nietzsche was not thinking much about psychology at this point.

Clearly, this Apollo hails not from Athens but from Basel or from Wagner's refuge, Tribschen. Despite Nietzsche, Apollo, though the leader of the Muses, was not primarily an aesthetic divinity; he was the patron of civilization as a whole, including public order. It has been authoritatively shown that he was not the god of dreams, nor was there in antiquity any deep opposition between Apollo and Dionysus.[24] As the sun god, he was indeed "the shining one," but it was unworthy of Nietzsche to play on the two meanings of *scheinen*, "seem" and "shine," in order to reduce Apollo to the level of beautiful appearance—that is, illusion. Surely Nietzsche knew better; and one cannot imagine Lessing or Goethe, Schiller or Burckhardt, deliberately manipulating the evidence in this way. At this point, obviously, Nietzsche had no interest in the authentic Apollo; it would have been far more logical to choose another symbol. Already a dangerous subjectivity appears: "words mean what I say they mean!" In any case, the Apollonian element soon disappears from the scene, being virtually absorbed by a broader concept of the Dionysian, as will appear.

Some lesser points are of interest. Anticipating later developments, Nietzsche is anti-Christian and anti-Semitic in a muted sort of way. The noble man or "Aryan" does not sin, whatever his offense; the Semite who does sin, as in his myth of the Fall, reveals a series of feminine traits (I, 56, 59). The train of thought "inferior"—"Semite"—"woman" is revealing. In his treatment of Euripides and to some extent of Socrates,[25] a strongly anti-rationalistic note is sounded; Nietzsche, like Wagner at the time, is still much under the spell of German romanticism. Unable to ignore the existence of Euripides' *Bacchae,* no doubt the most potent Dionysian work in existence, Nietzsche interprets it in a way to reduce Euripides—a great lyric poet in his choruses and the "most tragic" of dramatists according to Aristotle—to a mere propagandist (I, 70 f). In a very nostalgic way, Nietzsche laments the loss of myths as such—"the loss of the mythic homeland, the mythic womb"; one recalls the German "quest for myth," from Herder on.[26] In typical romantic fashion he contrasts the myth-informed life to "abstract education, abstract *mores,* abstract law, the abstract state" (I, 125). When he writes that at some point science (or scholarship) must become art (I, 84 f), he is obviously autobiographical. How often, alas, he fell between the stools! *The Birth of Tragedy* is certainly not scholarship; despite brilliant, even beautiful passages, it is not art either, for it has no focus, no center. Although he had turned away from Wagner, Nietzsche let himself be persuaded to devote the last sections of his book to that composer,[27] who was despite all a sort of father figure to him. Thus it turned out a three-headed monster: (a) The Birth of Tragedy, proper; (b) The Death of Tragedy, slain by the nasty, rationalistic Euripides and Socrates; (c) The Birth of Music Drama: *Richard Wagner über Alles.*

Since the last part of the book is propaganda in which the author himself did not believe, it is predictably enough of inferior quality. Nietzsche implies that his older friend is going to give a new birth to the myth, via music (I, 95), a rather complicated obstetrical metaphor. Dionysus will gain the upper hand over Apollo in the realm of musical drama (I, 109). References to Wagner abound as to Dionysus; some sort of deep bond between the two is obvious. Even Martin Luther is trotted out, compared to a bird, and labeled "Dionysiac" (I, 126). Who would have dared that to his face? The word "Dionysiac" occurs ever more often, not as a skillfully placed leitmotiv but apparently *faute de mieux.* The bird that converses with Siegfried is, although sober, a "Dionysian bird" (I, 128). Doubtless under Wagnerian influence, Nietzsche becomes uncharacteristically chauvinistic, using verbiage like "Aus dem dionysischen Grunde des deutschen Geistes"—from the Dionysiac depths of the German spirit (I, 109); and he holds that the German must fight for the return of everything German; he may need a *Führer* to guide him home (I, 128). References to Siegfried, Wotan, and so forth abound, and Nietzsche manages to get back to his main theme only by a *salto mortale* in the last paragraph, in which he restates his belief that Greek beauty and Greek suffering presuppose one another.

To return to Dionysus: in the later works he becomes ever more a universal symbol, freed from intimate connection with Greek myth and with the drama; he is no longer primarily an "art god." God is dead (I, 115); long live the god Dionysus! His positive character is the acceptance of all life (II, 253 *et passim*), which inevitably includes the negative, even death. He embraces cruelty and extreme sensuality, also the destruction of the noblest values in the name of the future (II, 59; III, 912), a tenet that would of course appeal to the Nazis and other extremists. Like Carlyle, whom Nietzsche despised (II, 718), Dionysus was a mighty yea-sayer. Indeed, "yea" must be stronger than "nays" and doubts; men must force themselves to a faith, presumably the Dionysian (II, 253). By 1886 the god is now the great tempter, ambiguous, a pied piper, a philosopher (II, 754f); shall we add, a former professor of Classics? He becomes increasingly Nietzschean in *Ecce Homo* (written 1888), where Zarathustra is identified with the superman and then with Dionysus (II, 1135f), all obviously aspects of the author, though the identification was not to become absolute as long as Nietzsche was reasonably sane.

In Nietzsche's *Nachlass* (work published posthumously) he gives a bombastic yet clear definition of what might well seem indefinable: the Dionysiac. The word expresses: "an urge to unity, a going beyond individuality, the everyday, society, 'reality,' beyond the abyss of perishing: the passionate-painful swelling over into darker, more abundant, more volatile conditions; an ecstatic yea-saying to the total character of life as the element that is equal in all charges, equally powerful, equally blissful, the great pantheistic communal joy, communal suffering, which sanctions and hallows even the most terrible and questionable aspects of life; the eternal will to procreate, to be fertile, to return; the unified feeling of the necessity of creating and destroying" (III, 791). This is purple prose indeed, and, as Irving Babbitt liked to say, "It sounds better in German." Goethe said it all infinitely better in one line: "Wie es auch sei, das Leben, es ist gut"—However life may be, it is [essentially] good.[28] Goethe however was writing poetry, not maintaining as a philosophical proposition that life, under all conditions, is good. We shall never know whether the disciple of Schopenhauer really believed in life as the absolute value, or whether this doctrine was a compensation for a personal life singularly lacking in success, beauty, or even a minimal amount of wealth or ordinary domestic happiness.

Since the late works of Goethe are often considered classical, and since Nietzsche maintains that the Dionysiac is also classical, he is able to ally the two. He draws an impressive sketch of Goethe as the Dionysian total man, the realist, the free spirit who accepted life (II, 1024 f).[29] But nothing is gained and much lost by pinning the label "Dionysian" on the poet who created "the spirit who denies" and who was also the poet of renunciation. Walt Whitman would have filled Nietzsche's bill—or even Lou Andreas-Salomé. This labeling seems all the more futile in view of Nietzsche's flat statement that Goethe did not understand the Dionysiac: *"Therefore Goethe did not understand the Greeks"* (II, 1031). We have here the curious phenomenon of a Dionysian poet who allegedly did not understand his own nature, and are aghast to see where bipolar thinking can lead us.

In Nietzsche's very private mythology, the successor to Dionysus is the prophet Zarathustra. One associates the historical Zoroaster or Zarathustra with the most extreme dualism, the cosmic battle between Light and Dark, absolute Good and absolute Evil. Nietzsche made Zarathustra a monist, believing that a complete dualist would be the first to see the error of his ways.[30] Like Dionysus, Nietzsche's prophet accepts the universe in a "holy yea-saying" (II, 294). Although only a man, he is not dwarfed by the memory of the God. He is the mouthpiece of Nietzsche's central doctrines: will to power, vitalism, the superman, eternal return, *amor fati,* and —against his will so to speak—nihilism. He says "yea" not only to life, but to the whole circular, eternally repetitious pattern of existence. *Thus Spoke Zarathustra* (1883–91) is accordingly probably the central work of Nietzsche; it is his best known and presumably his most influential work. In more than one generation it has proved to be a disease, indeed an epidemic, of adolescence, more widespread than say the vogue of Herbert Marcuse or R. D. Laing today. It is by no means Nietzsche's best book.

We are first struck by the utterly synthetic nature of the work. Nietzsche's Dionysus is still recognizable as a Greek god, even when linked with Wagner; Zarathustra is an ad hoc creation.[31] Having been up in the mountains for ten years, he comes down at the age of forty (Nietzsche was thirty-nine when the first and second parts of *Zarathustra* appeared) to preach to men. Thus the prophet is an extension of the philosopher. Yet what shall we say of the founder of a new weltanschauung, if not a new religion, who has to *invent* his own prophet? While brilliant insights and phrasings do indeed appear, not too frequently, in the almost three hundred pages of the book, it lacks the youthful verve of *The Birth of Tragedy* and, on the whole, the wit and sharpness of *Human, All Too Human* and *Beyond Good and Evil.* Unfortunately it is extremely repetitious, both verbally and in incident. The pseudo-biblical stance is doubly regrettable: it is pretentious—who was Nietzsche to compete with Luther? —and it took him too far from his real métier, "straight" prose. Some of Nietzsche's admirers have shared his delusion that he was a great lyricist, but he was rather the *poète manqué* than the *poète maudit*.

In style, Nietzsche deliberately parodies the Bible, in both a vicious and a more neutral sense, for example: "Unless we repent and become as the cows, we shall never enter the Kingdom of Heaven" (II, 506). Much of the vocabulary is biblical, as are the rhythm of many sentences and the instances of *Gedankenreim*—the statement of the same thought in two linked clauses or sentences. Compare "Lift up your heads, O ye gates; and be ye lift up, ye everlasting doors." At the same time there are, in harsh contrast, neologisms of Nietzsche's own invention, very prosaic words like "seasickness," and a good many puns. When Zarathustra makes a descent from the mountains, the term used is *Untergang* (also meaning downfall). Even the punctuation is hectic.

There is an abundance of imagery, mainly of a romantic flavor: a bridge over the abyss, mountains, brave mariners, ships, sea, and streams, war and warriors, arrow of longing for the other shore. The last is particularly revealing. While Nietzsche has been regarded as the great conqueror of romanticism, it is rather that he was a romanticist of a new sort. What could be more romantic than the concept of the superman itself? If we associate the term with science fiction, that is not unjust. As the Bible says, a man cannot add one cubit to his stature. Further, death must become a festival (II, 334); on the other hand, the familiar topos of the Happy Isles reappears. Zarathustra-Nietzsche, described as a wanderer, urges us to love what is farthest away, and stresses his own mountain loneliness, like Byron's Manfred. Nietzsche, though allegedly anti-romantic, enormously admired that drama (I, 1126). Like Wagner's operas, *Thus Spoke Zarathustra* is a belated product of German romanticism.

Of course this is a question of literary locus, not of rank

nor of quality. Nor does the fact that *Zarathustra* excellently conforms to Nietzsche's own definition of a decadent style necessarily say anything against it. In *The Case of Wagner* Nietzsche wrote: "What is characteristic of every literary *décadence?* The fact that life no longer resides in the whole. The word becomes sovereign and jumps out of the sentence, the sentence encroaches on the page and obscures its meaning, the page gains life at the expense of the whole—the whole is no longer a whole" (II, 917). Nietzsche claims that Wagner's music is decadent in this sense. However that may be, in reading the definition one cannot help remembering how a single italicized word often dominates a whole paragraph of *Zarathustra,* or how a single crassly sensational metaphor, like that of the shepherd who must bite off the head of a serpent intruded into his mouth, encroaches upon a whole chapter. Some striking, often brilliant formulations are equally aggressive, stylistically speaking, like the often repeated statement: "Man is something that must be overcome." In criticizing Wagner, Nietzsche is of course criticizing himself, and *Zarathustra* is probably his most Wagnerian, least subtle work. Small wonder that Wagner's most spectacular successor, Richard Strauss, was inspired by it to write a bombastic tone poem. In *The Wagner Case,* Nietzsche unsurprisingly calls Wagner a decadent (II, 903); it *is* surprising that he gives himself the same label (II, 903). Of course decadence is to be preferred to a stupid, bovine sort of health.

Doubtless, the central concept of *Zarathustra* is the superman (or overman), *der Übermensch.* It has been well shown how important compounds with *über-* are in the book:[32] We have for instance the superhero and above all the key verb *überwinden,* to surpass, transcend. Obviously, Nietzsche's view of life is still predominantly agonistic. Further, much as he looked down on Darwin (and on practically all other Englishmen), it is hard not to be reminded of doctrines of evolution when Nietzsche writes that the monkey is a source of painful shame to man; similarly, man will inspire such shame in the superman (II, 279). Nietzsche rejected the term "struggle for existence," preferring "will to power"; the factual difference between the slogans does not seem great, however.

Nietzsche puts it dramatically: "God died: now *we* [his emphasis] will—that the superman shall live" (II, 523).[33] How interesting that the willing of nonsupermen is so important in this process. Apparently Zarathustra, like his author, is not quite a superman but a John the Baptist, an "arrow of longing for the other shore." Real supermen are heroes of the caliber of Napoleon, Caesar, Goethe, or Frederick II of Hohenstaufen (II, 656f). One of the great virtues of the new man is to be instinctive good taste. Avoiding the "spirit of heaviness," he will know when to laugh, when to dance, as the rabble does not (II, 529). (One thinks of Stefan George's image "the Christian dancing.") At the same time, a man must keep alive "the hero in his soul" (II, 309), and, like Aristotle's great-souled man, he must practice the generous virtues (II, 336–338). Above all, man must remain "true to this earth," shunning any delusion that there may be another world, and consistently enough, true to the body (II, 280, 298f). Sick men of a dying culture sought redemption through "drops of blood": the reference to the New Testament is obvious. Supernaturally oriented persons are dubbed "backworldsmen," and the superman is sharply distinguished from the mere "higher man," who seems to be only a cultivated member of the old order. Zarathustra tells his disciples that the superman is and shall be the "meaning of earth" (II, 280), as it were the "far-off . . . event/Toward which the whole creation moves." Thus we are in a quasi-religious situation with Zarathustra as the none too secularized preacher. Precisely because of his eloquence, one suspects, he is more useful to Nietzsche than that earlier yea-sayer Dionysus: Greek gods do not deliver sermons. It is typically Nietzschean that he has presented us with a glittering faith in which no one really believes: what comfort are the next century's supermen to me in my personal, existential situation? It is done with mirrors, like the Rhine Maidens' singing under water. Santayana well said that the superman was not a possibility but a protest.[34] Goethe, who came as close to this lofty status as any modern, used the term only twice, in both cases ironically.[35]

In any case, another belief or obsession of Nietzsche's threatened to devalue the happy creed of Superman: the eternal return. This is a pre-Socratic notion, which Nietzsche in his ruthless euphoria claimed to be his original creation. If, Nietzsche and perhaps Heraclitus argued, there is an infinity of time but limited space, then everything literally returns, again and again. One remembers those monkeys who could allegedly type all the books in the British Museum, given enough time. Actually, Shelley anticipated Nietzsche on this point, writing in the chorus to *Hellas:*

> The world's great age begins anew,
> The golden years return,
> The earth doth like a snake renew
> Her winter weeds outworn.

Shelley ends however:

> The world is weary of the past,
> Oh, might it die or rest, at last![36]

In an impressive mathematical proof, not understandable to outsiders (including me), Georg Simmel has shown that the return is a quite impossible doctrine:[37] Nietzsche, then, fudged the evidence to gain something not worth the effort, a pathetically all-too-human act. Even the pope of American Nietzscheans, Walter Kaufmann, does not question Simmel's proof.[38] It is however to Nietzsche's honor that he let his two largely false concepts, superman (super-Nietzsche?) and eternal return, fight it out throughout *Zarathustra*, which in fact becomes overlong and repetitious, mainly because of this very duel. The drastic metaphor or parable of the snake who pushes his head into the shepherd's mouth refers directly to this matter: the snake is an emblem of return; compare the "serpent of eternity." As Zarathustra tells the shepherd: the only hope of survival lies in biting off the snake's head; a repulsive act, but the shepherd performs it and is saved. To Nietzsche, eternal return was a metaphor for accepting life, living gladly; he presumably cared less about its mathematical correctness. Nevertheless, his lack of candor, to put it very mildly, about the origins of this false notion is less excusable in him than in the relatively uneducated, largely submoral Wagner. Nietzsche was the spoiled child of the Establishment; Wagner was the outsider who landed his paratroopers on undefended brains. What Nietzsche was really getting at with his all too ingenious doctrine is expressed in the line that states that all pleasure, happiness, lust, or desire—*Lust* means any or all of these—aspires to last forever. *Denn alle Lust will—Ewigkeit* (II, 557). (He was a strange champion of "life" indeed. What is one to make of this undersexed Dionysus from Naumburg and Basel?) His most striking contribution is to say, against Schopenhauer, that life is a good. Very well: but had not Spinoza, Goethe, and Stendhal said this better, long before?

When Nietzsche's shepherd bit off the snake's head, it was an acceptance of reality, however repulsive, and thus an expression of what he called with increasing frequency *amor fati*. As Kaufmann points out, the words remind us of Spinoza and the Stoics, and this is not coincidental.[39] When the doctrine of eternal return leads man to despair—even superman will fall, as did Greek tragedy—then by a supreme effort of will he can accept fate and vanquish despair. More: "eternal return" can easily lead to the conclusion that life and the universe are utterly meaningless, with the cycle repeating itself throughout infinity, without any real change. In this sense Goethe's Werther complained that nature was an "eternally ruminating monster,"[40] and Zarathustra himself was filled with loathing. Like Dionysus as he appears in Nietzsche's mature works (III, 834) and like Zarathustra, *amor fati* is a symbol of total acceptance. In a somewhat tortured sense, it overcomes nihilism, for acceptance is not a nihilistic gesture. It came to be the philosopher's formula for greatness in man, and he called it the highest stage a philosopher can reach. Obviously it implies total acceptance of life, free of whining or lamentation. It is a sublime concept, but only a superman could fulfill it completely.

Nietzsche is really an aesthetic not a philosophic man; we owe him much for his aesthetic *aperçus*, still more for providing the insights, mainly psychological, that Thomas Mann and others were to incorporate into literature. "It should have sung—this soul"; and in Mann's books, Nietzsche's works are thus saved from the Bertrams and Rosenbergs and do sing, becoming components of works of art. In fact, they had contributed to German literature generally, from 1890 through the Nazi period, especially to the Expressionists. Only on a few authentically great artists like Mann, Rilke, George, Gide, and possibly Benn—"the poet of the economic miracle"[41]—was Nietzsche's impact really significant however, whereas he briefly influenced almost everyone writing in or near central Europe. It is like Byron's description of himself as "the grand Napoleon of the realm of rhyme." [42]

Since *Zarathustra*, from one point of view, is a series of sermons, it is naturally much concerned with morality. Clearly, it assumes the absolute division between slave and master, a morality that Nietzsche propounded in *Beyond Good and Evil* and *The Genealogy of Morals*. In the great contest to reach the superman, only superior men, aristocrats of the spirit, have the slightest chance. (Nietzsche had little interest in so-called race in a biological sense, but was considerably impressed by social rank.) On the whole, his ethic is that of sixth century Greece as he saw it. It is sternly aristocratic, with generosity offsetting hardness. This quality is like the discipline of the athlete; "Let whatever makes us hard, be praised!" Zarathustra exclaims. Hardness is linked with health, without which no great discoveries or achievements are possible (II, 404, 258). More, one must be hard to whatever is obsolete, rotten, or decadent and hasten its complete ruin (II, 455). Two forces, both Christian or Judeo-Christian in origin, threaten the Zarathustrian ethic: compassion *(Mitleid)* and the otherworldly. As will appear, Nietzsche was a far more compassionate person than is generally realized, also sensitive and easily upset; he turned to figures like Cesare Borgia and the notorious "beast of prey" as antidotes for his own softness. Compassion, to him, was the cross on which the lover of mankind was nailed (II, 281). Very late in his career, Nietzsche maintained that feeling pity robbed a man of power; it is or leads to nihilism (II, 1168). In the poem "Sternen-Moral" he pointed out that for the star, the higher man, compassion was a sin:

> Der fernsten Welt gehört dein Schein!
> Mitleid soll Sünde für dich sein!   (II, 32)

(Your radiance belongs to the world farthest away!/Compassion shall be, for you, a sin!) Yet as usual, he is not consistent, remarking a bit earlier that one must have strong powers of imagination in order really to pity: morality is closely bound to the intellect (I, 491). And almost his last free act, on the day of his collapse in Turin, was to throw his arms around the neck of a horse which had just been flogged by its driver. More drastically even than in Hölderlin's case, a long suppressed instinct seems to have risen from the depths of Nietzsche's psyche. However grotesque in form, the breakdown is a shattering thing to contemplate.

As mentioned, the other great threat to Zarathustra's ethic is otherworldliness. Zarathustra shoots sharp arrows, not of longing but of satire, at the "backworldsmen." Utterly rejecting the notion of another world, either religious or metaphysical (Kant's realm of *noumena*), Nietzsche had come to believe that belief in an "other" world was a sign of cowardice, stupidity, or both. "The world is deep, and deeper than the day has thought!" (II, 555). No need to invent another. Later, in less poetic language, he proclaimed that the world was "will to power and nothing else" (II, 601; III, 917). In two special sections of the book, and from time to time elsewhere, Zarathustra gets after the "despisers of the body" as well as the backworldsmen. The satiric parts of the work are generally the best, and these are no exception.

Nietzsche's hard ethics naturally lead him to a high estimation of war and warriors, in *Zarathustra* and elsewhere. The "gentle" Nietzscheans—to use Crane Brinton's term—explain his apparent militarism simply as imagery; the "tough" ones, like the gifted but very Nazi professor Alfred Bäumler, state that he meant what he said. Since they can stick to the text without indulging in dialectics or other fancy maneuvers, the "toughs" have a considerable advantage. To complicate matters, we must remember Nietzsche's ambivalence, his consistent inconsistency. Further, as has been pointed out, an author draws his imagery from realms that intrigue him; thus even if Nietzsche's every reference to war were metaphorical —which is by no means the case—it would still be very revealing that "this new soul" sang so much of martial matters.[43]

During the two world wars, Nietzsche was handled rather badly by Western writers. In the first, his name was linked with the notorious Prussian historian Heinrich von Treitschke —partly because the two names could easily be confused. Further, some of Nietzsche's gaudier notions, like the superman and the cult of power, do indeed seem to anticipate the Nazis. Again, who can honorably pretend that "power" to Nietzsche meant only intellectual, sublimated power? That would reduce him from a proto-superman to a professor, the last thing he wanted. Nietzsche, presumably, would not have become a Nazi; he is for example largely though not wholly philo-Semitic. Still less, however, would he have become a liberal, a democrat, or a socialist. That he rejected England (which he never saw), democracy (experienced to some extent in Switzerland), liberalism, and socialism (II, 720, 687, 1014) speaks clearly enough. We should not put a brown shirt on Nietzsche, but still less white shoes; he was not, even potentially, a liberal Ivy League professor.

Nietzsche's early studies of Greek literature favored hard, anti-democratic, warrior types; there is no evidence that this orientation ever changed. That he and Burckhardt wept when told—falsely of course—that the Louvre had been burned [44] puts them in a sympathetic light but does not mean that Nietzsche rejected the Franco-Prussian War, in which he served. Obviously the two Basel colleagues are vastly more attractive than Wagner, who rejoiced that the Parisians were reduced to eating rats.

At times it is perfectly evident that Nietzsche is using the term "war" quite literally. Thus he writes that substitutes for war are not enough; highly cultivated, slack people, like contemporary Europeans, need not only wars but the most terrible ones in order not to become too soft to survive (I, 688; II, 312). His notorious assertion that a good war hallows any cause should probably be read in this light. When he writes that war and courage have performed greater deeds than loving one's neighbor (II, 312), or prophetically states, in 1888, that man is entering the classical era of war, we have to take him at his word. Similarly, he called for men able to fight and women who could bear children (II, 457). At times "war" seems to denote any intense competition *(agon);* this would naturally include literal war. There is no reason, however, to suspect Nietzsche of harboring imperialistic plans. "Anti-Christian soldier/Marching *as* to war" would seem a fair description. Thus he referred to his literary campaigns against David Friedrich Strauss and Wagner as wars (I, 1113).

In some of Nietzsche's remarks, one notices an obsession with decadence and the remarkable belief that war is the appropriate antidote. Better dead than mauve! No fascist himself, Nietzsche gave the militarists a powerful if specious point: that there is something regenerative about war. Ernst Jünger's book "Storm of Steel" *(In Stahlgewittern,* 1920) is only one of many pernicious examples of this line of thought. Repeatedly Zarathustra warns against decadence and its end product nihilism. It is the superman who restores meaning to life and thus overcomes the decadence of those who despise it (II, 280).

An extreme type of decadent is the "last man," the end product of a civilization that cares only for comfort and physical well-being. His "life style" is anti-heroic and anti-romantic to the extreme; he is the ultimate bourgeois.

Look! I will show you *the last man* [spoke Zarathustra].
"What is love? What is creation? What is longing? What
is a star?"—so the last man asks and winks. Then the earth
became small, and on it hops the last man, who belittles
everything. His race is ineradicable like the earth-flea; the
last man lives longest.

"We have invented happiness"—say the last men and
wink. They have left the regions where it was hard to live,
for one needs warmth. [Compare the flight to Florida.] One
still loves his neighbor and rubs up against him, for one needs
warmth . . . .

A little poison: that causes pleasant dreams. And much
poison at the end, for a pleasant death. People still work, for
work is a pastime. But they take care that the pastime is not
too strenuous. People don't become poor or rich any more;
both are too much trouble. Who wants to rule any more?
Who to obey? Both are too much trouble.

No shepherd and *one* flock! Everyone wants the same,
everyone is the same; whoever feels differently, goes voluntarily to the madhouse.   (II, 284)

At the end of this speech, or rather parable, the people cry
for the last man—"Barabbas! Barabbas!"—and reject the
superman, one of the many echoes of the New Testament in
the book. Again, *Zarathustra* is most impressive as satire,
though one wonders how many of us would reject anesthesia
just to prove our heroic vitalism. Nietzsche has supplied a
fairly prophetic anti-Utopia, a completely egalitarian, ho-
mogenized society. A bit later, a "sage" who preaches sleep
and intellectual mediocrity—"the poor in spirit" (II, 296)—
makes essentially the same point.

Gradually the focus shifts from decadence to sheer nihilism. To Nietzsche that was the end point at which Christianity, democracy, and socialism converged. Because of
compassion and egalitarianism, all values are threatened or
have ceased to exist. In *Zarathustra* there is a fierce struggle
between nihilism and vitalism, with its slogan "Life above

all!" In the fragments written during the 1880s that later editors called "The Will to Power" [45] nihilism emerges vividly, even sensationally, the "uncanniest of all guests" (III, 881) at the European banquet. Either, we gather, "new tablets" will be created by the forces of life, or decadence and nihilism will take over. Given the eternal return, all this struggle seems futile: *che serà, serà*; but few Western philosophers, however fatalistic, urge man simply to fold his hands. Apparently, Nietzsche was increasingly aware that his highest goals were myths, like all goals; but he fought valiantly with and for his myths. In Nietzsche's view, the conservative Greek thinkers must have fought in much the same way against Socrates.

Nietzsche prefers the beneficent fiction or "vital lie" *(Lebenslüge)*, friendly to life, to the scientific, logical "truth" if and when the latter leads to nihilism and hence to death. Poets lie too much, he states, but must admit that Zarathustra is a poet, and even that gods and supermen (!) are brightly colored husks (II, 382f). Underneath the garish surface of Nietzsche's later work lurk despair and utter skepticism.

The only escape lies in a vitalism that has been called heroic but seems at times hectic, even desperate. The preface to *Human, All Too Human* reminds us that injustice is an integral part of life (I, 443). Nietzsche had long been persuaded that life is only aesthetically justifiable. In later works, cutting the Gordian knot completely, he established a complete opposition between life and morality (III, 887). Truth is often hostile to life, which depends upon will not intellect; the criterion of useful truth is will to power. In a preface to an unwritten book "The Greek State," Nietzsche proclaims, making our blood run cold like Dickens' Fat Boy, that "procreating, living, and murdering are the same" (III, 279). "Birth, and copulation, and death," T. S. Eliot, put it, avoiding Nietzsche's frantic overstating. However dreadful life may be, the good Nietzschean is to meet death with defiance: "Was that—life? I will say to death, Very well! Once more!" (II, 552). Given the eternal return, of course there will be "once mores" *ad infinitum* and literally *ad nauseam*. What raises this attitude above a merely instinctive desire to persist is the tenet that life is the element that must unceasingly overcome or surpass itself (II, 359, 372). Excellent, until we think of the eternal return. From this weltanschauung there is no exit; men are like squirrels in a cage; Nietzsche might well have gone mad even without his (presumable) syphilitic infection.

The term "life" oscillates, in a very uncontrolled way, between a neutral and a most honorific status. In German twentieth century literature, "life" and "youth," like later "blood," "soil," "race," are numinous terms, remaining so down to the Nazi defeat and in some cases even later. To the extent that Nietzsche's loose terminology and Zarathustrian eloquence misled highly seducible German "youth," he is to blame; but he is not really the pre-fascist type.

If truth is a threat to life, a nay-saying religion, like Christianity in Nietzsche's view, is far more so. There can be no doubt that is the main enemy, from *The Birth of Tragedy*, later described by the philosopher as radically anti-Christian (I, 15), to the last mad letters. Christianity is the enemy of normal love, health, strength, beauty, and truthfulness. With an assist from Judaism, it created slave morality and was thus ultimately responsible for the fall of Rome and the failure of the Renaissance: the whipping boy of world history. And yet, as Jaspers has shown, Nietzsche's thought grew out of Christianity and was spurred by Christian impulses.[46] Repeatedly, in *Zarathustra*, he implicitly appeals to a higher Christianity from a vulgar one. Do not repay evil with good, for that would shame your opposite number; rather, convince him that he has conferred a good upon you. Similarly, Zarathustra himself must repeatedly check, and thereby refine, his compassionate instincts. Obviously, Nietzsche, the son of a Protestant pastor, protests too much about his hatred. Yet Thomas Mann went too far in apostrophizing Nietzsche as a crypto-Christian, "who died for us all."[47] This appealing theory implies that Nietzsche deliberately incurred his illness and did so for the sake of mankind, but this view is not only psychologically improbable but self-contradictory.

Nietzsche's relation to Jesus, whom he considered the last and only Christian, is a very different matter. While he considered him a decadent, even in Dostoevsky's sense an idiot, he recognized Jesus' nobility (II, 1191f). Approvingly he views Christ as the overthrower of the law—that is, of codified morality—and the enemy of the hierarchy (II, 638; III, 658). Yet the dismembered Dionysus is still a symbol of life, while God on the Cross is a curse upon it; the contrast in interpretation is not really explained (III, 773). In the very late *The Antichrist* (1895) Nietzsche remarks that "we [gentlemen]" would avoid early Christians as we do Polish Jews: "they smell bad" (II, 1210). The reader is faced with a truly acute case of hate-love. Doubtless Jaspers is right in stating that Nietzsche identified himself with Jesus;[48] Kesselring seems equally correct, writing from a psychiatric point of view, to speak of jealousy.[49] *Zarathustra* includes both a tribute to Christ and a crass parody of the Last Supper.

Nietzsche's relation to the Jews, often debated, is at least as complicated as his attitude toward Jesus, but less ambivalent. On the whole he condemned Judaism as a life-denying, sin-obsessed religion that had given birth to that still more noxious creed, Christianity. On the other hand, broadly speaking, he considered Jewry one of the greatest races, and individual Jews he found far more interesting than Germans: "What a blessing to find a Jew among Germans!" he exclaimed (III, 806). (Possibly he stressed that point to punish his countrymen for ignoring him.)[50] While under the influence of Wagner, he was mildly anti-Semitic,[51] but thereafter wrote of anti-Semitism with the most biting scorn; this at a time when anti-Semitism was very chic in central Europe. Generally, he wrote admiringly of great Jewish figures like Spinoza and Heine; his nasty poem "To Spinoza" seems to be the product of one of those acute attacks of "agonistic" jealousy to which Nietzsche was prone.

Nietzsche's philo-Semitic statements are more numerous and more impressive than the hostile or lukewarm ones. The myth of the amoral, intriguing, greedy Jew leaves him virtually untouched; on the contrary it is the Jew as the representative of a "life-rejecting" religion whom he excoriates. In this sense he calls Plato a Jew (III, 564). Predictably, his comments are most consistently favorable in his "rationalistic" period. Thus he notes, not without a certain irony, that the Jews are the moral genius among nations; further, they have taught the Europeans to think more clearly and sharply (II, 132, 215). The Jews are the toughest and purest race, standing at the opposite pole to decadence, even though they lead all (!) decadent movements (II, 717, 1184f). Yet, Nietzsche implies, precisely the Jewish strengths stir up anti-Semitism; and he makes the shattering statement that he has never yet met a German who really liked Jews. As practical measures he proposes the cessation of Jewish immigration, combined with some intermarriage between the Prussian aristocracy and outstanding Jews (II, 717f)—in other words the partial fusion of two strong, superior "races."

In *Human, All Too Human* Nietzsche pays his most impressive tribute to the Jews. Perhaps, he concedes to the anti-Semites, "the young stock market Jew is the most repulsive invention of the human race"; that is no reason to make a scapegoat of the whole people. "Nevertheless I should like to know how much one should not forgive in a people . . . which not without the guilt of us all had the most sorrowful history of all peoples, and to whom we owe the noblest man (Christ), the purest sage (Spinoza), the mightiest book, and the most effective moral code in the world" (I, 685f).

We shall hear very different variations on this theme; the basic problem is that Nietzsche quite consistently opposed the biblical moral code, effective or not. Surely though, this quotation brings out a chivalrous side in his nature that is perhaps his most attractive trait. A late passage from *The Antichrist* makes the point that the Jews are the most remarkable people in world history: in order to survive at all, they had to live, consciously, against all the norms of nature (II, 1184). Here there is not bitterness, but it is claimed that the results were ruinous. Far more polemical, some passages from the *Nachlass* link the New Testament, which unlike the Old he loathed, with its Jewish authors and/or milieu and, by inescapable extension, with the Jews as such. (Although this *fleur du mal* is a growth of the 1880s, it cannot be excused as the product of derangement; it is lucid and, given Nietzsche's presuppositions, logical.) Possibly though, Nietzsche's inhibitions have weakened. To quote: "People of the lowest origin, in part rabble, outcasts not merely from good but even from [barely] respectable society, grown up far from even the *odor* of culture, without discipline, without knowledge, without any suspicion of the fact that there might be any conscience in spiritual matters, precisely—[these are] Jews" (III, 553). The Wagnerites could have said nothing more damaging, or as damagingly. On this vexed point it must be

said that Walter Kaufmann, impressive as a Nietzsche spe-
cialist, is far less responsible than Crane Brinton, whose
views on Nietzsche Kaufmann often rejoiced to correct.
Kaufmann explains away or ignores anti-Semitic passages;
possibly Brinton, writing in wartime, exaggerated their importance slightly, but I doubt it.

Little if any attention has been paid to Nietzsche's cata-
strophically anti-Semitic poems, one of which, in equating
Rome with a whore, uses Jewishness as a symbol of utter
degradation:

> Einstmals—ich glaub, im Jahr des Heiles Eins—
> Sprach die Sibylle, trunken sonder Weins:
> "Weh, nun geht's schief!
> "Verfall! Verfall! Nie sank die Welt so tief!
> "Rom sank zur Hure und zur Huren-Bude,
> "Roms Cäsar sank zum Vieh, Gott selbst—ward Jude!"
>   (II,486)

(Once—I think it was in A.D. One—/The Sybil spoke,
drunken without wine:/"Woe, now things are going wrong!/
Decay! Decay! Never sank the world so low!/Rome sank
to a whore and a whorehouse,/Rome's Caesar to a beast;
God himself—became a Jew!") Similarly, the "philosopher"
wrote about Spinoza's *Ethics*:

> Am Judengott frass Judenhass . . .
> Einseidler! hab ich dich erkannt? [52]

(Jewish hatred was eating away at the Jewish God . . ./Her-
mit! have I found you out?) Here Nietzsche's "unmasking
technique," recklessly applied, reduces the "purest sage's"
amor intellectualis dei to its opposite. As noted, jealousy of
Spinoza may well play its part too. Possibly the rhythm of
these rather crude verses helped to free unconscious prejudices. On the other hand, he invariably wrote favorably of

Heinrich Heine, perhaps because the poet was generally rejected by the "respectable" German public.

However Janus-faced Nietzsche's attitude toward the Jews may be, there is no ambiguity about his condemnation of anti-Semitism. The anti-Semite is a spiritual monstrosity, his views derive from *ressentiment* (roughly, the futile envy and resentment of the inferior for their betters; II, 1119, 814). In Wagner's case, anti-Semitism is indirectly linked with the composer's alleged decadence (II, 1054). A late note from the *Nachlass* puts things excellently: "The anti-Semites don't forgive the Jews for having brains [or "spirit"]—and money. The anti-Semites—a name for those who turn out badly" (III, 707). In his last, mad letter to Burckhardt, in which he identifies himself with Christ, Nietzsche states that he has "disposed of Wilhelm II, Bismarck, and all the anti-Semites" (III, 1352). (Bismarck, it should be noted, was in no sense anti-Semitic.)

Observing Nietzsche's career as a whole, we may be inclined to think of him primarily as a preacher, notably in *The Birth of Tragedy* and *Thus Spoke Zarathustra* but also in works like *Thoughts out of Season*, in which he delivers admonitory sermons. Zarathustra summons his brethren to preach through all the byways (II, 448). Kurt Hildebrandt, noting that Nietzsche wished, from his seventh to his fourteenth year, to become a preacher, suggests that he continued to look unconsciously for the great sermon that bowls the congregation over.[53] Although frequently addressed, the brethren remain indistinct. Undoubtedly Nietzsche felt a quasi-religious impulse, but how often he preached over his congregation's heads, confusing it with masks, paradoxes, and his Wildean flirtation with evil! While capable of great intellectual honesty, as in his excruciatingly painful break with

Wagner,[54] he became increasingly fascinated with lies: holy, honest, vital, and other varieties (Cf. II, 526).

If further we ask the meaning of the sermons, we find no consensus: Nietzsche has been seen as an aristocratic thinker, a Dionysian, a Heraclitean anti-idealist, a prophet of fascism, an existentialist.[55] In his vitalism, which denied that life could be judged by spirit or anything else, he commited the treason of the intellectuals, but there is something touching about the worship of life by an invalid.

In propagating the cult of life, Nietzsche depended largely on myths, as we have seen: Dionysus, Zarathustra, *amor fati* all signify about the same, the acceptance of life; the will to power is simply concentrated life. While Nietzsche could write fascinatingly about myths, he was not mythopoeic like Goethe, Hölderlin, or even Wagner. Siegfried has been compared to Tarzan,[56] but one can see him and believe in him, whereas Zarathustra is a construction. As Mann says: "with the rosy crown of laughter on his unrecognizable head, his 'Become hard!' and his dancer's legs, this faceless Zarathustra is not a creation, he is rhetoric, an excited play on words, tortured voice and dubious prophecy."[57] The superman is even less graphically presented. Apparently the realm of the superman will be a secularized paradise or better Valhalla on earth, where youths with Siegfried's looks and Nietzsche's brains—not, one trusts, the reverse—will vie agonistically in intellectual and physical sports.

These myths all imply or depend on the tough or aristocratic virtues: hardness, courage, grace. Except for courage, these were not Nietzsche's own qualities. Similarly, Nietzsche dwells at revealing length on the aristocracy, and his cult of the Renaissance reminds one rather of E. A. Robinson's Miniver Cheevy than of Burckhardt:

> Miniver loved the Medici,
> Albeit he had never seen one;

> He would have sinned incessantly
> Could he have been one.[58]

Curious also is his great scorn of the British, who could have taught him something about genuine power.

Increasingly, scholars are seeing Nietzsche in comparison with, not in contrast to, Wagner. This can easily be overdone, but when Brinton writes: "Nietzsche's prose always strives a little too hard, protests a little too much,"[59] the analogy is obvious. Both artists have a weakness for big bangs, effects for their own sakes. One of Nietzsche's dithyrambic poems—"The desert grows"—is a minor counterpart to the "sick" eroticism of *Tannhäuser* and *Parsifal*.

In Nietzsche's last works the contrast between a sense of mission and nihilism, between the superman (whom he now admits to be a fiction) and "unmasking" psychology, becomes more and more striking. Nietzsche, though keeping his skeptical, rational approach also open, became a great fount of mythical thinking, especially after 1890. Thus it is appropriate that we see him in mythical terms—if also skeptically. The name of Prometheus comes to mind, also that of Columbus, a special hero of his.

In this case though, we should think of Faust, in the original, completely tragic sense of the legend; and Nietzsche was Faustian long before Mann first conceived of basing his Faustian novel on him. He was an intellectual overreacher who never repented; one might see him as Faust and Lucifer combined. With his hubris, no pact with the Devil was needed. Almost four centuries ago, Marlowe—Faustian himself—pointed to the conflict between the drive of the Faust story and the ethos of the true scholar and intellectual:

> Cut is the branch that might have grown full straight,
> And burnéd is Apollo's laurel bough
> That sometime grew within this learned man.
> Faustus is gone.[60]

VI Greek and Germanic Myth in George

Sie werden selig unter hallen
Die unvergänglich neu und schön.

They attain bliss within halls
Imperishably new and fair.

—George

The latter half of the nineteenth century was a sterile period
for the German lyric and for most other genres. Then, in the
early nineties, three major poets emerged almost simultaneously: Stefan George, Hugo von Hofmannsthal, and Rainer
Maria Rilke, though Rilke did not achieve full stature until
well after 1900. In varying degrees, all these poets, like many
lesser ones,[1] shared the fascination with myth and symbol
characteristic of the fin de siècle in its revolt against naturalism. In German-speaking countries this revolt was strengthened by the precept and example of such works of Nietzsche
as *The Birth of Tragedy* and *Thus Spoke Zarathustra*.

Like hundreds of German writers, George was in Nietzsche's debt, but unlike all but a few of his most distinguished
colleagues, he was careful to maintain his independence. Thus
although he came to be associated with a type of "new man"
—*kalos kagathos*—he scornfully rejected the notion of the
superman,[2] as Thomas Mann did also. Whereas Nietzsche
preached the "will to power" with increasing fervor, George
simply incarnated it; there can be no question of influence
here. Both started from a basically aesthetic position—"the
world can be justified only as an aesthetic phenomenon"[3]—
but became increasingly concerned with moral, even political

questions. Like the philosopher, the poet believed that all
human societies should be hierarchically structured; like him
he rejected Christianity, largely from the point of view of
Greek values. The basic difference is that while Nietzsche
was essentially a dissolvent, a revolutionary of ideas, pro-
ceeding relentlessly from one position to another, George was
basically a conservative. From about 1900 to his death in
1933 he consistently remained a classicist in literature, a
devotee of a semi-Greek cult of handsome, intelligent youths,
and an aristocrat in his view of society. Compared to this
fundamental contrast, the fact that the two held similar positions about say, industrialism, democracy, and the emancipation of women is of minor importance. One must add that
George's taste was not as classical as were his principles.
Thus he put the nineteenth century painter Arnold Böcklin
on the level of Dante and Goethe, seeing in him a supreme
excellence that he does not possess.

George's specific criticisms of Nietzsche are often shrewd.
He commented, for instance, that the tone of the philosopher's
polemics against Christianity revealed that he was still close
to it.[4] His poem "Nietzsche" pointed out that this savior was
still far from salvation in his isolation and quoted the retrospective preface to *The Birth of Tragedy*; the author of that
lyrical work should have "sung not spoken."[5] Nietzsche, he
felt, was a prophet who warned in vain of disasters to come.
Also a prophet in aspiration, George regarded Nietzsche as
his great but tragic "ancestor";[6] a tortured romantic whose
Georgean descendants have surpassed him by reaching a
classical position. Yet like Hölderlin, Nietzsche had as it were
a phosphorescent nimbus, for George and his circle, which
not even Goethe possessed.

Nietzsche did not have any major impact on German culture until the nineties. During that decade, he, Strindberg,

and Oscar Wilde were perhaps the most influential figures in the literary life of central Europe. Attaining fame after Oscar Wilde, George soon surpassed him, both as a poet, and —obviously—as a manager of his own reputation. George was naive—or clever—enough to declare the youth he loved a god; surely Wilde was too sophisticated to apply that term to Lord Alfred Douglas. But in that age of Munich that was simultaneously golden and insane, madness or bizarre claims which simulated madness were revered. This is no exaggeration: one has only to consult Mann's early story "At the Prophet's," his *Doktor Faustus*, Franziska zu Reventlow's *Herrn Dames Aufzeichnungen*, or Peter Viereck's *Metapolitics* to realize that. The intellectuals in Munich, from about 1900 to 1933, were as shrill as those in the United States today; unlike the Americans, they could point to writers of genius, and not least to George, who as the peripatetic prince of German poetry had no fixed home but was primarily attached to Munich as his "residence." Here he attended many of the "cosmic" costume balls, at which persons of the magnitude of Friedrich Gundolf and Karl Wolfskehl appeared, decked out in a way to make them look like major figures of classical antiquity, gods, Dante, or whatever;[7] all this without a scintilla of humor or parody. That George dressed up as Julius Caesar is revealing, even frightening, but intellectual dictator though he aspired to be, he wrote great poetry.

As a young writer, George, while obviously searching for a myth, was plagued by radical skepticism. In his "Diabolical Stanza," significantly omitted from his collected works, he wrote:

> Noch jeder Gott war menschliches geschöpfe
> Die immer seligen sind allein die tröpfe
> Nur was die narren sprechen ist orakel
> Nur was nie war ist frei von jedem makel

Die tugend dankt am meisten dem vergehen
Die liebe kommt vom mangelhaften sehen
Kein heiliger ders nicht aus dem sünder wurde
Und ewige wahrheit bleibt nur das absurde.[8]

(Every God so far was created by men/Only the drips [sic]
are eternally blessed/Only what the fools say is an oracle/
Only what never was is free from all stain/Virtue is most
indebted to sin/Love comes from faulty vision/No saint who
did not begin as a sinner/And only the absurd remains as
eternal truth.) If one were to take these lines literally, one
might find that the whole structure of George's myth and
dogma had been erected on the foundation of an "As If," as
a compensation. More probably they express the quickly
passing mood of a young man, but they show at the least that
George, like Nietzsche (and perhaps Heine), felt the impact
of utter nihilism.

It will appear that George made his myths relatively tangible and credible by basing them on actual persons, institu-
tions, and so on. Thus while it was daring, to put it mildly,
to stylize his beloved Maximin as a god, he could at least
point back to the empirical Maximilian Kronberger, handsome and gifted, whom many of his associates had seen in
Munich before his premature death. Similarly, it was going
very far to suggest that the George "Circle" was the equal
of that centered on Socrates and Plato. But while George's
"aesthetic state" was a myth in the bad sense, his "Circle"
or "league" did include a few gifted poets besides himself,
and a number of brilliant scholars and essayists, among
whom Friedrich Gundolf was particularly outstanding. Of
course there were also mediocrities, hangers-on, and at least
one pompous, verbose charlatan, Friedrich Wolters. As in
Athens, beautiful youths seem to have abounded, though to
judge by the preserved photographs, this beauty existed at

times only in the eye of the beholder.[9] When the myth got too far from actuality it tended to lose credibility, as in the strange poem "Secret Germany."

Generally, however, George's myths hang together; in this sense they have integrity. Whereas George draws on a number of different cultures, he is not eclectic in the sense that Rilke is. His own ideals, interests, and tastes are at the center. While he turns to Greece, Rome, the Orient, or the Middle Ages, it is almost always the poet-prophet Stefan George who holds our attention.

Doubtless the most important traditional myth to George, as to almost all of his great predecessors, was that of the Greeks. Here men like Socrates and Plato were as significant to him as Apollo or Dionysus. Like various earlier Hellenists, he believed in the curious theory that there existed a unique spiritual bond between the Germanic peoples and the Greeks. In his prophetic poem "The War" a particular link between Apollo and the Norse god Baldur is posited. He was also fascinated by Rome, especially by the late Empire, as in his *Algabal*, but also by the majesty and dignity of the Roman Church.

Power is indeed a key to most of George's work and career. His Algabal is even more the autocrat than the artist; he is an aesthetic criminal, Nietzsche's superman seen through the eyes of Oscar Wilde, as it were. George as autocrat rules over his Circle, league, and *Reich*; and this is duly reflected in the poetry. The virtual exclusion of women from the Circle speaks for itself, as does the subordination of Aphrodite Pandemos to the "higher" but ambiguous Aphrodite Ouranos. It would be churlish to doubt the asseverations of the poet's friends that he could be charming, relaxed, and witty in personal relations,[10] but it would be naive beyond words to assume that George's genial side—many dictators have had that—altered in the least the basic pattern of his *Reich*, a realm of the spirit but still a monarchy, though not quite a dictatorship. In the poetry, however, the line of absolute rulers extends from Algabal (1892) to the barbarian conqueror in "The Burning of the Temple" (published in George's last book *The New Kingdom* (1928). Before he really developed his own myth—masters, devoted slaves, beautiful disciples—he made skillful use of the tales of Icarus and especially, most revealingly, of Narcissus; but such classical figures were not really his main interest. Unlike Rilke, he was too honest to *play* with such concepts as God, heroism, and so forth; he had to believe in them, or he kept silent. George was often wrong, sometimes disastrously so, but he has a certain crochety honesty one has to respect. For his part, Rilke was desperately involved, as his letters so embarrassingly show, in charming the "high society" of his day—Countess This, Duchess That. However strange George's sexual orientation was, there is no evidence known to me that he pursued young men because of their social prestige. Brains and beauty were his not unworthy ideals. Meanwhile Rilke operated on the thin line dividing a most gifted poet from a social climber. The point is, simply, that while some aspects of George's beliefs are repellent, they flow inevitably from his thought as a whole. If he is fond of striking gestures and poses, he is nevertheless basically sincere.

George's first strikingly successful poetry is also his first successful formulation of a myth, the cycle *Algabal*. Typically, George did not invent a mythic hero but combined stories dealing with the Roman Emperor Heliogabalus, who ruled for some four years, A.D. 218–222, with the decadent heroes of such writers as Baudelaire and Huysmans.[11] The historical Heliogabalus was a brave youth but cruel, an aesthete in the derogatory sense, and apparently handsome as well as bisexual. George has given his Algabal all these traits as well as the poet's own harsh imperiousness. As Victor Oswald well puts it, George's Algabal was not Heliogabalus but could not have been conceived without him.[12] Like his "decadent" French predecessors, Algabal has constructed an artificial realm of his own. In this sense he is an artist, no mere dilettante or epicure.

"The Clasp" ("Die Spange"), the brief poem standing just before *Algabal* in the collected works, gives a clear indication of George's ambitions and frustrations at this point. He had wished to form an ornament of cool iron, like a smooth, firm strip of metal; but the necessary ore was not procurable. Therefore his art shall be exotic, fiery, luxurious; the classic being unattainable, he turns to the baroque.

Algabal is dedicated to a French friend, the poet Albert Saint-Paul, and, very significantly, to the memory of Ludwig II of Bavaria, the famous half-mad king who befriended Wagner and had improbably spectacular castles built on the shores of various Alpine lakes. Like Heliogabalus, Ludwig was an artist *manqué;* like him (and like George) he had homosexual inclinations.[13] Everything fits together; there is almost an oversupply of objective correlatives. The cycle is learned poetry, deriving heavily from tradition, but its combination of the themes of art and power makes it peculiarly Georgean. If *Algabal* is rooted in strange soil, late Roman, plus Parisian, plus Bavarian decadence—what is worse than provincial decay?—its branches may rise so high precisely because of the superabundance of fertilizers around its roots.

The first poem of the subcycle "In the Underground Kingdom" ("Im Unterreich") in *Algabal* owes much to Baudelaire's "Paradis artificiel" but is essentially Georgean in its fusion of the themes of art and power. Thus there is an abundance of brightly colored jewels and ores—and an equally rich profusion of stylistic devices—but the Master's power is central:

> Wo ausser dem seinen kein wille schaltet
> Und wo er dem licht und dem wetter gebeut.   (I, 45)

(Where no will holds sway besides his own/And where he commands the light and the weather.) The poet glories in the sheer artificiality of his art: in his kingdom the birds are lifeless;[14] there is no need for air or warmth. Significantly, gloomy black colors predominate in the last poem of the group, in contrast to the gorgeousness that has gone before. The Master, a poet as well as a magician, wishes to bring forth in his sacred but apparently sterile kingdom a "dark great black flower"—"Dunkle grosse schwarze blume" (I, 47). This is the last line of the subcycle, obviously placed at the end for emphasis. Obviously too the "black flower" suggests a repudiation of the blue flower of German romanticism. Presumably Algabal's flower, with its overtones of exoticism and decadence, is no less romantic;[15] it is however the ideal of a very different, disillusioned generation.

In his best moods Algabal expresses the desire to turn from his largely subterranean *dolce vita* with all its fin-de-siècle allures to a new classicism:

> O lass mich ungerühmt und ungehasst
> Und frei in den bedingten bahnen wandeln   (I, 50)

(O let me, unpraised and unhated/And free, move in the allotted paths). Similarly, "Augury," the last poem of *Algabal,* contrasts the "clear, hot" wind to one that is "cold and clear"; the latter, the austere, is preferred, as in "The Clasp."

Such aspirations may well come from Algabal's "angel" or higher self.[16] Normally, however, the spirits of Ludwig II, the not yet chastened Oscar Wilde, and the Stefan George who still espoused *l'art pour l'art*, prevail in him. He is a

200 percent aesthete who, if he must murder, kills in beauty —shades of Hedda Gabler—by smothering his potential enemies under rose petals.[17] He is well aware that as a single person he is as important as the entire populace together but admits, reluctantly, that he cannot hate the people "deeply" (I, 52). Probably his attitude toward women is the most revealing. Whereas he seems generally most attracted by youths and boys, he has on one occasion been so impassioned by one of the Vestal Virgins that he tore her away from the altar to be his bride but rejected her on finding that she had, like the others, a blemish: "Sie hatte wie die anderen ein mal" (I, 57). The episode is partially historical: according to Dio Cassius, Heliogabalus spurned a certain Cornelia Paula, who "had some blemish on her body."[18] George's Algabal, however, scorns the priestess because she had a mark *(mal)* "like the others": in other words, presumably the normal female genitals. If *Algabal* were only the presentation of an individual, it would perhaps be unnecessary to examine the hero's views on such matters, but he is held up as a model not only for poets, but for the aristocratic life generally. Aside from his aesthetic gifts, the Georgean of the aristocratic type should be suave, implacable, imperious, cruel but not unnecessarily brutal, and keep women and the other "lower" ranks in their place.

Of course the cycle, in true symbolist fashion, is primarily a poem about poetry: the Underground Kingdom is a metaphor for a kind of poetry relatively new in Germany: deliberately artificial, amoral, hard, rich, and *ungemütlich*. *Algabal* makes its point brilliantly; it is one of the two or three finest of George's achievements. At the same time, since the poet-magician is also an emperor and a priest, his figure points beyond poetry to the state and to life generally; otherwise it would have been inartistic of George to have presented

Algabal's total personality. Increasingly, George was to go
beyond poetry to play the role of lawgiver and prophet. Alas,
as Eric Bentley implies, it is far better to be the "greatest of
minor poets"—perhaps "minor" is harsh here—than "one of
the most meretricious of minor prophets."[19] In dealing with
the literature and history of Germany, one is often dealing
with the attainments, frequently brilliant, of outlandish out-
landers, beyond the Roman wall or "limit" that divided
southern and western from northern and eastern Germany
for centuries. This division was later largely eliminated, but
it is curious that George, who was so proud of living within
wine-growing, classic "Roman" Germany should so often appear romantically outlandish in his later years.

The tension between poet and prophet in George becomes
obvious only late in George's career; C. M. Bowra feels that
the prophetic message does not gain the upper hand until
"The Star of the Covenant"—*Der Stern des Bundes* (1914).[20]
Yet it appears from *Algabal* on at least, and it accurately
reflects the duality of George's nature. Now there is no intrinsic reason why the poet should not also be a prophet or
vice versa; one thinks of Isaiah, of a few Greek writers, of
Hölderlin. Yet several gifted persons who knew George personally felt that his peculiar combination of lyricist and seer
was sinister, and that his egregious lust for power, yoked with
real genius, was dangerous indeed. Thus Hofmannsthal
wrote, in his sonnet "The Prophet":

> In einer Halle hat er mich empfangen
> Die rätselhaft mich ängstet mit Gewalt
> Von süssen Düften widerlich durchwallt
> Da hängen fremde Vögel, bunte Schlangen . . .
>
> Er aber ist nicht wie er immer war.
> Sein Auge bannt und fremd ist Stirn und Haar.
> Von seinen Worten, den unscheinbar leisen

Geht eine Herrschaft aus und ein Verführen
Er macht die leere Luft beengend kreisen
Und er kann töten, ohne zu berühren.[21]

(He received me in a hall that enigmatically frightens me, re-
pulsively pervaded with the violence of sweet odors, there
hang exotic birds, bright-colored serpents . . . But he is no
longer as he always was. His eye enchants and strange are
brow and hair. From his words, plain and quiet, emanates a
domination, a seduction. He makes the empty air circle op-
pressively and *he can kill without touching.*)

A minor but sensitive and attractive figure like Herbert
Steiner had the same reaction. His "Encounter with Stefan
George" is written with the greatest respect, even with awe,
but with a basic sense of fear. Borrowing a phrase of Balzac's,
he designates George as one of the family of Cain; he also
compares him with Burne-Jones's "Merlin"[22]—an analogy
that may well owe something to Hofmannsthal's sonnet but
seems just in its own right.

To sum up: one finds most of George's major myths in
Algabal, though mainly in rudimentary form. Surveying his
work as a whole, one finds that what makes his structure of
myths consistent and relatively tangible is that it centers on
one point, the personality and ideas of Stefan George. As
we shall see, the boy-god Maximin is only an apparent exception. Like Algabal, the poet fused the artist with the love
of power; the two entities are inseparable. Told that Napoleon had said, "J'aime le pouvoir comme artiste," George
retorted instantly, "J'aime l'art comme pouvoir."[23] Although
it is not until after *Das Jahr der Seele* (1897) that women
(virtually) disappear from his poetry, the process of system-
atically degrading the female sex for a variey of reasons,
including aesthetic ones, begins in *Algabal:* "Sie hatte wie die
anderen ein mal." Not homosexuality as such but the down-

right hostility toward half the human race is shocking here. Women are to become just another object of the will to power. Of course George speaks primarily *pro domo*, but the belief that he was in the line of Socrates, Plato, and Alcibiades —and for that matter of Nietzsche—must have strengthened his allegiance to the doctrine of male superiority.

Less exciting than *Algabal*, George's next volume, *The Books of Pastorals and Eulogies, of Tales and Songs and of the Hanging Gardens* (1895), makes its contribution to George's myth by developing the twin theme of mastery and service. As is often the case with George's books, it is tripartite in structure. In the second part—medieval in subject matter, as in the third, which is set in the Orient—this dual theme is of central importance. Obviously, it too is an aspect of the dominant motif: power.

As one would expect, the medieval knight or page is seen as following his master with utter self-surrender. This celebration of complete devotion goes back to *Algabal*, in which a slave "gladly" kills himself because he inadvertently startled the emperor. In "Vigil" ("Sporenwache") a young man about to be knighted expresses his total, exclusive devotion to the cause. "Errant Troop" evokes a dedicated band, reviled by the majority, which nevertheless attains the highest goal: "They attain bliss among halls/Imperishably new and fair" (I, 88). Quite possibly this is a metaphor for George, his followers, and their achievements. Like the knight in "The Companion in Arms," they are bound together by the closest ties of comradeship.

The poem "Kingliness in Childhood" adds the complementary theme of leadership to that of service. Here the future ruler is mysteriously singled out while a mere boy; this is genuine elitism. His playmates realize that it would be sweet to die for him—a typically Georgean notion. C. M. Bowra remarks that George's stress on obedience and devotion "aggravated a deep disease in the German nation."[24]

George's next volume of poems, *The Year of the Soul (Das Jahr der Seele*, 1897), is less concerned than is most of his work with setting up a mythic or didactic system. The cycle is gentler and softer than George normally is; as the title implies it is "inward" poetry, modern and self-conscious rather than classical in intention.[25] Being at least relatively close to ordinary human experience, it is his most accessible and most popular book.[26] Although the relevance of *Das Jahr der Seele* to this study is limited, it does have aspects that invite our attention. First, nature, banished in *Algabal*, now becomes an important part of the Georgean world. To our surprise, moreover, we find that nature largely serves as a mirror and symbol of the soul, in the characteristic romantic fashion. On the whole, the tone of the cycle is melancholy; accordingly, the symbolical year it presents has only three seasons: spring, the most hopeful time of year, has been expunged. Further, as has been observed, nature has been tamed; the setting is a park, and "park" appears in the first line of the cycle, doing much to set the tone. Here civilized, introspective persons play their parts within a civilized, stylized setting.

More relevant to George's weltanschauung is the appearance in *Das Jahr der Seele* of one of the first of his "pictures" of beautiful youths. This is the poem "Do you still remember the lovely image?" Whereas the poems about or addressed to women are usually quite pale, this is one of his finest, despite a certain preciosity at the end. George's ideal youth is not only handsome but himself devoted to beauty. Undoubtedly, we are to envision him as *kalos kagathos*. A brave hunter, he is also a thoughtful human being. Apparently he

has a charisma worthy of Orpheus; even a swan is drawn to
him. Shades of Rossetti and Burne-Jones!

With *The Tapestry of Life and The Songs of Dream and
Death, with a Prelude* (1900) we are back in the realm of programmatic poems like "The Clasp." In the very first poem,
a naked angel—George's higher self? [27]—approaches the poet
as the messenger of "Beauteous Life," "das schöne Leben."
A bit later we hear of the "Great" or "Magnanimous Life,"
das grosse Leben (I, 187). George's criteria are now by no
means merely aesthetic. Such a life, to judge by the book as
a whole, would be a work of art in every sense, aristocratic
and above all pagan. The last point is borne out by the ending of one of George's most central poems:

> Eine kleine schar zieht stille bahnen
> Stolz entfernt vom wirkenden getriebe
> Und als losung steht auf ihren fahnen:
> Hellas ewig unsre liebe.   (I, 176)

(A little band marches along silent ways/Proudly apart from
bustling activity/And as a slogan stands out on its banners:/
Hellas our love forever.) George is the last important poet,
at least in Germany, to stand firmly by the classic Winckelmannian doctrine of the absolute ethical and artistic hegemony of the Greeks. Of course he knew Nietzsche's ideas
and was indebted to them, but basically his sympathies were
with Apollo rather than Dionysus.

Part of the "Beauteous Life" consists of utter indifference
to the value judgments of the populace. Thus the natural
aristocrat, unconcerned with sin or custom, makes the noble
choice "without difficulty" (I, 176), like Schiller's "beautiful
soul." (What Schiller would have thought of George's
"tough" Nietzschean ethic is another matter.) Those who try
to apply obsolete Christian moral standards appear dis-

traught, hollow-eyed, like Savonarola, though George does not name any individual figure here.

Gradually the idea of a unified group or *Bund* begins to emerge. Of course the notions of devotion, service, and mastery are fundamental; beyond that, the idea of solidarity becomes important. George writes also of a Circle and later of a *Reich* to designate his poetic state; the latter term indeed has nationalistic overtones but is by no means Nazi in this context. In *The Tapestry* the poet addresses his "pupils"; actually, they are disciples. As we have seen, the Hellenophiles are a "little band." A drastic ethic holds the Georgean confederation together, in poetry as in life.[28] In one poem (I, 187) the "children" of the Master are proudly prepared to die, not for him as such but for his glory. Here, alas, we are reminded of Nazi heroes like Horst Wessel and Hitlerjunge Quex: "the flag means more than death!" Yet the splendor and dignity of his language make it seem almost blasphemous to mention George in the same breath with these persons. Some of his ideas were nevertheless lethally close to theirs. "The Disciple" (I, 197) is an expression of unconditional surrender to "the Master"; the word *Herr* occurs eleven times in sixteen lines. Only persons utterly ignorant of George's "days and deeds" could doubt that these verses are autobiographical. In line with George's emphasis on the *Bund* is his new awareness of the national past, of the so-called *Volk*. Thus the powerful poem "Primal Landscape" closes:

> Archfather dug archmother milked,
> Nourishing the destiny of a whole folk.   (I, 191)

Having remarked that George is basically Apollonian, one should add that he could write superbly Dionysian poetry when he chose, thus paying his tribute to the most potent of Nietzsche's mythical innovations. The last poem of *The*

Tapestry begins: "Glanz und ruhm! so erwacht unsre welt"
—Splendor and glory! thus our world awakes—and ends
magnificently: "Glanz und ruhm rausch und qual traum und
tod" (I, 223)—Splendor and glory ecstasy and torment dream
and death. For lines like these one can forgive George almost
any number of proclamations.

Whereas *The Tapestry* contains several programmatic
poems, *The Seventh Ring* (1907) seems to aim at nothing less
than the establishment of a new religion or cult.[29] Here it is
necessary to consider a chapter of George's biography. Early
in 1902 he encountered the fourteen-year-old Maximilian
Kronberger in Munich. Very moderately gifted as a poet,
Maximin—so George came to call him—was apparently an
exceedingly handsome youth, of great charm. Raised as a
Catholic, he had little interest in George's neo-pagan doctrines.[30] Whether or not George literally thought him a god
—as the poems repeatedly imply or state—he surely found
in him, *mutatis mutandis*, his Beatrice. For his part, Maximin
refreshingly believed, on first seeing George, that he was one
of Wedekind's cabaret singers, "The Eleven Executioners." [31]
As Heine said, "God is the Aristophanes of heaven."

Maximin died when he was barely sixteen. Only in death,
after all, could he be preserved as an immortal mythic figure,
let alone a god. Further, it is clear that the adored image of
the beautiful youth was already present in George's psyche—
as in the poem "Do you still remember?"—*before* he met the
empirical Maximilian Kronberger.[32] The poem "Knights
Templar" pits a masculine league against nature; the males
force her to "make the body divine and the god incarnate"
(I, 256), a line that expresses the very center of the poet's
paganism, without reference to Maximin. To make these
points is not at all to detract from George's devotion to him.

George's friendship with Maximin coincided roughly with

a very bitter schism among the Munich intellectuals and pseudo intellectuals who had clustered about him. When compared to the "Cosmic" wing of this highly colorful group, George appears rational, even Apolline. (It must be recalled however that Apollo was, or is, a very cruel god.) The leading Cosmics, especially Ludwig Klages and his ally Alfred Schuler, proclaimed that the intellect or spirit *(Geist)* was the antagonist of the soul; therefore intellect was bad. Although at the very best deceived deceivers, Klages and Schuler were not stupid; they seem to have threatened the security and prestige of the Georgian *Reich;* after all, they claimed to have something "deeper" and more extreme to offer than he. Probably one cannot tell for sure whether the Cosmics were George's followers or his uneasy allies; presumably the latter. In any case, the George-Klages-Schuler axis did not last. Perhaps it was sheer coincidence that George discovered Maximin as a god just in time to enable him to trump the Cosmic aces with a far greater attraction of his own. Perhaps. Again, George's posthumous use of Maximin in this feud need not suggest the slightest insincerity on his part; in fact, the fervor of these "religious" verses suggests quite the opposite. And who would bother with the *chronique scandaleuse* of Bavarian bohemia were it not for the fact that fascinating poetry and challenging (if often ruinous) ideas originated there?

With surprising tact, George presents his new, not to say ad hoc god primarily in terms of Christian not Greek myth. Whereas Claude David, generally the clearest and most perceptive of George critics, tells us that the poet did not really believe Maximin to be a god,[33] the poems themselves say the opposite. (Perhaps even David projects French rationality onto the Germans. As Heine warned us over a century ago, that is something no one should do.) In the second line of the subcycle "Maximin" George announces: "I see in you the God"—the last word capitalized, contrary to his habit (I, 279). A bit later, the reader is ordered to "praise your city [Berlin not Bethlehem] in which a god [lowercase this time] was born! Praise your time in which a god lived!" (I, 284). "Gott ist ein Berliner," he might have put it. George has wandered all too far from his French masters; when he does so, he is exposed to the danger of sinking to the level of yet another German eccentric. Munich is not really an ideal city for artists; it is too uncritical. When George wrote: "RE-TURNENT FRANC EN FRANCE DULCE TERRE" (I, 236), he was close to the source of his original inspiration; when he insistently compared Maximin with Jesus (I, 284 f), he had never strayed further from it. A climax of sorts is reached in the poem "Incarnation": the poet feels that he is linked to Maximin in a "most secret marriage," and that indeed he is the "creature of his own son" (I, 291)—a rather confusing bit of theology. In any case, Maximin had the special nimbus of heroes who die young, like Achilles, Alexander the Great, or Jesus.[34] Thoughts of resurrection surround his memory, as does the term *glorie,* meaning not secular glory, but aureole, halo, or nimbus (I, 287, 285). Apparently, the youthful god will return "in the red dawn" (I, 341). Still the neopagan, however, George manages to apply the Apollo-Dionysus cliché to the now defenseless Maximin (I, 290).

No doubt, the cult of Maximin was at the most a private religion for George; and probably Claude David is right when he warns us not to take it too literally. At the same time we might well be on our guard against personalities who invent quasi-religious cults of their own. Who could imagine T. S. Eliot confusing himself with Apollo or identifying one of his followers with St. Paul?

Whether or not George thought Maximin divine, it was he,

George, as prophet-poet who stood at the center of the poetic state, regarded at varying times as circle, ring, *Bund*, or hierarchical order. To some extent Maximin, like the Angel and the allegorical figure Beauteous Life, is a projection of George's own ideas and desires. The basic opposition of center versus periphery does much to shape the imagery as well as to define the theme. Thus a union of young men *(Bund)* is centered on a single star. Whoever has circled around the sacred flame shall remain the flame's satellite (I, 382).

In view of certain other tendencies in twentieth century Munich, one is relieved to find George free of anti-Semitism. On the other hand, it may seem surprising that Jews of the intellectual caliber of Friedrich Gundolf and Karl Wolfskehl became impassioned Georgeans. The reasons are not far to seek: aside from fervent admiration for the poems, these figures showed the German tendency, strong since the eighteenth century, to adulate the great cultural Master; and they were no more immune to the infection of mythical thinking than were their gentile contemporaries.

Seven years later, in 1914, appeared *The Star of the Covenant* (or *of the League: Der Stern des Bundes*.) Not surprisingly the "league" represents the poet's own phalanx, tautly ruled by him and inspired by the god or the "star"—Maximin of course, though the adored youth, no longer a gestalt, is sinking more and more to the status of a mere symbol. The linked themes of decay and renewal predominate. Roughly, decay is the characteristic of anti- or non-Georgean forces; renewal, needless to say, can emanate only from the poet's own army. By 1914 it was a formidable host.

George is first and foremost the lawgiver here. It is appropriate that *The Star* is a concentrated, clear, highly integrated whole, with relatively little ornament, but much biblical imagery. It is outspokenly didactic. In emulation of

Dante, no doubt, George has divided the 100 poems of the
book into a strict mathematical order: 9 + 30 + 30 + 30 +
1—the last unit being a triumphal chorus, reading in part:

> Gottes krieg ist uns entzündet
> Gottes kranz ist uns erkannt.   (I, 394)

(God's war has been kindled for us/God's wreath has been
awarded to us.) Just who "God" is here is an open question;
something more than Maximin seems to be intended. And
as George writes in the preface to the definitive edition of
The Star, the volume was written without any conscious
reference to the coming European war; probably "God's war"
refers to the metaphorical smiting that the Georgean warriors
were to inflict on philistines, Cosmics, democrats, feminists,
and other lesser breeds without the Munich law. Yet unconsciously, as in the famous line prophesying that the "holy
war" must strike down tens of thousands, George like other
German poets seems to have sensed that a genuine catastrophe was imminent (I, 361). When it did come, public
interest in *The Star* greatly increased—somewhat to George's
embarrassment (I, 347).

In stressing that decay and even catastrophe were overwhelming Europe, George is part of a long and motley line
of German "prophets," running from Wagner over Nietzsche
—a breath or rather blast of fresh air—and Max Nordau to
Oswald Spengler and beyond. Expressionists like Georg
Kaiser, critics like Karl Kraus, have apposite things to say.
Except for his impressive prophecies in "Der Krieg," George
was one of the least perceptive of these soothsayers; indeed,
his "verdicts" on Austrian and French culture are based on
the assumption that he is the sole possessor of the whole
truth. He wished to reverse the verdict of *Götterdämmerung*
as far as Germany was concerned; only such "lesser" nations

as England and France were decadent. At his best, he was the
poetic equal of Baudelaire, Verlaine, and Hofmannsthal. Yet
he contrived to look down on them—as indeed he rather
condescended to Goethe, and even to Shakespeare.[35]

In the first poems a sense of general decay prevails. It is
closely linked to a feeling of religious crisis, and since crises
can be resolved, hope is not lacking. One poem, appropriately set at one of the Cosmics' mystical costume parties, describes the attempt to draw great figures of the past back into
life.[36] Apparently it was unsuccessful (I, 352). Some satiric
verses present the attitude of the bourgeois of the early twentieth century, spiritually starving in the midst of the greatest
cultural riches (I, 360). Persons of the same era try frantically
to build higher and higher; it is as it were a Tower of Babel
situation; the structure is tottering. One thinks of such impressive yet ultimately futile technical achievements of the
time as the zeppelin and the S.S. *Titanic*. For George, such
progress *is* decay; and the time for patchwork and medicine
is past:

> Zehntausend muss der heilige wahnsinn schlagen
> Zehntausend muss die heilige seuche raffen
> Zehntausende der heilige krieg.   (I, 361)

(Ten thousand must the holy madness strike/Ten thousand
must the holy plague snatch away/Tens of thousands the
holy war.) Yet when literal war broke out, the poet regarded
it coldly. Nor does one have to share in his complete rejection
of modern technology to find these lines powerful. Less so
is a poem celebrating a Jesus or anti-Jesus of George's own
invention who believed that only total destruction of all the
works of man could save life as a whole (I, 363).

Appropriately enough, the theme of renewal is tied closely
to the figure of the deified Maximin. Perhaps when he appeared in the flesh he seemed to be already the incarnation of

a classical god. He is "Lord of the Turning"—the notion that culture had reached a decisive turning-point was particularly strong among German intellectuals from about 1900 on—and he appears "in naked radiance" as a good neopagan should. See also: "The image rises in the light, naked and free" (I, 367). Borrowing an idea from Nietzsche, George hails Maximin for saving his followers from the "torment of duality": in other words, flesh and spirit are but two aspects of one substance, and flesh is as sacred as soul or mind. On departure, Maximin speaks of his kiss, "which shall burn deep into your souls"—a rather typical touch (I, 351). Maximin is the son "whom the new center bore out of the spirit" (I, 354). Clearly, "the new center" is a metaphor for George's new classicism; that he is born of the spirit (masculine in German) may imply that he was brought forth without benefit of a woman, like Pallas Athena. Unlike Swinburne's "creeds that refuse and restrain," Maximin's creed guides his followers to joy. At the very beginning of the neopagan movement, Winckelmann had asserted that Greek life was joyous; this charming illusion was effectively refuted by Heine, Burckhardt, and Nietzsche. Basically conservative and in some senses reactionary, George swept away the skeptics and scholarly heretics and went back to the orthodox if largely false dogmas of the eighteenth century Hellenists. The hundreth poem of the book, "Final Chorus," achieves a crashing climax with its insistent repetitions, its hammering rhythm, its persistent assertion of the triumph:

> Gottes band hat uns umschlossen
> Gottes blitz hat uns durchglüht
> Gottes heil ist uns ergossen
> Gottes glück ist uns erblüht. (I, 394)

(God's bonds have surrounded us/God's lightning has glowed through us/God's salvation has been poured out for

us/God's happiness has blossomed for us.) This god remains
as intangible as Nietzsche's superman and as little credible.
Since George had it on very high authority that God was
dead, he did his best to create a new one, but it would have
taken rather more than a mixture of Winckelmann, Nietzsche,
Maximilian Kronberger, and the poet himself to perform that
miracle.

As its title implies, *The Star of the League* has to do with
the setting up of an ideal state, however abstract and non-
political. From a very great distance, *The Star* does look back
to the *Republic:* it proposes a hierarchical society and a myth
of its own. The differences are not to be ignored: George as
a thinker is at best a transalpine mini-Plato; Munich, at that
time a world center for beer, dachshunds, writers, intellectuals, and pseudo intellectuals, had no discernible affinity
with Athens. One cannot imagine Thomas Mann at a Cosmic
costume party, though he lived in Munich for some forty
years; one cannot imagine a Cosmic inviting him—the author
of *Death in Venice* was too bourgeois, too conventional, for
either the Cosmics or the Georgeans. Aside from George, the
very few really great writers in Munich were not allied with
the antirationalist establishment. *Res ipsa loquitur!*

George describes his "*Reich* of the Spirit" quite concisely.
Everyone who joins it is "reborn"—one thinks of the so-
called encounter groups—and forgets his home. "Fathers
mothers are no more" (I, 382). From those whom he has come
to call his sons he will choose his "masters of the world."
Obviously, George had no interest in the *realpolitische* plots
that were being prepared at the very time *The Star* was
written. It is equally obvious that he stoops here to the vulgar, aggressive vocabulary of Kaiser Wilhelm II—"masters of
the world"—even though his conscious aim must have been
the education of masters of the spirit.

The League is to be made up of a new nobility drawn from all social levels; as a totality it will be greater than the sum of its parts (I, 389). Women serve merely to bear children, and it is quite clear that none could join the favored circle. Woman is mere material; cf. *mater, materia*. As George puts it, "woman bears the animal"; whatever makes the child human is taught him by men. When the lawgiver warns against polluting one's body with women "of an alien sort," he is hardly thinking of race (I, 383, 387).

Whereas these poems often mention Jesus with respect, he is in effect a person of George's own creation, more Nietzschean than Christlike. Lesser Christians are haggard and distraught. As noted, the ensouled body (*Leib*)[37] is as holy as the spirit. When the poet states that he who has never thrown himself away never need fear the flesh or regret his acts on earth (I, 388) he is tautological indeed: those—if any —who have no awareness of having sinned have no pangs of conscience nor need of forgiveness. One might ask whether such sub- or supermen have ever truly lived, for that matter. Again the extremely theoretical quality of George's ethics is apparent.

As time went on George became more and more nationalistic in orientation, the *Blätter für die Kunst* published fewer non-German writers; and the Circle, despite the adherence of such figures as Albert Verwey, was more and more a purely German affair. Remote though they tried to be from merely mundane affairs, the Georgeans were obviously influenced by the worsening international situation. Thus while a brief poem on France begins with thanks to poets like Mallarmé who helped him long before, it quickly sinks to the level of chauvinistic insult, and George himself descends to the moral level of Wagner. The French are degenerate, like mongrelized dogs (I, 364). Perhaps the worst thing about these lamentable verses is that they illuminate a particularly stupid cliché. Apparently the next poem in *The Star* is a polemic against Hofmannsthal and other Austrian writers.[38] It is equally indiscriminate, equally hostile, ending: "and what comes is night" (I, 364). At one point Maximin shrinks from godlike stature to being the "spirit of the holy youth of our folk" (I, 353). As so often in nationalistic German writing, the implication is that no other "youth" is as holy as the German. One might well wish that George had avoided both politics and literary criticism.

Because of its basically thematic approach, this book has largely neglected imagery—perhaps too much so. In the case of *The Star of the League*, however, a quick glance at certain images may prove rewarding. Sexual imagery is as important here as are colors and jewels in *Algabal*. Generally, George uses figures and terms borrowed from the realm of heterosexuality to illustrate an entirely male, often homosexual, situation. Thus the prophet-priest who is generally the "I" of these one hundred poems bears or bore within him the seed implanted by the god (I, 356, 376). In the most powerful poem of the whole cycle, the "I"—Maximin speaking through George—describes his essence by reciting a series of opposites. This is a familiar mystical device, aimed at describing the indescribable.

> Ich bin der Eine und bin Beide
> Ich bin der zeuger bin der schooss
> Ich bin der degen und die scheide
> Ich bin das opfer bin der stoss . . .
> Ich bin der reiche bin der bare
> Ich bin das zeichen bin der sinn
> Ich bin der schatten bin der wahre
> Ich bin ein end und ein beginn.   (I, 359)

(I am the One and am Both/I am the begetter and the womb/ I am the sword and the sheath/I am the victim and the thrust/

. . . I am the rich am the deprived one/I am the token am the sense/I am the shadow am the true one/I am an ending and a start.) The poem can be read not only as an exercise in defining a god through contradictions but as an expression by the prophet-priest of the most enormous egotism imaginable. "I am" occurs twelve times in twelve lines; George begins to sound like Jehovah. Finally there is the erotic imagery, apparent in the first four lines, even in the translation, but utterly inescapable if one realizes that the second, quite common meaning of *scheide* is "vagina," which fact causes one to take *degen* in two senses; this in turn casts new light on *stoss*.

Now it could be said by Georgeans that this approach "lowers" an immortal bard to the level of Freud. The poet, however, was no prude; he proclaimed that the highest knowledge could be obtained only by him "with whom the god slept" (I, 387). This is stated in a context from which women have been rigorously excluded. Of course it is a metaphor, but to think it a mere metaphor would be to underestimate George's almost frightening sincerity. Similarly, the novice who is destined for acceptance carries the mark of election "kissed upon him" (I, 389); differently put, those who will become pillars of the order have been "impregnated" by the god who awakes men to true life (I, 393). Like the Spartans, or like the Knights Templar, who particularly fascinated George, the members of his league are to combine the greatest hardness toward outsiders with the most extreme intimacy among themselves.

The Star of the League is a remarkably controlled, consistent collection, but in this case George has gained unity at the cost of richness and variety. The *Bund*, with its laws, individual members, their loves and ideals, remains very much in the center. The didactic note has largely pushed aside the lyric. Instead of the cosmopolitanism of the earlier volumes one finds a national emphasis, in line with a general narrowing of George's interests. There is an amazing sense of infallibility, of triumph, of being elected. However specious, it must have contributed a great deal to the élan of the *Bund*.

George's next and last volume of verse *Das neue Reich* (*The New Kingdom*) did not appear until 1928, and was thus his only book of poetry to appear in the last twenty years of his life. Clearly it was not a case of his lyric talent simply running dry, as Hofmannsthal's had, for a few of the poems in the last book are among his finest; nor was he one of those who could not write during the war. Perhaps it was rather the case that he felt himself a prophet who had already laid down the laws, delivered the holy message. Certainly his view of the world, once he turned aside from belief in art for art's sake, changed very little; there was not a great deal to add.

The book is as variegated as its predecessor is unified. Much of it is taken up with cultural criticism in verse, dealing with a variety of topics; four brief works of this type are in semidramatic dialogue form. Several then important poems are focused on the war. As in earlier collections, there is a series of brief epigrams addressed to and characterizing specific individuals; not all of them are flattering, by any means. Finally, there is a handful of songs; one of them, "Thou pure and slender like a flame," which closes the book, is as lovely a lyric as George ever achieved.

The long poem "The War," published separately in 1917, consists for the most part of a very severe criticism of the Germans, their leaders,[39] especially the Kaiser (I, 412), and their naive views of both war and peace. No pacifist, George was nevertheless aware that "the old God of battles is no more"; modern war is sickness and mechanized nastiness.

Yet the poet, at the end, makes a *salto mortale* into myth
and manages to close optimistically. After claiming that Germany is so beautiful a country that no alien force could lay
it waste—was France then ugly?—he evokes the return of
the old gods, summoned by youth. Wotan and Zeus, Christ
and Dionysus appear in a syncretic union; Apollo tells Baldur
that when the "night" (the long period of alienation from
the gods, as in Hölderlin) is over, this time the light will not
come from the East. After suggesting that there is a unique
link between the Germans of the early twentieth century and
the ancient Greeks, George ends with the implication that the
Germans will be the masters of the future. In a curious way
he has used the greatest of the gods to make nationalistic
propaganda. A worthier reason for invoking the gods is ex-
plicit in the poem, however: "A folk is dead if its gods are
dead" (I, 414).[40] Such baldly expressed statements are typical
of George's didactic verse.

Another war piece conjures up a time when contemporary
Germany will have cast off the fetters of the oppression and
purged itself of shame. Then the dead, "the Sublime, the
Heroes" (I, 455) will return. Then the royal standard with
the "true symbol"—obviously the swastika—will flutter in
the breeze. Heavily alliterative in the manner of Old High
German poetry, the poem is barbaric in both form and content but effective, even powerful. It marks George's closest
approximation to the Nazi point of view.

Somewhat less repellent but still sinister, "To a Young
Officer [*Führer*] in the First World War" expresses in the
word "first" a threat in its very title. With great empathy
George shows the courageous bearing of the young leader,
actually a member of the *Bund*.[41] With his comrades he had
reached the very portals of victory. Now he is warned not
to turn his back on his martial ideals but to maintain his be-

lief in a meaning, to be a meaning himself. Another conflict will come, and already a crown may be descried on the young officer's head. Although it is free of hate, the poem is the expression of a "higher" revanchism, impersonal but still suggesting that the results of the war could and should be reversed.

Of the many poems concerned with general cultural criticism, a few are helpful in illuminating the structure of George's myth. Thus "Goethe's Last Night in Italy"[42] is a dramatic monologue. "Goethe" speaks in a stiff, pompous, most un-Goethean way. He describes his own achievement in a rather derogatory manner, but states his delight that a miracle of marble and roses would be performed, obviously by the Georgeans. Knowing of this coming miracle, Goethe can leave Italy without unhappiness. To grasp the enormous hubris of this monologue, one would have to imagine Walter Savage Landor or Swinburne condescending to Shakespeare. Just as Nietzsche tried to demonstrate his superiority over Socrates, Plato, and Jesus, George (whose horizon was quite narrowly German once his *Wanderjahre* were over) puts his "competitor" Goethe in the role of a "forerunner" of the George Circle.

Similarly, a poem with the enigmatic title "Secret Germany" alleges that the god Pan poked the poet with his foot and urged him to return to his "holy homeland" (I, 426). The poet ends this homily—one of all too many—with the notion that only the forces that have survived in long, historical hibernation will shape the destiny of the future. As so often, the prophecy is vague enough to be almost meaningless. The title implies the existence of an esoteric, so to speak latent German tradition, nobler and deeper than the Germany that meets the eye and stretching from the Hohenstaufen emperors to the George Circle itself.

To turn to the miniature dramas: they are "cultural criticism" and rather abstract, but at least one of them, "The Burning of the Temple," has been successfully performed. "The Hanged Man" makes the point that any criminal dies a vicarious death to some extent; he has acted out passions that the respectable, to their regret, have never been able to satisfy. Thus he will become a hero, a god; his gallows will be bent into "the wheel"—almost certainly the swastika. The psychology of this unpleasant piece is worthy of the Cosmics at their worst,[43] but it is interesting that George, perhaps involuntarily, has linked criminality to the symbol of the swastika.[44]

In "The Man and the Faun,"[45] the faun embodies the qualities of sheer, raw, animal nature. If man cuts his ties to the animal and the soil, civilization as a whole will perish. "Only through magic does life stay awake" (I, 432). The poem takes a position somewhere between Rousseau and the ecologists of today.

In "Conversation of the Lord with the Roman Captain" the Roman approaches Christ, hoping to gain insight and instruction. "Jesus" however answers with the arrogance and in the terms of the George Circle: thus he states: "The world's salvation comes only from inflamed blood" (I, 433)—meaning in context Dionysian ecstasy rather than some disease. In fact, Jesus says that he takes part in sacred dances, but the people are not aware of this side of his nature. "For aeons [the Son's] banner must fly over the nations/Before anyone shall see the fulfillment of the covenant: Christ's[46] dancing" (I, 434). Here George joins in the tradition of a Third Kingdom reconciling Christianity with paganism, found in a long series of mystics from Joachim of Floris down, in Goethe's "The Mysteries," and on an earthier level in Heine.[47]

"The Burning of the Temple" reminds one of the world of

Spengler and the late Nietzsche. Nothing can save a thoroughly decadent culture, but barbarism or a series of wars may harden individuals as in a "bath of steel." In such a case, the ruthless conqueror may be the only possible savior. Thus when the barbarous "Ili" (presumably Attila) conquers a civilized country, it soon appears that cruel though he is, he is morally superior to the nation he has conquered. Incorruptible, clear-eyed, chaste, he will wipe out any person, culture, or religion that is no longer vital or effective:

> Ich bin gesandt mit fackel und mit stahl
> Dass ich euch härte nicht dass ihr mich weichet. (I, 440)

(I have been sent with torch and steel/To harden you, not that you weaken me.) George does not explicitly glory in this Nietzschean harshness; still less does he reject it. At the end of the brief play the temple burns; it will not be rebuilt for five hundred years. One thinks of Hofmannsthal's prophecy of coming tyranny in his tragedy *The Tower*, of Yeats's "The Second Coming." With its highly dubious doctrine of possible rebirth through barbarism, George's work is the least pessimistic of the three.

The lyric "Thou pure and slender as a flame" that closes the collection is deliberately simple but not banal. It is a sheer love song and vastly more appealing than George's versified proclamations on cultural matters. By no means the last poem George wrote—it reflects the death some years before of his disciple Bernhard Uxkull—it closes the volume on his characteristic note of praise.[48] Appropriately, it returns to the archetype of the beautiful youth, as found in *The Year of the Soul* and many of the Maximin poems:

> Du blühend reis vom edlen stamme
> Du wie ein quell geheim und schlicht
> Du schlank und rein wie eine flamme
> Du wie der morgen zart und licht. (I, 468)

(Thou flow'ring branch of noble stem/Thou secret and simple
as a spring/Thou pure and slender as a flame/Thou bright
and tender as the dawn.)

Regarding George's life and work as a whole, one may
wonder why a friend, the English musician Cyril Scott, called
his short book about him *The Tragedy of Stefan George*.
Primarily he refers to the perversion of George's ideas, not
only by the Nazis; blind adulation of the "master" proved
ruinous. As Scott rightly puts it, the poet would never have
been deified had he been an Englishman, but he fails to note
that an English George might well have shared the fate of
Oscar Wilde.[49] In sexual matters Germany seems to have
been much the freer country. Secondarily, Scott finds it regrettable, from one point of view, "that he let himself be
enticed from the path of true poetry and undertake the role
of the herald of a philosophy."[50] With this judgment, I believe, virtually all observers will agree, except for the few
survivors of the Circle and their intellectual descendants.

Closely related to the matter of adulation is George's obsession with authority and power. Far from being merely an
aspect of his private life, this drive affected his thought and
the structure, even the rhythm of many of his poems. Like
Adrian Leverkühn in Mann's *Doctor Faustus*, he was determined to impose a rigid, highly disciplined order on art. Yet
like Leverkühn, he was no fascist: he shunned demagoguery,
mass action, racism. Whereas Gottfried Benn allied himself
with the Nazis, however briefly, and Ezra Pound broadcast
for Mussolini, George scorned both the Nazi tiger and the
Fascist hyena. Refusing, through a Jewish intermediary,[51]
the highest honors the Third Reich could offer him, he left
Germany to die in voluntary exile. One can forgive the poet
a great deal for his stubborn integrity. One of the great
heroes of the Circle was Julius Caesar. Obviously George

knew the difference between a basically civilized dictator and a bloody tyrant.

It is unfortunate that George, with his very real achievements, should find it necessary recklessly to magnify them, placing himself by clear implication on the level of Plato and Dante, well above Goethe. (Aside from Burckhardt and Heine, the major figures of this book are marked by an enormous immodesty; and in George's generation the tendency to inflate reputations was particularly strong. The poet had the double egotism of artist and prophet. Other overrated figures of his generation were Max Klinger, Arnold Böcklin, Richard Strauss, Gustav Mahler, the minor poet Richard Dehmel, and not least Wilhelm II, German Emperor and King of Prussia.)

Unlike these personages, George deliberately addressed himself to a small audience. As time went on, his range and scope narrowed, his interests grew more elitist. While he always looked down on popularity, such early cycles as *Algabal* and *The Year of the Soul* were not written for a clique, and could be read by any reasonably intelligent person. The young George was a European poet whose literary ancestry was mainly French; after 1914 he was primarily a German writer appealing first of all to his own group and to other connoisseurs. Max Weber and his wife made the sound if obvious criticism that the Circle excluded women and ignored the masses; Weber also pointed out that it was made up of *rentiers*.[52] Since most European academics and other intellectuals presumably had some sort of outside income, the latter objection does not seem cogent.

That George remained devoted to the eighteenth century vision of Greece as found in Winckelmann, Goethe, and Hölderlin was another factor that limited his appeal. Classicism has never been a cult for the crowd; and Winckel-

mann's cult of Greece, after the researches of the nineteenth
century philologians and Nietzsche's iconoclastic attacks upon
it, had been largely pushed to one side. In fact, George himself disclaimed interest in "mere" humanism, proclaiming
that the "Greek" equation of the beautiful body with the god
was the greatest and boldest of all insights.[53]

Often George has been charged with being cold and magis-
terial; not without reason. Yet the finest of his poems are
very far from being as "sounding brass or a tinkling cymbal."
In his own imperious, at times harsh way, he had love.

VII Rilke, Mythology, and Myth

Götter von Alleen und Altanen,
niemals ganzgeglaubte Götter, die
altern in den gradbeschnittnen Bahnen

Gods of avenues and balconies,
never wholly believed gods, who
age in their straightly trimmed paths

—Rilke

With the possible exception of Yeats, no major poet of the twentieth century has been more concerned with myths than Rainer Maria Rilke.[1] He progressed from a rather facile manipulation of traditional mythology in his early works to the impressive reinterpretation of mythical figures in his *New Poems,* and from there to the use of myths largely of his own devising in the late poetry. The angels of the *Duino Elegies* are very clearly his own creatures; the Orpheus of the *Sonnets* is more familiar but still basically Rilkean, just as Nietzsche's Zarathustra bears little resemblance to the historical Zoroaster. Let the reader beware: when he reads about Christ or Leda in the *New Poems,* he is often reading about Rilke's highly subjective reaction to these figures, beautifully presented. The Duino angels are actually anti-angels, as will appear. Undoubtedly Rilke was astute in pouring new wine into very old bottles. Whereas George shocked readers by declaring that a contemporary youth was a god, Rilke disarmed them by the use of familiar terms. Similarly, instead of stating bluntly that he did not believe in love, he constructed a doctrine of keeping one's distance from one's partner, and called it love. Rilke played with some myths, debunked others, and used still others purely for aesthetic effect, as in "Annunciation." On the other hand he can take the symbolic value of some mythical figures very seriously, as in "Archaic Torso of Apollo" and the late poems. Presumably influenced by Nietzsche, he wrote that the "serenely happy Greece" dreamed of by the German classicists had never existed.[2] At times he "mythified" himself, as in "Self-Portrait of the Year 1906,"[3] in which he rather pathetically claims to be the descendant of an ancient noble family.

This study has no aspirations to biography, and in no case would Rilke's private experiences explain the surpassing quality of his best poems. Perhaps an unhappy family life like Rilke's can be a stimulus to productivity, as in writers so enormously different as Byron and Kafka. But Rilke's upbringing was so skewed, so perverse, that one wonders how he managed to survive it. His mother and two other relatives were definitely pathological; his hypochondria and neurasthenia were not caused by the war of 1914–1918 but at the most aggravated by it.[4] He himself attributed his inability to love to his resentment of his mother,[5] for which he had excellent reasons. She wished he had been a girl, and for five years treated and dressed him as one. (See his very "sweet" cult of maidens.) His survival shows great strength, but it could well be that his distorted childhood in turn distorted his thought, as in his un-Christlike Christ figure, his angels, and so on. This is a matter, though, of speculation, which at best casts some light on the intellectual thrust of his poems.

Whereas Rilke's use of traditional myths is eclectic, exploitative, and at times even frivolous, his treatment of new mythic entities, largely self-devised, is very different. Death, "art things," love, and sex are the subjects of his most intense artistic and intellectual endeavor. The last theme has been relatively neglected, probably because it does not fit into the basically false image of the saintly Rilke, the "seraphic doctor." It was natural that such an image was inferred from many of his poems, his ineffably "sensitive" letters, and his exquisite manners; but he had a very earthy side. He was not at all interested in the "mystical renunciation of the world."[6] At one period, he behaved very much à la Don Juan.[7] Indeed, his whole elaborate theory of love, as will appear, is in effect the rationalization of his inability to love any one person over a protracted period of time. He was capable of friendship—a very different matter of course. At any rate, Rilke drew a sharp distinction between unceasing love, impossible except for a few dedicated women, and sex, which while terrifying at times, is needed. In his *Letters to a Young Poet,* he stresses the necessity for the poet of "a thousand forgotten nights of love."[8] Thus, sex is real and basic, love an almost impossible achievement. Obviously, his attitude is shared by many members of the "counter culture" today.

Rilke fits in with the tendency to emancipate literature and often life from sexual taboos that is largely a nineteenth and twentieth century phenomenon. Among its great precursors were Walt Whitman and Nietzsche.[9] One thinks of the "fleshly school" of English poets, of Wagner's more erotic operas, of tendencies in various German youth movements, of many minor poets around 1900. Thus Richard Dehmel published a cycle called "Metamorphoses of Venus," Max Dauthendey a collection of novellas called *Lingam.* These men were not only vastly less gifted than Rilke; despite their use of sensational titles, they were on the whole less outspoken, less erotic. Believing that every organ of the human body, however taboo, could be evoked and metaphorically described in poetry, Rilke did precisely that. And his metaphors are unmistakable: not even the most determined anti-Freudian could miss the significance, in context, of "trident," "ravine," and so on. It would seem that Rilke's mastery of rhythm, simile, and metaphor make his erotic passages even more persuasive than Lawrence's.

While there are a few outspokenly sexual passages in the early poems,[10] this aspect of Rilke becomes prominent only in the *New Poems* (1907–1908), his first great collection of lyrics. Here his strategy is to sexualize the traditional myths, usually by focusing, in a couple of lines, on a significant detail. (If the basic story is already erotic, as in the poem "Leda," his deft emphases make it more so.) In "Orpheus. Eurydike. Hermes" he writes of Eurydike, who is rather loath to be rescued from Hades:

> ihr Geschlecht war zu
> wie eine junge Blume gegen Abend   (I, 544)

(Her sex was closed/like a young flower toward evening). Similarly, in "Birth of Venus" he writes first of the genitals of the sea, whatever that means, and then turns to the goddess:

> wie ein Bestand von Birken im April
> warm, leer und unverborgen, lag die Scham   (I, 550)

(like a stand of birches in April/warm, empty, and unconcealed, her sex lay). How skillfully Rilke offsets the graphic terms with lovely similes—"young flower toward evening," "birches in April." Later, he was less concerned about such balancing, but even in the potentially rather sordid poem "Hetaeras' Graves" he introduces flowers and pearls. Using one of his favorite female symbols, he speaks of the courte-

sans as "river beds" (I, 541). (There is no point in listing all
the sexual images in this poem; they are quite obvious.) In
treating biblical subjects he is more reticent, but he does
evoke the youthful David's envy of Saul's amorous experiences—"Your nights, o King, your nights" (I, 488)—and has
Mary Magdalene lament that she and Jesus were never lovers
(I, 494; "Pietà").

Rilke's "Seven Poems" (1915) are more drastic and must
constitute a grave embarrassment to those who believe in
Rilke the saint. Like the "Correspondence in Verse with Erika
Mitterer" (see below) they were not published in the poet's
lifetime and hence do not have the full validity of the works
that did then appear. In imagery, however, they have much
in common with the more outspoken of the *New Poems;* only
Rilke could have written them, and it would be silly to ignore
them. These "phallus poems" deal with the pleasures of sex
and above all celebrate the bodies of the lovers. Avoiding
anatomical terms, Rilke is nonetheless anatomically precise.
Among the masculine symbols one finds "abrupt tree" (*Baum;*
Rilke connects the word with *bäumen,* to rear up), "column,"
"tower." When he writes "This is my body, which is rising
up" (II, 438; the German word used connotes the Resurrection), he is blasphemous. Female images include "nocturnal
arch," "inwardly spacious one," "vault," "counter-heaven,"
"primal mountain of joy." Marcel Kunz, who has discussed
these poems, finds Rilke's expressions for coitus too "mon-
strous" to mention;[11] but there seems to be no qualitative or
moral distinction between "womb-dazzling rockets" or "deep
ascension to heaven" and the images noted above. Clearly,
Rilke is not using sexual imagery to express religious feeling,
as so many mystics have done. Rather, in his own way, he
is trying to put into practice George's famous line "Den leib
vergottet und den gott verleibt," make the body godlike and

the god into a body. Differently put, he is not celebrating sex for its own sake, but elevating it into a sort of god. In a later letter, he wrote of the need of a phallic divinity for modern man.[12]

While the "Seven Poems" have undoubtedly shocked some readers, they are not "dirty" in any sense. Yet they are deliberately one-sided, in that the lovers are utterly cut off from everything but their own physical rapture. Both writing these erotic verses and the experiences that presumably underlay them must have had cathartic value for Rilke.

In the third *Duino Elegy* the poet put sex into the framework of society and time; the result was a far more impressive treatment of the theme. Broadly speaking, he contrasts the fierce sexual drive of the male with the far gentler, more selective, but by no means weak passion of the young woman. To the man, sex is a frightening, overwhelming, but somehow magnificent force: "O des Blutes Neptun, o sein furchtbarer Dreizack" (I, 693)—O Neptune of the blood, o his dreadful trident. The man has a "primal forest" within him; part of him goes back to the most savage times. For some reason the woman is not cursed with the "older blood" of prehistoric ages. Instead of rejecting the partly primeval male, she is implored to save him by granting him an "overweight of nights"—a superabundance of love.

Rilke's correspondence in verse with the young Austrian poet Erika Mitterer returns to the sphere of relatively private poetry. These poems—roughly half of them by Fräulein Mitterer—were written and exchanged as letters in 1924–1926 but not published until 1950. The erotic note is strong but not nearly as pervasive as in "Seven Poems." Rilke[13] compares his role to that of the rain and the wind; "flowery valley" and "meadow" signify his correspondent (II, 292, 300). A rather embarrassing piece, not included in the collection of 1950, tells of his sexual excitement while writing to Fräulein Mitterer and inquires if she has analogous reactions while reading his letter (II, 492).

In "The Letter of the Young Worker" (1922; published in 1934), the focus is primarily on Christianity; the main charge brought against it is hostility to sex. Operating with Nietzschean concepts, the fictitious worker echoes Rilke's own resentment toward Jesus: "who is then this Christ who interferes with everything?" He also rejects the Cross as a symbol (VI, 1111f). It is quite possible, though hardly demonstrable, that Rilke like Nietzsche thought of Christ as a rival. Christianity degrades the here and now and refuses to acknowledge the happy friendliness of the earth (VI, 1114, 1116). Above all, the worker scores the Christian denunciation of sensual love—"as they call it with an unbearable mixture of scorn, lust, and curiosity." Thus an experience which all creatures find blissful and which lies "at the roots of all experience" has been defamed. Paraphrasing Nietzsche almost literally,[14] he proclaims that "our pure fountain" has been poisoned (VI, 1123f). Doubtless Rilke realized that this account of things is very one-sided, but by using the mask and voice of the young worker, he was able to write in a simplistic, almost simple-minded way.

Obviously, concentrating on the sexual theme in Rilke, on perhaps a score out of hundreds of poems, could be seriously misleading. He was not primarily an erotic poet; still less was he a pornographic one. Yet it is necessary to redress the balance, over against the persistent myth of the seraphic doctor. Even as intelligent a woman as Lou Andreas-Salomé could write that Rilke "calls down each of these words from the cross to which he is nailed."[15] (Perhaps she saw herself as Mary Magdalene.) That Rilke was far from being a pure seraph or cherub would seem to make him more tangible and acceptable as a human being. In the earthier sense of the term, Rilke was far more the "great lover" than Goethe.[16] More important: lines extend from Rilke's notions of sex to his concepts of love, religion, and even of aesthetics; one has to understand all of these if one is to grasp his view of life as a whole.

Curiously, Rilke's clear and direct treatment of sex has been generally played down or ignored, whereas his precious, evanescent, and ultimately unsatisfactory concept of love is often discussed. (Of course the two concepts usually do and should overlap—but very rarely in Rilke.) The term "intransitive love," implying that the true lover should not depend on the return of his or her emotions, indeed expresses a truth. Some two centuries after Spinoza proclaimed: "He who loves God cannot strive to have God love him in return," a pert wench in *Wilhelm Meister's Apprenticeship* told the protagonist: "If I love you, what business is it of yours?" In Rilke's eyes, to love is splendid; to be loved is oppressive or worse. Yet a love that radically excludes mutuality had better be called by another name; one critic has described Rilke's approach as ultimately a matter of auto-eroticism.[17] Writing from a Freudian point of view, Eric Simenauer exclaims in understandable indignation: "What sort of creature is this who teaches us that real love is renunciation?"[18] In a brief essay on the letters of the nun Marianna Alcoforado, one of his "saints of love," the poet maintained that "the essence of love does not lie in what is shared [*im Gemeinsamen*], but in the fact that one compels the other to become something, to become infinitely much, to reach the ultimate of which his powers are capable." And a bit later he quotes Marianna's words to her faithless lover: her love no longer depends on how he treats her (VI, 1001f; cf. 1016f, on the Comtesse de Noailles, who also exemplified Rilkean love). Similarly, the hero of the autobiographical novel *The Notebooks of Malte Laurids Brigge* (1910) does not want to be loved; at the end, Rilke's re-interpretation of the parable of the Prodigal Son makes virtually the same point. Brigge resolves never to love, lest someone be placed in "the hideous position of being loved" (VI, 941). As the novel implies, there *is* something selfish about wanting to be loved. That such a wish is, however, as inevitable and important as the desire for food is not noted. For a largely self-contained person, a "Narcissus," certain elemental human needs obviously have no relevance.

At least Rilke practiced what he preached. His marriage to the sculptress Clara Westhoff, while never legally ended, resulted in virtual separation after about a year and a half, though the two corresponded frequently and saw each other occasionally. To be sure, there were strong professional and economic reasons for this arrangement, but what shall one say about his refusal to attend the wedding of his own daughter?[19] He was after all the laureate of "maidens" and young women, a reverse sexist, who professed a strong belief in female superiority. *Cherchez la mère!* As we have seen, Phia Rilke kept her son in girl's clothes until he was five and otherwise gave him a bad time. Unsurprisingly, he avoided seeing her after he was fifteen; perhaps the warm praise of mothers in his works[20] represents a rather pathetic compensation. There seems to be no reason to question Simenauer's generalization that a split between love and desire is typical of men with "mother-fixations";[21] in any case, it fits Rilke perfectly. He admitted that perhaps because he did not love his mother, he was not a loving person.[22]

If "intransitive" love represented a complex rationalization of Rilke's own inability to love—openly admitted in many of his letters[23]—it also fitted in with his artist's need for privacy, indeed isolation. He was no Bach, who could create while surrounded by a small army of children, and he cannot be faulted for following the style of life his genius demanded. If only he had spared us his theory of nonlove, disguised as its reverse!

Whether or not his relations with his mother lay behind Rilke's emotional troubles, there is no doubt of the mythical symbol that best represents them: it is the self-isolated figure of Narcissus, who occurs in Rilke's poetry with significant frequency. In Ovid's version he falls in love with his own reflection in the water, rejecting the nymph who is enamored of him, the potential "thou," to whom he might otherwise have responded. (As Rilke-Brigge would put it: to be loved is shameful!) Self-love of course eliminates the question of transitive versus intransitive passion; it is literally reflexive. As Kunz[24] and—to a lesser extent—others have shown, the image of Narcissus is related to a whole series of related symbols like the swan in *Poèmes Français*, "tout entouré de lui-même" (II, 540), and the angels of the *Elegies*, glorious figures who mirror themselves. Then there is the rose, which:

> se caresse en soi-même
> par un propre reflet éclairé.
> Ainsi tu inventes le thème
> du Narcisse exaucé   (II, 576)

(caresses itself in itself/illuminated by its own reflection./By this you find the theme/of Narcissus fulfilled). It is relevant to note that the rose is a classic erotic symbol. When Narcissus appears, he reminds us that the mirror figures again and again in Rilke: it gives a purer reality than does the empirical world,[25] the poet thought. Finally, one recalls his poem "Self-Portrait from the Year 1906" where the portrait seems to describe an image in the mirror (I, 522f).

Two complete poems and a sketch (all of 1913) testify directly to Rilke's fascination with the figure of Narcissus. In

one we read "Er liebte, was ihm ausging, wieder ein" (II, 56)
—What emanated from him, he brought back within himself,
by loving. Surely this is the height of autarky. If Narcissus,
like so many figures in Rilke, stands for the artist, then it is
for one who avoids all communication. In the second poem,
the youth contrasts the dangerous impression his beauty
might make on a woman to his calm, aesthetically distanced
image on the water. "I could think that I might have a lethal
effect" (II, 57), he sums up, with only a trace of concern. Life
is problematic, art serene; isolation is the only sound position
for the artist.

Whereas Rilke fled emotional involvement with women,
his attitude in other contexts was very different. Women,
especially "maidens," are superior to men as a class,[26] partly
because they can love without requital. Apparently annoyed
by his cult of women, Miss Butler wrote that he always regarded them as "potential or actual martyrs to men."[27] (Possibly there is some autobiographical experience behind Rilke's
theory.) Goethe also put women "on a pedestal," sometimes
almost literally, throughout his career, but in his works there
appear also a number of female characters who are not glorified. For his part, Rilke has a whole gallery of feminine saints
of love—the Portuguese Nun, Louise Labé, and so forth, and
even such unlikely candidates as Sappho and Bettina Bren-
tano, whose adolescent and unrequited infatuation with
Goethe he elevated into an instance of love at its most intransitive. As for Rilke, he could offer women not human devotion—except briefly—but immortality in the framework of his
poems; true to his aesthetic theory, he changed his loves from
"things" to "art things" which would perhaps endure forever. At the least, he would link them with "art things" in
the dedication of a poem or a whole book. Understandably

enough, many women preferred this sort of love-making to the more conventional kind.

Thus if Rilke, on the level of sexual behavior, was at times almost a latter-day Don Juan, he was simultaneously an Orpheus[28] who tried to save his loves from oblivion, a *Frauenlob* ("Lady-Praiser," sobriquet of a German minnesinger) whose great theme was the exaltation of women. In his poetry Rilke paid reparations, as it were, to those who had loved him and from whom he had compulsively fled.

Even in some of his most moving love lyrics, the theme of avoidance occurs. Thus "Love Song" begins:

> Wie soll ich meine Seele halten, dass
> sie nicht an deine rührt?   (I, 482)

(How shall I hold my soul, so that/it does not touch yours?) Throughout, he uses the image of the violin: some god (perhaps) holds it in his hand; from the two strings a lovely sound arises. The bow touches both simultaneously, but the strings must never touch each other.

In "Du im Voraus/verlorene Geliebte"—to a lover lost before the poet had seen her—intransitive love reaches its height. The speaker links "the one who never came" with images, landscapes, and other "things" significant to him but admits that he does not know what sounds are dear to his imagined love. "Who knows if the same/bird did not sound as it flew through us/yesterday, in the evening, when we were alone?" (II, 79). The last question reflects Rilke's notion of *Weltinnenraum* (cosmic inner space)—the idea that since reality is within, true events and objects are also within the individual, within the poet essentially.[29] Thus any object—here the term includes animals and even human beings—becomes real only in art. Rilke writes about a tree:

> Erst in der Eingestaltung
> in dein Verzichten wird er wirklich Baum.   (II,168)

(Only when shaped into form/within your renunciation does it really become a tree.)[30] Rilke's attitude toward love and his theory of art are one and the same: both imply the absolute triumph of the aesthetic over vulgar reality. Again, one may regret that he clothed both in quasi-philosophical garments.

Like Nietzsche, Rilke has sometimes been compared by his admirers to Christ; he would not have been flattered by this. From quite early days he rejected the concept of the mediator and felt that "the greatest one" was yet to be born (I, 273). In his younger years, at least, he was much attracted by Nietzschean ethics, and it may well be that his fascination with the poor and the blind had very little to do with compassion. That for instance is the impression given by his unforgettable but rightly notorious line: "Denn Armut ist ein grosser Glanz aus Innen" (I, 356)—For poverty is a great radiance from within. E. M. Butler even charges him with "cruel fastidiousness." [31] His attitude here is in line with the fashionable aestheticism of the nineties, and few creeds could be more opposed to Christianity than the idolatry of art. While there is much confusion about what Rilke meant by "God"—he was hardly sure himself—and while no consensus exists about the significance of the angels in the *Elegies*, his image of Christ is unambiguous: a pathetic, at times rather noble, but hopelessly misled person, the champion of otherworldly values, and thus in Nietzsche's sense an enemy of life. One must agree with Eudo Mason that were it not for the *Sonnets to Orpheus*, one might conclude that Rilke was a Luciferian figure like Leopardi or Nietzsche; his frequent references to love and humility seem "almost dishonest." [32]

Whereas Frank Wood holds that Rilke's Orpheus is "in many ways modeled after the Christ of the Gospels,"[33] probably Erich Heller is closer to the truth in seeing in the mythical singer a mingling of Dionysian and Apollonian elements.[34]

In his early prose sketch "The Apostle" (1896; IV, 452–459), Rilke confronts Christian with exaggeratedly Nietzschean notions; the latter are completely victorious. After presenting, impressionistically, a fashionable party at an expensive hotel, Rilke draws our attention to a mysterious stranger, later called "the magnificent man." He alone opposes a project to aid the victims of a great fire, radically rejecting the ethic of love and compassion: "the law of love was given us too early." Man was not ready for the "ridiculously childish nobility" of the Nazarene. Christianity is poison for the weak, and modern man is like a beast of prey whose claws and teeth have been filed down; the world has become one great hospital.[35] Only the great man with his unconquerable will and a "victorious smile" can prevail. Let the weak die! "I go into the world to kill love." Suddenly, mysteriously, the "apostle" vanishes. Is he Nietzsche? the Antichrist? Both?

While the vocabulary is Nietzschean, the tone and content are so extreme that they go far beyond that philosopher, except for the wildest passages of his very late works. "The Apostle" can well be contrasted with Mann's "At the Prophet's," where a similarly outré figure is presented, but satirically. Rilke has written a parody of Nietzsche, yet the tone of the story makes it clear that the apostle is seen as admirable and at least largely correct; the caricature must be involuntary.

Probably Mason was right to hold that Rilke had a secret Christian within.[36] This would account for his vehemence here as a "compensation" and similarly explain such later expressions in his letters as "my rabid anti-Christianity" or the "telephone Christ into which one calls: who is there, and nobody answers." [37] "Telephone" reminds us that Rilke particularly disliked the concept of Christ as the mediator.[38] In contrast, Stefan George wrote of Christianity with far more balance and objectivity precisely because he could hardly be charged with possessing a secret Christian within. "Cross, thou shalt long remain the light of the earth!" [39]

Two series of poems, "Visions of Christ" (1896–1898), are much less vehement. At times half-serious or downright comic, they are somewhat reminiscent of Hans Sachs's Shrovetide plays and Goethe's early farces; there is also an echo of Gerhart Hauptmann's once-renowned tearjerker *Hannele* (III, 129). In these poems Jesus is presented with considerable if intermittent sympathy, but he appears throughout as a rather unhappy man, with no trace of divinity. At one point he identifies himself with the Wandering Jew; he specifically denies being God; and he holds that his blood (his influence?) is poison not wine (III, 148, 151). (The last touch recalls the bitterness of "The Apostle.") He appears as a charismatic "fool" who appeals to children, and as a proletarian; when an artist paints him as a coward, he defends himself well (III, 135, 140f). In true Rilkean fashion he rejects love but has no objection to spending the night with a Magdalene figure. The last poem points toward the triumph of passion over asceticism (III, 166–169). Jesus does not appear here; that would be redundant, for to Rilke asceticism was Christianity and vice versa: it was one of the great enemies.

In the *New Poems*, the function of saints, angels, and Christianity itself is mainly a decorative one; it hardly bears more intrinsic weight than do the poems about Buddha or Mohammed, to whom I believe Rilke was not particularly devoted. With a very few exceptions like the magnificent "Archaic Torso of Apollo," this collection is made up of morally neutral "art things" (*Kunstdinge*), which often present other art things, such as a statue or dance, or treat the nature of art itself, or both. Generally, the poems are symbolic, but only the aesthetic symbolism matters. Who would be philistine enough to object? It is all the more remarkable then that Rilke's hostility toward and even scorn of Jesus persist in these relatively objective, distanced poems. In this one case he gives us not an image but a most tendentious exposé.

It is not that Rilke presented Jesus as merely a man—scarcely a new idea—or even as a defeated man; rather, he is portrayed as one who has failed because he committed a gross moral error. In the poem "The Olive Garden" (I, 492–494) Jesus complains poignantly that he can no longer find God and doubts his existence. Jesus feels himself a deceived deceiver: "O nameless shame." No angel came: "For angels do not come to such prayers." Those who lose themselves are abandoned by all, repudiated by their fathers, excluded from their mothers' wombs.

Sic Rilke, with devastating scorn and feline cruelty; yet it is not Jesus but the poet whom these lines devastate. "When you strike at a king you must kill him," as Emerson said.[40] As in "The Apostle," Rilke has used an exaggerated Nietzschean notion; Nietzsche generally wrote of Christ in a very decent way. One recalls George's much more moderate statement that he who has never thrown himself away need never repent (above, p. 139).

Two other poems are similar in attitude. "Crucifixion" (I, 581f) portrays the event most unedifyingly: "Far in the background Maria screamed/and he roared like an animal [*brüllte*] and decayed." "Nun's Complaint" (II, 31–34) is a sort of dramatic monologue spoken by a devoted but very limited woman—again, an ordinary person is treated scornfully—who states that Jesus' mother is now a "fine lady [*Dame*] in heaven" and that he himself now has all the women he could possibly want. Sexually frustrated, she wonders whom she was really calling, when she called to Jesus. Written in 1909, the poem may show the influence of Freud, via Lou Andreas-Salomé. While it is much less abrasive than "The Olive Orchard" and "Crucifixion," it remains rather trivial.

Until his late poetry, Rilke has a good deal to say about God; it is significant that in his greatest work the figure of the deity, generally unconvincing in the early writings, virtually disappears.[41] "God" would often appear to be a limit concept: he may or may not exist, but by definition there can be nothing beyond him. From the beginning, Rilke's God seems vague, shifting, impossible to pin down. Is this predominantly an emerging "art god,"[42] or a personification of art, like Orpheus? Sometimes God is seen as an ancient tower (I, 253), suggesting the Judeo-Christian divinity; often as an unfinished god of the future in quasi-Nietzschean terms. In some moods, Rilke felt that men were creating God.[43] As we have seen, he was to maintain later that a phallic god should be created for modern man. Bewildered by these shifts, one may ask: was God, to Rilke, a being who does not exist, like the unicorn in the *Sonnets to Orpheus*? "O dieses ist das Tier, das es nicht gibt" (I, 753). Knowing, thanks especially to Erich Heller,[44] how much Rilke had in common with Nietzsche, one is tempted to believe that he too "knew" that God is dead but felt as free to discuss the deity in aesthetic terms as to deal with any other idea or image. To Rilke nothing was too sacred to be subordinated to the demands of art; nor was anything too profane to be raised to the level of art. From a strictly aesthetic point of view, an image of God may well be as religiously neutral as, say, Cézanne's apples. This may seem amazing in view of the frequent references to the deity in *The Book of Hours;* but as Mason points out, they prove nothing about Rilke's personal beliefs.[45]

Rilke's *Stories of God* (1900) proved to be very popular, perhaps because of their combination of seeming piety, charm of style, humor, and a certain artfully calculated childlikeness. Thus the notion that "Russia borders on God" is discussed at length. (A slightly condescending Russophilia was much in vogue with German writers around 1900.) Actually, *Stories* is a triumph of the "false naive," the precious disguised as the simple, and it is to the poet's credit that he later repudiated the book.[46] "God" is a very human, fallible fellow. As one would expect, he is essentially an artist. It was for aesthetic reasons, we are told, that he created poor people—a thesis that anticipates the meretricious glorification of poverty in *The Book of Hours.* In short, the spiritual value of *Stories of God* is rather less than zero.

Like the *Stories, The Book of Hours* (1905) is superficially theocentric and overtly pious; basically it is neither. Thus it is not really incongruous that Rilke dedicated the work to the free-thinking, radically emancipated Lou Andreas-Salomé. She was a semi-Nietzschean, at least, and Nietzsche lurks behind these glorifications of monks, poverty, and death. That philosopher, it may be recalled, held that life was justifiable only as an aesthetic phenomenon; that was precisely the justification of God in Rilke's eyes though he was too politic to say so outright.[47] When the "I" of most of these verses (a monk) addresses God directly, he is the least religious. Thus he solemnly announces: "I circle round God, round that ancient tower" (I, 253), as if he were doing the Almighty a favor by these maneuvers. When the monk asks God what he would do if he died, adding a bit later "Was wirst du tun, Gott? Ich bin bange" (I, 275f)—What wilt thou do, God? I am worried—he has reached the peak of coyness. To be sure, Angelus Silesius wrote, in the seventeenth century, "Ich weiss dass ohne mich Gott nicht ein Nu kan leben" [48]—I know that God cannot live an instant without me—which represents a strange amalgam of Christianity, pantheism, and philosophical egotism; but at least the baroque poet believed what he was saying. This is a far cry from flirtation with a divinity half believed in, at best. Again, we encounter the "false naive."

Aesthetically, *The Book of Hours* is more satisfactory than *Stories of God*. If its melodious verses betray an almost fatal facility, making one wonder at times why a given poem stopped when it did, rather than running on still longer, there are also a few fine lines and passages, like the ones expressing exhilaration at the beginning of the century (I, 257). Two contrasting lines express the decadence of the time, which is by no means limited to monarchs:

> Die Könige der Welt sind alt
> und werden keine Kinder haben.   (I, 328)

(The kings of this world are old/and will have no children.) At times God is a neighbor, at others ineffably distant (I, 254f). Once he appears as an ancient tower; elsewhere he is only now being constructed by men, like a cathedral (*God is ripening,* I, 261f; cf. 268). In other words God may be a perhaps obsolescent relic, but equally he may be a God of the future, "ripening" in time, like a Hegelian idea. "In this night, all cats are gray." Generally speaking, *The Book of Hours* consists of random thoughts on God, artistic creation, and poverty. Its most challenging concept, a "death of one's own," will be treated below.

In *New Poems*, the sonnet "God in the Middle Ages" similarly uses the concept of a deity gradually developing through the efforts of men (I, 502f). Half-humorously, the poet relates how, when God "really got under way," the startled mortals who created him fled in terror. While *New Poems* contains numerous representations of divine or mythical figures—Greek gods, Old Testament heroes, Buddha, Mohammed, poems about or rather against Christ—it avoids God, with the exception just noted. The reason is clear: Rilke was now aiming to reproduce in art tangible, solid "things," comparable to the works of Rodin and Cézanne. Such "art things" are generally symbolic,[49] but first of all they must be densely real. Thus the Virgin Mary or Apollo might very well inspire an art thing, but an abstract or invisible God could not.

In his strange anti-novel *The Notebooks of Malte Laurids Brigge* (1910)—the title has also been translated as *The Journal of My Other Self*—[50] the protagonist makes certain rather mordant references to God. He is amazed that people believe they can have a god without "using" him (VI, 728); a purely formal religion is none. Very revealingly, he writes: "Do let's be honest: we have no theater any more than we have a god: for those a sense of community is needed" (VI, 922). It is no accident that the theater is mentioned before the deity. Generally speaking, the specifically religious element plays a much less important role in Brigge's life than do his neuroses, his horror of Paris—to him the city of *Angst* not light—or even his fascination with ghosts, provided they are of aristocratic origin. When however, at the end of the *Notebooks* he makes the great refusal, completely reversing the parable of the Prodigal Son by interpreting it in the light of "intransitive love," he has made a definitive negative religious statement. He does not love; One might love him, but "he did not yet wish to" (VI, 941–946). And it seems highly improbable, in the light of the book as a whole, that God is truly existent for Brigge, though he does struggle toward some sort of faith.

In general, Rilke's approach to religious figures of less than divine status is psychological, decorative, or—occasionally—humorous. Thus a prophet, a martyr, a personage of the New Testament may be transmuted into an art thing; or the focus may be on the narrative. (The angels of the *Elegies* are a different matter entirely.) Usually, such figures are the subjects of poems, but they also appear occasionally in his prose, like the Prodigal Son in *Brigge*. Often, as in this instance, Rilke tends to reinterpret the accepted version of a story or parable, sometimes radically.

"The Saint" (I, 383f) might well be called Freudian today. A young woman is unable to find water until she thinks of the youth whom she loves; then her divining rod becomes alive, as does her own blood. "Annunciation" (I, 409f) gives the words spoken by the angel to the Virgin. He is dazzled and bewildered but manages to convey his message through imagery:

> ich bin der Tag, ich bin der Tau,
> du aber bist der Baum.

(I am the day, I am the dew,/but still, you are the tree.) The second line is repeated three times. It is a pretty poem, perhaps too pretty. "The Three Kings" (I, 411–413) is a spoof of the New Testament account, too lighthearted to be in any way offensive. "St. Sebastian" (I, 507f) is a perfect example of the change of religious legend or myth into a sheerly aesthetic entity. The saint scorns his persecutors not because they are heathen or cruel; rather they are "die Vernichter eines schönen Dinges"—the destroyers of a lovely thing. This, incidentally, is a fine illustration of how Rilke stretched the meaning of "thing." Probably the twin sonnets "Adam" and "Eve" (I, 583–585), with their elaborate parallelisms, are the most self-consciously virtuoso of all these pieces. Rilke has not only changed the motivation of these primal figures; he has obviously transformed them into works of art. The poems do not deal with the biblical originals but with statues on the outer wall of a cathedral, "near the rose window." He further distances Eve by portraying her "with the apple in the apple-pose," reminding us both of the conventions of medieval art and of the model who presumably posed for the sculptor. The sonnets are closer to Montmartre than to the Book of Genesis.

The poems dealing with Old Testament figures are generally darker. Saul, whose desperate and problematic nature seems to have fascinated Rilke, screams and curses in order to give David more time to escape. After the encounter with the ghost of Samuel, he suffers a complete breakdown, described in a very modern way; it is almost like an episode from *Malte Laurids Brigge* (I, 564–566). In "Esther" (I, 570f) Rilke's method is more conservative: he does not change the biblical tale, but expands it, giving an account of Esther's intense fear while approaching King Ahasuerus in defiance of the law. Here Rilke's aim, like Mann's in *Joseph and His Brethren*, is to flesh out the story, not to change it drastically.

To mention only one more of Rilke's many treatments of more or less sacred themes: his highly representative "Birth of Mary" (I, 667) starts on the familiar note of the "false naive": "O how much it must have cost the angels,/not suddenly to burst out in song." They are "beside themselves with busybodiness [*Getue*]," which last word rhymes with the equally comic *Gemuhe*—the mooing of a cow. Even Voltaire could hardly have deflated the event more effectively— the tone of these verses implies that it was a non-event—but Rilke, typically, has provided enough sweetness and archness to keep his seraphic image intact, at least in the eyes of his more sentimental readers. Where Voltaire used acid, Rilke often employed whipped cream.

Rilke's early portrayal of angels in his poetry is generally rather conventional. At times his angel figure is mainly decorative; it may also be treated with a trace of irony, as in "Annunciation" (I, 409f). In the more serious "The Angel" (I, 508f) he remains largely within the tradition, using the biblical motif of wrestling with a celestial stranger. But in "L'Ange du Méridien" (I, 497), written six years before his first inspired beginning of the *Duino Elegies* in 1912, he stressed the great chasm separating angels from men—"Was weisst du, Steinerner, von unserm Sein?" (What do you know, creature of stone, of our being?)—as he was to stress it repeatedly in the *Elegies*. Other short poems of the period strike the same note. Whereas Stefan George's famous angel is the fair messenger of Beauteous Life, reminding one of Art Nouveau figures, the angels of Rilke's mature poetry are far more complex, far harder to comprehend.

It seems convenient to follow first the "negative road" and establish what these beings are not. Above all they are not messengers—thus in the etymological sense they are not angels at all—nor are they mediators, saviors, or guides.[51] Nor are they visible, though Rilke makes it clear that they are beautiful and convinces us that they are gloriously so. Yet they are not merely concretions of beauty (or art things); their sublimity is frightening, and the sublime is not merely an aesthetic quality.[52] As completely transhuman, they are nonmoral from man's point of view. Being mirrors of themselves, they are utterly self-contained. This is reminiscent of Rilke's remark that the eyes of Rodin's statues never look at the viewer.[53] Mason holds that the angels are Narcissistic to the highest degree,[54] an extreme judgment, since they do have a positive function. There can be no communication with them, yet on occasion the poet may "praise the world to the angel" (I, 719). Since no one can tell or sing the deeds of invisible, inaccessible beings, the angels are beyond mythology and constitute as it were a metamyth. Yet their function as preservers of beauty, in eternity, is a mythic one. An ancient analogy is Plutarch's "Mothers," divinities equally inaccessible to man (except belatedly to Goethe's Faust), who guard the abstract forms or patterns in a realm outside of space and time.

Speaking of the aversion of the Hebrews to making works of plastic art, Herder attributed it to the loftiness of their religious concepts: "The most perfect has no image." [55] Yet of course Rilke found an abundance of images for these angels of his own devising—an almost impossible task. As Goethe remarked: "Everything perfect in its kind must transcend its kind," and Rilke's art has done just that in the *Elegies*. Like van Gogh or better Blake, he managed, in his own phrase, to "say the unsayable." Rilke is able to evoke these invisible beings so that we believe, impossibly enough, to be seeing them:

> Frühe Geglückte, ihr Verwöhnten der Schöpfung,
> Höhenzüge, morgenrötliche Grate
> aller Erschaffung,—Pollen der blühenden Gottheit,
> Gelenke des Lichtes, Gänge, Treppen, Throne,
> Räume aus Wesen, Schilde aus Wonne, Tumulte
> stürmisch entzückten Gefühls und plötzlich, einzeln
> *Spiegel:* die die entströmte eigene Schönheit
> wiederschöpfen zurück in das eigene Antlitz.   (I, 689)

(Early perfected, you pampered children of creation/High ranges, dawn-reddish ridges/of all creating—pollen of flowering godhead/joinings of light, ways, stairs, thrones,/spaces of being, shields of delight, tumults/of stormily ecstatic feeling and suddenly, singly,/*mirrors*, which draw their own beauty,/back again into their own faces.) Along with the magnificent crescendo of metaphors, one notes how deftly Rilke has kept this passage from being too visual, by balancing abstract against concrete terms. Thus "godhead" offsets "pollen," "being" is contrasted to "spaces," and so on. We cannot really envisage "shields of delight," but the so-called inner eye, or the imagination, has perceived tremendous images; we have a subliminal grasp of these figures.

The first thing we learn about the angels is that they are arrayed (I, 685) in ordered ranks,[56] like the traditional Heavenly Hosts. They are awesome—"almost deathly birds of the soul" (I, 689)—precisely because of their inhuman beauty and perfection, and "endowed with an overwhelming fullness of being which to us appears 'terrible'," as Holthusen puts it.[57] We would be blinded by them, could we see them, just as Faust was dazzled when he looked directly at the sun. Yet they exist, and a very few persons, as we shall see, can apparently send messages to them though they receive no answers.

Primarily the angels are storehouses and symbols of beauty, which exists invisible within them. Not merely aesthetic in function, they appear as guardians of all that is valuable in the human tradition, indeed of perfection. In the poem "Turning" ("Wendung," II, 82–84), Rilke implied very clearly that he was turning away from art things to a more inward sort of poetry: "Work of the eye is done,/do now heart-work/on the images in you, the captured ones." Written about two years after the inception of the Elegies, these lines clearly imply a shift from the mood and method of New Poems. The late poetry returns, on a far higher level, to the soulfulness of works like The Book of Hours but avoids the garrulity and softness of the early verse.

To return to the angels: they also "do heart-work." For

them "all towers are existent, *since* they have long since become invisible." To quote further Rilke's letter to his Polish translator, Hulewicz: "The angel of the Elegies is that being who takes the position of recognizing in the invisible a higher grade of reality."[58] In his turn, man, or rather the poet, will praise to the angel "things" the latter cannot see—simple objects like trees or houses—so that these, transformed, can enter the eternal angelic sphere. "We are the bees of the invisible," Rilke wrote in the same letter. Differently put, "things" are to become more inward; externalities increasingly disappear.[59] In other words, poets (and artists generally?) must transform the raw reality of an empirical tree to the evocation of that tree in a work of art, which will then become part of the angels' realm. Precisely this transformation the angels cannot effect, and in this one sense poor, tortured man—if he is a poet—is superior to them.

Assuming, as of course one must, that this whole fascinating construction is very seriously meant and radically different from the playfulness of works like *Tales about God*, one feels impelled to venture two criticisms. First, the denigration of the outer world in favor of the inner is in line with a long, dangerous German tradition extending from various medieval mystics via Luther to the romantics, especially Novalis, and thence to the late Rilke and beyond. Its most characteristic result is a dangerous split between a man's actions and his "inner" thoughts and intentions. All may be excused if the latter are pure. It is particularly paradoxical that an artist, whose work after all appeals first of all to the senses, should glorify the invisible. Possibly Rilke was influenced by the fact that the "things" evoked in his writing are not literally visible; but this is a very lame conjecture, for one of his great aims, often brilliantly achieved, was to make them *seem* visible. Second, we note the extreme exclusivity of Rilke's aesthetic world. It contains angels; an ultra-remote "God" is mentioned once or twice; on earth there are a handful of poets, a few lovers and heroes, and untold millions of the disinherited, the "many too many." Despite some of the early verse, Rilke was far from sympathetic to ordinary people; in fact, he was a snob of the first water,[60] as his pretensions to noble birth and above all his ineffable letters to highborn ladies reveal. Actually, Rilke was more of an elitist than Stefan George, who was proud of his descent from Rhenish peasants and explicitly stated that the "new nobility" whom he wished to train did not depend on birth. George's dislike of "the masses" was almost as strong as Rilke's or Heine's, but unlike Rilke, he was honest about it.

The angels, like most of Rilke's figures, have a dual aspect. On the one hand, as bastions of aestheticism, they are unassailable. Rilke has raised the doctrine *l'art pour l'art* to *l'art, c'est l'ange.* Yet since the angels are inaccessible, they confirm man's essential loneliness. Even the poet, whose role is praise and "saying the things to the angel" (cf. I, 719), cannot be sure that he is heard. His evocations of them, like his statements to them, are based on faith alone. Thus it is appropriate that the *Elegies* are a mixture of praise and lament; both strains are found mingled throughout the work as a whole. The Sixth and Seventh are the happiest, the Fourth, Fifth, and Tenth the most sorrowful. (It will not do at all to dismiss the Tenth as an "afterthought"; it was begun in 1912, and was always planned as the last.[61] Aesthetically, it is one of the finest: Rilke's "City of Pain" can well bear comparison with the evocation of London in *The Waste Land.*)

The final lines of the last (Tenth) Elegy, which is largely devoted to death, are particularly difficult:

Und wir, die an *steigendes* Glück

> denken, empfänden die Rührung,
> die uns beinah bestürzt,
> wenn ein Glückliches *fällt*.   (I, 726)

(and we, who think of happiness as *rising*, would feel compassion which almost dismays us when a happy being *falls*).
To Rilke, every happiness reaches a peak from which it must
decline; this may be a melancholy event but should not be
thought of as a shattering one.[62] In context the lines refer to
death and suggest that it should not appall us; man reaches
the top of a parabola, as it were, and inevitably starts down-
ward. Thus read, the lines quoted form a bridge to the far
brighter *Sonnets to Orpheus,* in which life and death are seen
as halves of one great entity. The *Elegies* end neither as lament nor as praise but on a slightly muted note of acceptance.

As we have seen, the mythical role of the poet is to trans-
mute raw experience into art, which then contributes to the
timeless aesthetic order guarded by the angels. This would
hardly seem to have much of an existential appeal—except to
poets. When Rilke wrote that as a poet he was radically cut
off from men, he overstated, but the implied lack of interest
in the average person was quite real.[63] This may well limit
the intellectual and human value of the *Elegies,* perhaps also
their ultimate value; but their aesthetic appeal remains enormous. Similarly, despite the sinister cult of power it implies,
Algabal is still splendid poetry; Wordsworth remains great
despite his inanities about babies and children. Those who
would make a great philosopher out of Rilke are unwittingly
the enemies of his reputation, not those who try soberly to
note his limitations as well as his poetic virtues.

Critics are fond of speaking of the "dialectical reversal"
(*Umschlag*) that led from the generally melancholy *Elegies*
to the exuberant *Sonnets to Orpheus.*[64] Broadly speaking this
view is correct, although some of the *Elegies* do strike that

note of praise that is central to the later work. It is interesting that the *Sonnets* were the product of the second great creative breakthrough—in 1922—which brought about the completion of the *Elegies*. The *Sonnets* were occasioned by the death of a gifted young girl, the dancer Wera Ouckama Knoop, and must have been intended, in part, as a consolation to her mother. It seems clear, however, that Rilke's glorification of the poet, of song, would have been written in any case. Thus E. M. Butler's remark, "All his life Rilke had been . . . following young girls and women down into the shades and trying to rescue them from oblivion," [65] while characteristically witty, is characteristically reductive.

Orpheus is the most convincing and attractive mythological figure Rilke ever shaped. Although of course descended from the Greek singer, he stands primarily for the lyrical impulse as such:

> Ein für alle Male
> ists Orpheus, wenn es singt.   (I, 733)

(Once and for all/it's Orpheus when there's song.) Yet "he comes and goes"; inspiration cannot be continuous. That there is an intimate bond between the late Rilke's image of himself and his Singer-God hardly needs to be mentioned. This Orpheus is not narcissistic; he is communicative by definition, as it were, and he is far more comprehensible than the angels. As a singer he is "*the* representative of man," in Rilke's eyes; in fact, he is a sort of non-Christian savior.[66] His "double sphere" (*Doppelbereich*) embraces life and death, this world and the other. Since the two spheres are closely interrelated, Orpheus is the lord of transmutation, a god of death as well as life: "Ist dir Trinken bitter, werde Wein" (I, 770), If you find drinking bitter, become wine. Death does not mean an end, but a metamorphosis. Since Orpheus accepts the "double sphere," his special mode is hymnic, his motto is praise. Although it is quite true that Orpheus has Apolline traits and was linked by the Greeks to Dionysus Zagreus, who was also torn to bits, he is not primarily a Nietzschean synthesis of those deities but, to repeat, the quintessence of song. In his serenity he is a god of healing, perhaps because he represents the principle of metamorphosis. To some extent, perhaps, he will heal the wounds inflicted by the girl's death.

Orpheus, then, is both an aesthetic divinity and more than that. The famous statement "Gesang ist Dasein," Song is existence (I, 732), seems a bit simplistic if read in isolation, but Rilke is making the point that poetry is not concerned with the desire to obtain something but is a form of existence in its own right. This is not far from Kant's position in the *Critique of Judgment*. Precisely because of the disinterested purity of song, the *Sonnets* imply, it is able to afford consolation though that is not its inherent aim.

The figure of the young dancer, so recently dead, is the most impressive of the long series of "maidens" whom Rilke glorified at excessive length. Unlike most of them she was an artist and a person not a fiction. In terms of the myth the poet almost had to link her with Eurydice (I, 759).[67] Wisely, he did this in a brief, almost casual way, for the dancer has almost nothing in common with the Greek matron. It is far more significant that the girl is aligned with Orpheus by the idea of metamorphosis. In Rilke's eyes a great dancer transmutes motion, rhythm, and body into a new work of art. This occurs earlier in the especially fine poem "Spanish Dancer" (I, 531f); and the theme of dancing is frequent in the *Sonnets*. The bold line "Dance the orange" (I, 740) indicates his belief that the art could attain almost any effect. Of course metamorphosis is not limited to art. Man must

welcome change, both in life and beyond it, though Rilke did
not commit himself to any concept of immortality:

> Wolle die Wandlung. O sei für die Flamme begeistert,
> . . .

> Wer sich als Quelle ergiesst, den
> erkennt die Erkennung   (I, 758f)

(Will transformation. Oh, be ardent for the flame . . . Whoever pours himself out as a fountain, him perception shall
perceive.) The intention of these appropriately orphic lines
can be most succinctly given in three words from Goethe's
"Holy Longing": "Stirb und werde," die and be reborn.
Neither poet pretends to know what will happen after rebirth; Rilke is generally the less sanguine of the two. That
the Orphic cults believed in immortality may have somewhat
influenced his choice of the mythical hero of the Sonnets; but
he does not mention them in these poems.

If the question of eternal life is left open, death remains
very much a fact for Rilke. Even Orpheus, who was at least
a demigod, was killed by angry devotees of Bacchus; Rilke's
personal maenads were much kinder. Like John Webster,
Rilke "was much possessed by death";[68] the rather irrelevant
criticism has been made that he was unduly afraid of it.[69]
For a person of his sensibility, that would be hardly unnatu-
ral; and in any case the approach to death in the Sonnets does
not seem to be based on fear.

Rilke has come to accept death as the other side of life,
invisible to us like the other side of the moon but indubitably
real.[70] Thus if a poet praises life, as Rilke does in the Sonnets,
he must celebrate death as well. Only he who has sung
"among the shades," as the mythical Orpheus did, may
glorify existence as a whole (cf. I, 736). It is no longer a
question of a "death of one's own" but of the common fate

of mankind. When Rilke speaks of the ideal attitude that one can attain, he employs the words "clear . . . awake and transparent, ambiguous, sunny, earthy, here" (I, 739). "Ambiguous" (*doppeldeutig*) has a positive meaning in this case; it signifies the awareness of both halves of the double sphere. Possibly it is the dead who furnish the living with strength (I, 740).[71]

This view of death and the dead leads to a total acceptance of existence; Rilke has moved a very long way from the neurotic world of Malte Laurids Brigge. Now he can write:

> Alles ist ausgeruht;
> Dunkel und Helligkeit
> Blume und Buch.   (I, 745)

(All has found rest:/darkness and brightness/flower and book.) Although men are compelled to drive forward restlessly, enduring, indeed divine patterns persist (cf. I, 769). Shortly before his death, he maintained that life is glorious.[72] The word "optimism" would be trivial here; Rilke's position is more like Nietzsche's "tragic acceptance of life." The *Sonnets* end on a new note of synthesis:

> Zu der stillen Erde sag: Ich rinne.
> Zu dem raschen Wasser sprich: Ich bin.   (I, 771)

(To the quiet earth say: I am flowing./To the rapid water speak: I am.)

To sum up: one must distinguish sharply between Rilke's use of traditional mythology and the myths that were largely his own creation. (In the figure of Orpheus we have a fusion, for he is both the ancient singer and the concretion of modern poetry, mainly the latter.) In *The Book of Hours* Rilke is playing with the myth: it is not too much to speak of his flirtation with God. If "poverty is a great radiance from within," it must be noted that Rilke did his best to avoid that gleam. The *New Poems* make extensive use of myth as raw material; Rilke consistently (and of course legitimately) subordinates the accepted tales and figures of the past to his aesthetic aims. Thus his St. Sebastian is explicitly called "a beautiful thing"; his Eve has very little to do with the biblical original; his Christ is a miserable, deluded creature. Perhaps the greatest of the *New Poems*, "Archaic Torso of Apollo," does not seem specifically Apolline but is a magnificent evocation of the Greek ethos as well as Greek beauty; one has to go back to Winckelmann to find its equal.[73] Here Rilke's "negative capability" is enormous; unlike Stefan George, for example, he was not a classicist nor particularly devoted to Hellas, yet these few lines surpass anything that George wrote about Greece. "You must change your life" is electric in context, whereas George's "Hellas eternally our love" is only a concise, impressive statement of a program.

How desperate Rilke's search for a myth was may be seen from his "Five Hymns" (II, 86–92), written in August 1914 to celebrate the "most distant, incredible War-God." Of course Rilke was one of the least military of men, and it would be grossly unfair to attack him for succumbing to an enthusiasm that swept away far wiser persons than he. (Not only on the German side, though the Germans were, typically, more thorough and extreme in their patriotic frenzy than others.) Rilke's approach is characteristic: he is obviously ambivalent about the War God, but writes "Hail unto me, that I see people deeply moved." With less excuse, Gottfried Benn "hailed" the Nazis—briefly—for similar reasons. Rilke is very frank about his: he is well aware that war is terrible, but it fuses individuals into one communal whole; personal motives are overcome. His martial mood was of very brief duration, and at the end of "Five Hymns" he focuses not on the exhilaration evoked by war but on the sorrow it causes.

In the late poetry, creatures of Rilke's own imagination predominate. Rather, one might say that these new mythic beings, like the angels and the "Laments" of the *Elegies*, are more obviously his own creations than are Apollo and Eve in *New Poems*. While the mythical "persons" of the later poems are very difficult to comprehend, one should bear in mind that their predecessors often are also radically different from the archetypal figures of the same name found in the Bible, the *Acta Sanctorum*, or Ovid. Rilke's saints and heroes are to a large extent his own invention.

In an extended sense, one may speak of Rilke's concepts of love and death as myths. His notions are based not on empirical evidence but on a mixture of truth and falsehood, thought and feeling. "Intransitive love," like "free love," is a contradiction in terms; it neatly excludes any thought of mutual commitment. Although the idea of "a death of one's own"—*der eigene Tod*—is more plausible, it also is basically fallacious.[74] To be sure, other things being equal, it would be pleasant to say that a friend's death grew out of his life, "like the fruit from the flower." But who can decide just which death is authentic? When, for instance, the dramatist Ödön von Horváth, who had fled from Hitler, was killed in Paris by a falling tree, was his death inauthentic because accidental or was it his "own" in symbolizing the blackly absurd fate of the emigré? One cannot make treaties in advance with death or expect poetic justice from it; and Rilke's concept is, characteristically, an aesthetic and rather exclusive one. That he later sees death as the other half of life rather than an evil is a relatively credible view though hardly one that might comfort the bereaved. On this point one can find keener insights in the New Testament that Rilke, like Nietzsche, despised.

One cannot read Rilke carefully without realizing that

there is something very unusual, almost unique, about his whole mode of thinking and feeling. Thought and emotion, imagination and observation, are inextricably fused. Holthusen's phrase "monism of feeling" rightly implies that feeling dominates here; thought is only ancillary, and "the myth of omniscient and omnipotent feeling" is central.[75] Mason puts it bluntly: "His [Rilke's] thinking is ultimately directed against thinking itself."[76] Such judgments do not diminish the value of his poems, but do help to establish their kind. Compared to the genuinely philosophical poetry of Lucretius or Dante, Rilke's is a "mélange adultère du tout"; in that regard he is close to Shelley and Novalis. In the late poetry, a sort of cosmic system emerges, but it is a cosmos of unclear ideas.

Arguing against T. S. Eliot, Erich Heller has maintained that one cannot split off the thought of a given writer from his poetry: if the ideas are bad, the poem is bad.[77] In extreme cases this is undoubtedly true, but one can certainly reject Dante's notions of eternal punishment or Goethe's attitude toward nature without in the least reducing the stature of these poets. If however the ideas presented are outrageous, as in Nazi and Stalinite "literature," then the work fails aesthetically as well as intellectually. But it is only as the (youthful) laureate of poverty that Rilke sets one's teeth on edge; even the doctrine of intransitive love has some truth in it, and disbelief can be suspended. That his ideas are generally unconvincing rarely detracts from the artistic effect of his work.

Rilke was a supremely gifted poet, by no means merely a superb master of technique. He was capable of such flights of imagination as the evocation of the angels quoted above (p. 173), and could also render his art things almost tangibly real. Why then do many critics hesitate to call him a "great" poet without reservations? Some words of Friedrich Gundolf may be pertinent: Rilke was intellectually porous, without a firm point of view, penetrated by every experience, broken by God; he was also hectically erotic.[78] No doubt Gundolf, a sworn supporter of Stefan George, exaggerates Rilke's defects, and he seems irritated by the fact that Rilke had far greater aesthetic sensitivity than George. To put things more dispassionately, Rilke was possessed of "negative capability" to the highest degree. The defect of this virtue is that one searches in vain for a center, a firm core in his work. It is not a question of agreeing with his ideas. Not everyone accepts the convictions of T. S. Eliot, still fewer those of Stefan George; but one knows where these poets stand. Few readers, one likes to think, approve of Baudelaire's Satanism, yet who would question that he has a center? But to end on a note of praise: it has been very well said that Rilke's great aim was to express inwardness in a monumental way.[79] That he certainly attained, and it is his highest poetic achievement.

Epilogue

This study does not seem to call for formal conclusions, but a few final remarks may be appropriate. In recent decades the function of myth in German literature seems to have become a somewhat secondary one. Often it is half-serious or playful, as in much of Thomas Mann or Friedrich Dürrenmatt; or myths may be employed in an eclectic, almost random manner, as in Rilke and Gottfried Benn. Perhaps the most useful function of myth in the twentieth century has been as an integrative structural device in long, complex works like Joyce's *Ulysses* or Mann's *Doctor Faustus*.

Since 1945, German literature has been largely nonmythical in tone. Disillusion with Nazism, which operated largely with myths and symbols, may mainly account for this development. The Hitlerites manipulated such fictions as the superman, the blond beast, Siegfried, and the Aryan race very adroitly; they had also a truly Wagnerian flair for spectacle. Whereas the neo-romantics owed much to Wagner, the expressionists and others to Nietzsche, contemporary writers like Heinrich Böll, Hans Magnus Enzensberger, and Uwe Johnson emphasize social and political conditions. Günter Grass plays most skillfully with mythology; he is anything but mythic. Elisabeth Langgässer was perhaps the only notable postwar German novelist to employ myth with the utmost seriousness. One wing of the recent lyric poets, descended largely from Rilke, Georg Trakl, and Benn, makes much use of mythology but without any profound intellectual commitment. If the influence of any one figure predominates, it is probably that of Bertolt Brecht; Voltaire and the Enlightenment generally are also held in high regard, though seldom really emulated. The political stance of contemporary German writers tends to be either a rather skeptical, sophisticated liberalism or Marxism. Neither of these positions is conducive to the making of myths—at least not to creating those of a poetic sort.

Looking back to the writers considered in this book, one can observe how each of them has modified the concept of myth generally, and specifically the myth of the Greeks. Heine contributed the elements of wit and heterodox, often saucy imagination. At the same time, he refused to admire the Greek divinities or to grant them any tangible reality. With vast scholarship and intellectual courage, Burckhardt argued that the historical Greeks were neither virtuous nor happy, nor were their gods admirable. Wagner utilized certain notions he held about the Greeks in building the vast complex of the *Ring*. By rediscovering the Dionysiac element in Greek culture (already beautifully evoked in Goethe's "Prometheus Fragment") Nietzsche infused new life into the discussion of Greek mythology and culture. The extreme subjectivity of his views did not detract from their impact on literary men. In sharp contradistinction, George returned to a disciplined, Apollonian Greece. His fervor for Hellas recalls Winckelmann or Hölderlin; it is as if Burckhardt had never written. Characteristically, he holds up Greece as an ideal for the few, for a rigidly exclusive elite. Whereas Rilke is largely devoid of genuine enthusiasm for Hellas as such, his Greek figures have a magical attraction which his New Testament persons generally lack.

In that connection, it is remarkable that the writers considered in this book, all of them neopagan to some extent, generally regard Jesus with respect, admiration, and often affection. Heine remarks on his charisma in a tone amazingly free of irony; Nietzsche writes of Jesus' ethical nobility. He was the first and last Christian, Nietzsche held. Even Wagner planned a drama on Jesus. Whereas the archpagan George writes of Christ with measured respect, the "sweet" Rilke has a very different attitude. He is the only exception, calling Jesus "God's telephone" and heaping shrill, even hysterical invective upon him.

Looking back on many years of interest in German Hellenism, I find it surprising that the one figure who emerges as authentic from all this welter of myths is precisely Jesus Christ. My original bias, stemming from classical studies and a continuing admiration for Winckelmann and the Greek aspect of Goethe, was mildly neopagan. No one need apologize for such an approach. It would be a thick-skinned person indeed who was not fascinated with Winckelmann's Apollo, Goethe's Helena, or Nietzsche's Dionysus within their context, in literary works of art. It would be absurd, however, to claim that these figures—to say nothing of Wotan—are even remotely as real today as Jesus Christ. This is not a matter of religious belief; it is simply an observable fact, evident in the texts of the great German writers, from Herder and Hölderlin to our own time.

Yet perhaps because of Jesus' unique fascination, it is excruciatingly difficult to present authentic "Christ figures" in literature. Jesus is of course not the only divine figure to rise again after being slain; but he is unique, at least in the West, in undergoing sacrifice voluntarily and in suffering vicariously. This gives his life and death an inimitable poignancy. To some extent Prometheus did sacrifice himself for men, but who can imagine Adonis or Dionysus doing so? Such a concept would and did seem absurd to the pagan mind: "But we preach Christ crucified . . . unto the Greeks foolishness" (I Corinthians 1:23). To this point it must be added that the life of Jesus is documented in the Gospels, in vastly more detail, however problematic, than is that of any "straight" mythical figure. Even D. F. Strauss had to admit that the New Testament contains more than fiction. Jesus *is* more real than Apollo—no doubt the most attractive Greek deity. Jesus remains a controversial fact; Apollo, alas, a dream.

Jesus then being *sui generis,* it is obvious that evoking his personality in literature is an almost insuperable task. If a perfect figure is represented in a work of fiction, it is apt to be unbelievable; or sentimentally sweet; or, as in Klopstock's *Messias,* impossible to imagine vividly. Some writers, like Gerhart Hauptmann in *Emanuel Quint,* present him as downright neurotic. A third approach, even more reductive, tends in the direction of parody, even of scurrility. In Theodore Zielkowski's excellent *Fictional Prefigurations of Jesus,* many such "Jesus figures" are listed, but few of them are really both impressive and convincing. In the literature of the last century, roughly speaking, only two basically successful Christ figures are known to me: Melville's Billy Budd and Hofmannsthal's "Children's King," in *The Tower.* They are charismatic, but neither author tries to push us into believing that they are in any sense equivalent to Jesus; credibility is not sacrificed.

The way of the mythical writer is hard, in the latter half of the twentieth century. Who is to go beyond Mann's *Doctor Faustus* or Joyce's *Ulysses?* On the one hand, triteness threatens; on the other, sheer travesty. Whereas a private myth may seem to be almost a contradiction in terms, one sees why it was that Yeats, George, and Rilke were impelled to fashion mythical figures of their own invention.

Bibliography, Notes, and Index

Bibliography

PRIMARY SOURCES

Burckhardt, Jacob. *Gesammelte Werke*. 9 vols. Basel: Schwabe, 1955—.

———— *Gedichte*, ed. K. E. Hoffmann. Basel: Schwabe, 1926.

———— *Griechische Kulturgeschichte*, ed. Rudolf Marx. 3 vols. Stuttgart: Kröner, 1948–1952.

———— *Historische Fragmente*. Basel: Schwabe, 1942.

———— *Briefe*, ed. Max Burckhardt. 7 vols. to date. Basel: Schwabe, 1949—.

———— *Briefe*, ed. Fritz Kaphahn. Leipzig: Kröner, 1935.

———— *Briefe*, Insel-Bücherei Nr. 336, 1946.

George, Stefan. *Werke*. *Ausgabe in zwei Bänden*, Munich and Düsseldorf: Küpper, 1958.

Heine, Heinrich. *Sämtliche Werke*, ed. Ernst Elster. 7 vols. Leipzig and Vienna: Bibliographisches Institut, 1887–90.

———— *Briefe*, ed. Friedrich Hirth. 6 vols. Mainz: Kupferberg, 1950–1957.

———— *Gespräche mit Heine*, ed. H. H. Houben. Frankfort on the Main: Rütten and Loening, 1926.

———— "The First Draft of Heine's 'Für die Mouche,' " ed. Stuart Atkins. *Harvard Library Bulletin*, 13 (1959): 415–443.

Nietzsche, Friedrich Wilhelm. *Werke in drei Bänden*, ed. Karl Schlechta. 2 Aufl. Munich: Hanser, [1960].

Rilke, Rainer Maria. *Sämtliche Werke*, ed. Ernst Zinn. 6 vols. Wiesbaden: Insel, 1955–1966.

———— *Briefe und Tagebücher aus der Frühzeit, 1899–1902*. Leipzig: Insel, 1931.

———— *Briefe an einen jungen Dichter*. Leipzig: Insel, 1929.

———— *Briefe aus Muzot 1921–1926*. Leipzig: Insel, 1935.

———— *Briefe aus den Jahren 1907–1914*. Leipzig: Insel, 1939.

———— *Duineser Elegien. Die Sonette an Orpheus*, ed. Ernst Zinn. [Wiesbaden]: Insel, 1950.

Wagner, Richard. *Gesammelte Schriften und Dichtungen.* Fifth
edition. 10 vols. Leipzig: Breitkopf and Haertel/Siegel, n.d.
———— *Nachgelassene Schriften und Dichtungen.* Leipzig: Breitkopf and Haertel, 1895.
———— *Mein Leben.* Munich: List, 1963.

Boeckh, August. *Die Staatshaushaltung der Athener,* 2nd ed. Berlin: Reiner, 1851.
Goethe, Johann Wolfgang von. *Gedenkausgabe der Werke, Briefe
und Gespräche,* ed. Ernst Beutler. 24 vols. Zurich: Artemis,
1948–1954.
Herder, Johann Gottfried von. *Sämtliche Werke,* ed. Suphan. 33
vols. Berlin: Weidmann, 1877–1913.
Hesse, Hermann. *Gesammelte Dichtungen.* 7 vols. N.p.: Suhrkamp,
1958.
Hofmannsthal, Hugo von. *Gesammelte Werke.* 15 vols. Stockholm
and Frankfort on the Main: Fischer, 1946–1959.
Mann, Thomas. *Gesammelte Werke in zwölf Bänden.* Frankfort
on the Main: S. Fischer, 1960.
Schiller, Friedrich. *Sämtliche Werke,* ed. Eduard von der Hellen.
16 vols. Stuttgart and Berlin: Cotta, 1904–1905.
Schlegel, Friedrich. *Friedrich Schlegel 1794–1802: seine prosaischen Jugendschriften,* ed. Jacob Minor. Vienna: Konegen,
1882.

SECONDARY MATERIALS

I. Jacob Burckhardt
Gass, Alfred L. *Die Dichtung im Leben und Werk Jacob Burck-
hardts.* Bern: Francke, 1967.
Kaegi, Werner. *Jacob Burckhardt.* Basel: Schwabe, 1947.
Knittermeyer, Hinrich. *Jacob Burckhardt.* Zurich: Hirzel, 1949.
Martin, Alfred von. *Nietzsche und Burckhardt.* 3rd ed. Basel:
Reinhardt, 1945.
Neumann, Carl. *Jacob Burckhardt.* Munich: Bruckmann, 1927.
Rehm, Walther. *Jacob Burckhardt.* Frauenfeld/Leipzig: Huber,
1930.

Salin, Edgar. *Jacob Burckhardt und Nietzsche.* Heidelberg: Schneider, 1948.

Wenzel, Johannes. *Jacob Burckhardt in der Krise seiner Zeit.* Berlin: Deutscher Verlag der Wissenschaften VEB, 1967.

II. Stefan George

Boehringer, Robert. *Mein Bild von Stefan George.* Munich and Düsseldorf: Küpper, 1951.

David, Claude. *Stefan George: Sein dichterisches Werk.* Munich: Hanser, 1967.

Goldsmith, U. K. *Stefan George: A Study of His Early Works.* Boulder: University of Colorado Press, 1959.

Gundolf, Elisabeth. *Stefan George.* Amsterdam: Castrum Peregrini, 1965.

Gundolf, Friedrich. *George.* Berlin: Bondi, 1930.

Kronberger, Maximilian. *Nachlass.* Zurich: Privately printed, [1937].

Meessen, Hubert J. "Stefan Georges Algabal und die französische Décadence," *Monatshefte,* 39 (1947): 304–321.

Morwitz, Ernst. *Kommentar zu den Werken Stefan Georges.* Munich and Düsseldorf: Küpper, 1960.

Oswald, Victor A., Jr. "The Historical Content of Stefan George's *Algabal,*" *Germanic Review,* 23 (1948): 193–205.

Salin, Edgar. *Um Stefan George.* 2nd printing. Munich and Düsseldorf: Küpper, 1954.

Scott, Cyril. *Die Tragödie Stefan Georges.* Eltville am Rhein: Hempe, 1952.

Steiner, Herbert. *Begegnung mit Stefan George.* Aurora, New York: Wells College Press, 1942.

Weber, Max. *Wirtschaft und Gesellschaft.* Tübingen: Mohr, 1922.

III. Heinrich Heine

Butler, E. M. *Heinrich Heine.* London: The Hogarth Press, 1956.
———— *The Saint-Simonian Religion in Germany.* Cambridge, Eng.: At the University Press, 1926.

Fairley, Barker. *Heinrich Heine. An Interpretation.* Oxford: Clarendon Press, 1954.

Filtso, Maria. *Heinrich Heine und die Antike.* Diss. Munich, 1928.

Fleischmann, Jakob. "Heine und die Hegelsche Philosophie," *Deutsche Universitäts-Zeitung,* 14 (1959): 418–426.

Friedemann, Hermann. *Die Götter Griechenlands von Schiller bis Heine.* Diss. Berlin, 1906.

Galley, Eberhard. *Heinrich Heine,* 2nd printing. Stuttgart: Metzler, 1957.

Hirth, Friedrich. *Heinrich Heine. Bausteine zu einer Biographie.* Mainz: Kupferberg, 1950.

Hofrichter, Laura. *Heinrich Heine.* Oxford: Clarendon Press, 1963.

Iggers, G. "Heine and the Saint-Simonians," *Comparative Literature,* 10 (1959): 289–308.

Kurz, Paul Konrad. *Künstler, Tribun, Apostel, Heinrich Heine's Auffassung vom Beruf des Dichters.* Munich: Wilhelm Fink Verlag, 1967.

Lichtenberger, Henri. *Henri Heine Penseur.* Paris: Alcan, 1905.

Marcuse, Ludwig. "Heine and Marx, A History and a Legend," *Germanic Review,* 30 (1955): 110–124.

Prawer, S. S. *Heine the Tragic Satirist.* Cambridge, Eng.: At the University Press, 1961.

Puetzfeld, Carl. *Heinrich Heines Verhältnis zur Religion.* Berlin: Grote, 1912.

Rose, William. *Heinrich Heine. Two Studies of His Thought and Feeling.* Oxford: Clarendon Press, 1956.

Sandor, A. I. *The Exile of Gods.* The Hague and Paris: Mouton, 1967.

Spann, Meno. *Heine.* London: Bowes and Bowes, 1966.

Strich, Fritz. *Kunst und Leben.* Bern and Munich: Francke, 1960.

Weigand, H. J. "Heine's Return to God," *Modern Philology,* 18 (1920–1921): 309–342.

IV. Friedrich Nietzsche

Beithan, Ingeborg. *Friedrich Nietzsche als Umwerter der deutschen Literatur.* Heidelberg: Carl Winters, 1933.

Bernoulli, Carl A. *Franz Overbeck und Friedrich Nietzsche.* Jena: Diederichs, 1908.

———— *Nietzsche und die Schweiz.* Leipzig: Haessel, 1922.

Bertram, Ernst. *Nietzsche: Versuch einer Mythologie*, 7 Aufl. Berlin: Bondi, 1929.

Brinton, Crane. *Nietzsche*. Cambridge: Harvard University Press, 1941.

Campbell, T. M. "Nietzsche's *Die Geburt der Tragödie* and Richard Wagner," *Germanic Review*, 16 (1941): 185–200.

———— "Nietzsche–Wagner, to 1872," *PMLA*, 56 (1941): 544–577.

Ellis, Havelock. *Affirmations*. Boston and New York: Houghton Mifflin, 1915.

Else, Gerard F. *The Origin and Early Form of Greek Tragedy*. Cambridge: Harvard University Press for Oberlin College, 1965.

Hildebrandt, Kurt. *Nietzsches Wettkampf mit Sokrates und Plato*. Dresden: Sybillen, 1922.

Hollingdale, R. J. *Nietzsche*. London: Routledge and Kegan Paul, 1965.

Howald, Ernst. *Friedrich Nietzsche und die klassische Philologie*. Gotha: Perthes, 1920.

Jaspers, Karl. *Nietzsche und das Christentum*. Hameln: Seifert, n.d.

Kaufmann, Walter. *Nietzsche*, 3rd ed. New York: Vintage Books, 1968.

Kerényi, Karl. *Apollon*. Vienna: Franz Leo, 1937.

Kesselring, Max. *Nietzsches "Zarathustra" in psychiatrischer Beleuchtung*. Affoltern: Aehren Verlag, 1954.

Klages, Ludwig. *Die psychologischen Errungenschaften Nietzsches*. Leipzig: Barth, 1926.

Lonsbach, Richard M. *Nietzsche und die Juden*. Stockholm: Bermann-Fischer, 1939.

Rosenberg, Alfred. *Friedrich Nietzsche*. Munich: Eher, 1944.

Salin, Edgar. *Jacob Burckhardt und Nietzsche*. Heidelberg: Schneider, 1948.

Schlechta, Karl. *Der junge Nietzsche und das klassische Altertum*. Mainz: Kupferberg, 1948.

Simmel, Georg. *Schopenhauer und Nietzsche*. Leipzig and Munich: Duncker and Humblot, 1923.

Vogel, Martin. *Apollinisch und Dionysisch.* Regensberg: Bosse, 1966.

Wilamowitz-Moellendorf, Ulrich von. *Erinnerungen, 1848–1914.* Leipzig: Koehler, [c. 1928].

V. Rainer Maria Rilke

Andreas-Salomé, Lou. *Rainer Maria Rilke.* Leipzig: Insel, 1929.

Blume, Bernhard. "Ding und ich in Rilkes *Neuen Gedichten*," *Modern Language Notes,* 67 (1952): 217–224.

Buddeberg, Else. *Rainer Maria Rilke: eine innere Biographie.* Stuttgart: Metzler, 1955.

Butler, E. M. *Rainer Maria Rilke.* New York: Macmillan, 1941.

Gundolf, Friedrich. *Rainer Maria Rilke.* Vienna: Johannes-Presse, 1937.

Holthusen, Hans Egon. *Rainer Maria Rilke: A Study of His Later Poetry,* trans. J. P. Stern. New Haven: Yale University Press, 1952.

Kunz, Marcel. *Narziss: Untersuchungen zum Werk Rainer Maria Rilkes.* Bonn: Bouvier, 1970.

Mason, Eudo C. *Lebenshaltung und Symbolik bei Rainer Maria Rilke.* 2nd printing. Oxford: Marston, 1964.

————— *Rainer Maria Rilke.* Göttingen: Vandenhoeck and Ruprecht, 1964.

————— *Rilke's Apotheosis.* Oxford: Blackwell, 1938.

Pongs, Herman. "Rilkes Umschlag . . . ," *Dichtung und Volkstum,* 37 (1936): 75–97.

Salis, J. R. von. *Rainer Maria Rilkes Schweizer Jahre.* Frauenfeld: Huber, 1952.

Simenauer, Erich. *Rainer Maria Rilke: Legende und Mythos.* Frankfort on the Main: Schauinsland-Verlag, 1953.

Steiner, Jacob. *Rilkes Duineser Elegien.* Bern and Munich: Francke, 1962.

Weigand, H. J. "Rilke's 'Archaïscher Torso Apollos,'" *Monatshefte,* 51 (1959): 49–62.

Wood, Frank. *Rainer Maria Rilke: The Ring of Forms.* Minneapolis: University of Minnesota Press, 1958.

VI. *Richard Wagner*

Carlsson, Anni. "Das mythische Wahnbild Richard Wagners," *Deutsche Vierteljahrsschrift für Literaturwissenschaft und Geistesgeschichte*, 29 (1955): 237–254.

Donington, Robert. *Wagner's Ring and Its Symbols.* New York: St. Martin's Press, 1969.

Hildebrandt, Kurt. *Wagner und Nietzsche.* Breslau: Hirt, 1924.

Newman, Ernest. *The Life of Richard Wagner.* 4 vols. New York: Knopf, 1933–1946.

Petsch, Robert. "Der Ring des Nibelungen in seinen Beziehungen zur griechischen Tragödie und zur zeitgenössischen Philosophie," *Wagner-Jahrbuch*, 2 (1907): 284–330.

Schadewaldt, Wolfgang. "Richard Wagner und die Griechen," in his *Hellas und Hesperien.*² Zurich and Stuttgart: Artemis, 1970.

Shaw, George Bernard. *The Perfect Wagnerite.* London: G. Richards, 1898.

Stein, J. M. *Richard Wagner and the Synthesis of the Arts.* Detroit: Wayne State University Press, 1960.

Stein, Leon. *The Racial Thinking of Richard Wagner.* New York: Philosophical Library, 1950.

Wallace, William. *Richard Wagner as He Lived.* London: Kegan Paul, Trench, Trubner, 1925.

VII. *General*

Babbitt, Irving. *Rousseau and Romanticism.* Boston and New York: Houghton Mifflin, 1919.

Béguin, Albert. *L'Ame romantique et le rêve.* Paris: J. Corti, 1939.

Bentley, Eric. *A Century of Hero-Worship.* Boston: Beacon Press, [1957].

Bowra, C. M. *The Heritage of Symbolism.* London: Macmillan, 1943.

Butler, E. M. *The Tyranny of Greece over Germany.* Cambridge, Eng.: At the University Press, 1935.

Chase, Richard. *Quest for Myth.* Baton Rouge: Louisiana State University Press, 1949.

Eissler, K. R. *Goethe: A Psychoanalytic Study 1775–1786*. 2 vols. Detroit: Wayne State University Press, 1963.

d'Harcourt, Robert. *La Religion de Goethe*. Strasbourg: F.-X. Le Roux, 1949.

Hatfield, Henry. *Aesthetic Paganism in German Literature*. Cambridge: Harvard University Press, 1964.

Heller, Erich. *The Disinherited Mind*. Philadelphia: Dufour and Saifer, 1952.

Killy, Walther. *Wandlungen des lyrischen Bildes*. Göttingen: Vandenhoeck and Ruprecht, 1958.

Kolnai, Aurel. *The War Against the West*. London: V. Gollancz, 1938.

Lang, Paul Henry. *Music in Western Civilization*. New York: Norton, 1941.

Lerner, Max. *The Mind and Faith of Justice Holmes*. Boston: Little, Brown, 1943.

Levin, Harry. *James Joyce*. Norfolk, Conn.: New Directions, 1941.

Rehm, Walther. *Orpheus: der Dichter und die Toten*. Düsseldorf: Schwann, 1950.

Robertson, J. G. *The Gods of Greece in German Poetry*. Oxford: Clarendon, 1924.

Rosteutscher, J. H. W. *Die Wiederkunft des Dionysos*. Bern: Francke, 1947.

Santayana, George. *Egotism in German Philosophy*. London and Toronto: Dent, n.d.

Silesius, Angelus [Scheffler]. *Cherubinischer Wandersmann*, ed. Georg Ellinger. Halle a.S.: Niemeyer, 1895.

Simmons, Ernest J. *Leo Tolstoy*. Boston: Little, Brown, 1946.

Strich, Fritz. *Die Mythologie in der deutschen Literatur von Klopstock bis Wagner*. 2 vols. Halle: Niemeyer, 1910.

Tolstoy, Leo. *What is Art?* New York: Scribner's, 1904.

Notes

Chapter I. Introduction

1. See Theodore Ziolkowski, *Fictional Transfigurations of Jesus* (Princeton: Princeton University Press, 1972), and esp. his "Der Hunger nach dem Mythos" in *Die sogenannten Zwanziger Jahre* (Bad Homburg: Gehlen, 1970), pp. 169–201. Also Harry Levin, "Some Meanings of Myth" in *Myths and Mythmaking* (New York: Braziller, 1960), pp. 103–114; Henry Hatfield, "The Myth of Nazism," *ibid.*, pp. 199–220; John J. White, *Mythology in the Modern Novel* (Princeton: Princeton University Press, 1971).

2. Ziolkowski, *Fictional Transfigurations of Jesus.*

Chapter II. Heine and the Gods

1. See Heinrich Heine, *Sämtliche Werke*, ed. Ernst Elster (Leipzig and Vienna: Bibliographisches Institut, 1887–1890), VI, 83. This edition cited hereafter by volume and page only. Here and throughout translations are my own unless otherwise noted.

2. E. M. Butler, *Heinrich Heine* (London: The Hogarth Press, 1956), p. 11.

3. Maria Filtso, *Heinrich Heine und die Antike* (diss., Munich, 1928), p. 18. On the general subject see also Hermann Friedemann, *Die Götter Griechenlands von Schiller bis Heine* (diss., Berlin, 1906).

4. Filtso, pp. 20–22.

5. A. I. Sandor, *The Exile of Gods* (The Hague and Paris: Mouton, 1967), p. 16; see also Carl Puetzfeld, *Heinrich Heines Verhältnis zur Religion* (Berlin: Grote, 1912), pp. 15f.

6. See Henry Hatfield, *Aesthetic Paganism in German Literature* (Cambridge: Harvard University Press, 1964), pp. 6f.

7. Heinrich Heine, *Briefe*, ed. Friedrich Hirth (Mainz: Kupferberg, 1950–1957), I, 62f. Letter to Immanuel Wohlwill. This edition cited hereafter as Hirth.

8. Hirth, I, 228 (October 1825).

9. Eberhard Galley, *Heinrich Heine*, 2nd printing (Stuttgart: Metzler, 1957), p. 19.

10. Letter of January 9, 1826. Hirth, I, 250.

11. See Jakob Fleischmann, "Heine und die Hegelsche Philosophie," *Deutsche Universitäts-Zeitung*, 14 (1959): 421.

12. *Ibid.*, p. 422.

13. E. M. Butler, *The Tyranny of Greece over Germany* (Cambridge, Eng.: At the University Press, 1935), pp. 263f.

14. See Hatfield, *Aesthetic Paganism*, pp. 30, 122–124.

15. See also the sarcastic ending of this poem (I, 531), withdrawn by Heine after its appearance in his *Reisebilder*.

16. Barker Fairley, *Heinrich Heine. An Interpretation* (Oxford: Clarendon Press, 1954), p. 164.

17. See Paul Konrad Kurz, *Künstler, Tribun, Apostel, Heinrich Heine's Auffassung vom Beruf des Dichters* (Munich: Wilhelm Fink Verlag, 1967), pp. 54f.

18. See Hatfield, *Aesthetic Paganism*, pp. 116, 197, 230.

19. Goethe, *Gedenkausgabe der Werke, Briefe und Gespräche*, ed. Ernst Beutler (Zurich: Artemis, 1948–1954), XIX, 85.

20. Nietzsche, *Werke*, ed. Karl Schlechta (Munich: Hanser, 1956), II, 834.

21. See Meno Spann, *Heine* (London: Bowes and Bowes, 1966), p. 51.

22. See William Rose, *Heinrich Heine, Two Studies of His Thought and Feeling* (Oxford: Clarendon Press, 1956).

23. Cf. V, 218.

24. A hierarchy of preachers, scholars, and industrialists was to dominate society. See Henri Lichtenberger, *Henri Heine penseur* (Paris: Alcan, 1905), p. 107; also Laura Hofrichter, *Heinrich Heine* (Oxford: Clarendon Press, 1963), pp. 63f.

25. For a vivid account of Saint-Simonianism in its relation to German literature, see E. M. Butler, *The Saint-Simonian Religion in Germany* (Cambridge, Eng.: At the University Press, 1926).

26. G. Iggers, "Heine and the Saint-Simonians," *Comparative Literature*, 10 (1958): 289–308, differs from Miss Butler in sharply limiting Heine's dependence on Saint-Simonianism.

27. Hirth, II, 22; letter of May 1832.

28. Thus Fritz Strich in *Kunst und Leben* (Bern and Munich: Francke, 1960), p. 136.

29. Schiller, *Sämtliche Werke*, ed. Eduard von der Hellen (Stuttgart and Berlin: Cotta, 1904–1905), XII, 249.

30. Butler, *Tyranny*, pp. 254, 268f.

31. The much briefer version of 1833, entitled *Zur Geschichte der neueren schönen Literatur in Deutschland*, was based on a series of articles published the same year in *L'Europe littéraire*.

32. Hatfield, *Aesthetic Paganism*, p. 117.

33. Contrast Butler, *Tyranny*, esp. p. 269.

34. The passage is dated August 6, 1830.

35. The passage has been quoted very often but should not be ignored.

36. See letter of April 24, 1849; Hirth, III, 170.

37. Butler, *Tyranny*, pp. 286f. See also Sandor, *The Exile of Gods*, pp. 37–41.

38. For a somewhat different reading of "The Goddess Diana," see Sandor, *Exile of Gods*, pp. 30–33.

39. H. J. Weigand, "Heine's Return to God," *Modern Philology*, 18 (1920–21): 309–342.

40. *Gespräche mit Heine*, ed. H. H. Houben (Frankfort on the Main: Rütten und Loening, 1926), p. 757. Conversation of October 1850.

41. S. S. Prawer, *Heine the Tragic Satirist* (Cambridge, Eng.: At the University Press, 1961), p. 162.

42. Prawer, p. 166. Walther Killy gives a much darker interpretation of the poem in his *Wandlungen des lyrischen Bildes* (Göttingen: Vandenhoeck und Ruprecht, 1958), pp. 111–114.

43. The best generally available text can be found in the second (incomplete) edition by Elster, often known as E^2. See also Stuart Atkins' superb edition of the Harvard MS of "Für die Mouche," *Harvard Library Bulletin*, 13 (1959): 414–443. (The version available in E^1 suffers from cuts made by Alfred Meissner, who first published the poem.)

44. V, 217. See above, p. 40.

45. Thomas Mann, *Gesammelte Werke in zwölf Bänden* (Frankfurt on the Main: S. Fischer, 1960), III, 685.

46. Cf. Robert d'Harcourt, *La Religion de Goethe* (Strasbourg: F.-X. Le Roux, 1949).

47. In "Heine and Marx: A History and a Legend," *Germanic Review*, 30 (1955): 122. For a detailed treatment of Heine's relationship to Marx, see Friedrich Hirth, *Heinrich Heine. Bausteine zu einer Biographie* (Mainz: Kupferberg, 1950), pp. 117–131.

Chapter III. The Burgher and the Greeks: Burckhardt

1. See Walther Rehm, *Jacob Burckhardt* (Frauenfeld–Leipzig: Huber, 1930), p. 13.

2. See Alfred von Martin, *Nietzsche und Burckhardt*, 3rd ed. (Basel: Reinhardt, 1945), p. 63.

3. Cf. Hinrich Knittermeyer, *Jacob Burckhardt* (Zurich: Hirzel, 1949), pp. 234f.

4. Jacob Burckhardt, *Briefe*, ed. Max Burckhardt (Basel: Schwabe, 1949—), I, 164. Letter of 5.IV, 1841. This edition hereafter cited as *Briefe*.

5. Werner Kaegi, *Jacob Burckhardt* (Basel: Schwabe, 1947), II, 170, 171f.

6. *Ibid.*, I, 515f.

7. *Gedichte*, ed. K. E. Hoffmann (Basel: Schwabe, 1926), p. 72.

8. *Briefe*, I, 80; to Riggenbach, 26.VIII, 1838.

9. *Ibid.*, VI, 290f; to Preen, 9.XII, 1878.

10. Jacob Burckhardt, *Briefe*, ed. Fritz Kaphahn (Leipzig: Kröner, 1935), p. 451, 13.IV, 1882, and p. 485, 24.VII, 1889; both to Preen. (The comprehensive edition of Burckhardt's letters is not yet complete; one must rely on selections for his later years.)

11. *Briefe*, I, 164; to Louise Burckhardt, 5.IV, 1841.

12. *Ibid.*, V, 110f; to Preen, 27.IX, 1870.

13. *Ibid.*, p. 265; to Preen, 31.XII, 1874.

14. Johannes Wenzel, *Jacob Burckhardt in der Krise seiner Zeit* (Berlin: Deutscher Verlag der Wissenschaften VEB, 1967).

15. See Alfred L. Gass, *Die Dichtung im Leben und Werk Jacob Burckhardts* (Bern: Francke, 1967).

16. *Briefe*, I, 84, and II, 60; letters to Riggenbach (28.VIII. 1838) and Beyschlag (14.I, 1844) respectively.

17. Kaegi, *Burckhardt*, I, 580.

18. *Gedichte*, pp. 100f.

19. Jacob Burckhardt, *Gesammelte Werke* (Basel: Schwabe, 1955—), V, 10. This edition quoted hereafter by volume and page only.

20. *Jakob Burckhardt und Nietzsche* (Heidelberg: Schneider, 1948), p. 183.

21. Cf. Kaegi, *Burckhardt*, II, 136. On Herder, see Hatfield, *Aesthetic Paganism*, p. 54.

22. *Historische Fragmente* (Basel: Schwabe, 1942), Nr. 123, p. 217.

23. Knittermeyer, *Burckhardt*, p. 158.

24. *Briefe*, I, 225 (7.XII, 1842); to Gottfried Kinkel.

25. Knittermeyer, *Burckhardt*, p. 152, quoting *Historische Fragmente*, Nr. 1, p. 1.

26. Rudolf Marx in the Afterword to his edition of the *Griechische Kulturgeschichte* (Stuttgart: Kröner, 1948–1952), III, 492.

27. *Briefe*, I, 208; to Fresenius, 19.VI, 1842.

28. Cf. Gass, *Dichtung*, p. 38.

29. I have used S. G. C. Middlemore's translation of this passage (*The Civilization of the Renaissance in Italy*, London: Harrap, 1929, p. 54).

30. Jacob Burckhardt, *Briefe* (Insel-Bucherei Nr. 331, 1946), p. 94; to L. Pastor, 23.I, 1896.

31. *Briefe*, VI, 55; to Preen, 19.IX, 1875.

32. *Briefe*, V, 119; to Preen, 31.XII, 1870.

33. *Briefe*, II, 210; to Schauenburg, 5.III, 1846.

34. Kaphahn, p. 451; to Preen, 13.IV, 1882.

35. See Carl Neumann, *Jacob Burckhardt* (Munich: Bruckmann, 1927), pp. 155f.

36. August Boeckh, *Die Staatshaushaltung der Athener*, 2nd ed. (Berlin: Reiner, 1851), I, 792.

37. Marx in his Afterword to the Kröner edition, III, 514.

38. *Briefe*, III, 228; to A. v. Brenner, 11.XI, 1855.

39. *Nietzsche*, 3rd ed. (New York: Vintage Books, 1968), p. 28.

40. Kröner edition, III, 505.

41. *Friedrich Schlegel 1794–1802; seine prosaischen Jugendschriften*, ed. Jacob Minor (Vienna: Konegen, 1882), II, 227.

Chapter IV. Aestheticism and Myth in Richard Wagner

1. Thomas Mann, *Gesammelte Werke*, X, 182f.

2. Harry Levin, *James Joyce* (Norfolk, Conn.: New Directions, 1941), p. 211.

3. Friedrich Nietzsche, *Werke in drei Bänden*, ed. Karl Schlechta (Munich: Hanser, n.d.), I, 398; II, 242, 925.

4. Jacques Barzun, *Darwin, Marx, Wagner* (Boston: Little, Brown, 1941), p. 287.

5. I am indebted to the late Professor Ernest J. Simmons for this information. See also his *Leo Tolstoy* (Boston: Little, Brown, 1946), pp. 68, 312, 726.

6. Leo Tolstoy, *What is Art?* (New York: Scribner's, 1904), p. 119.

7. See Aurel Kolnai, *The War Against the West* (London: V. Gollancz, 1938); Peter Viereck, *Metapolitics: From the Romantics to Hitler* (New York: Knopf, 1941); Konrad Heiden, *Geschichte des Nationalsozialismus* (Berlin: Rowohlt, 1932).

8. Nietzsche, *Werke*, II, 931.

9. Paul Henry Lang, *Music in Western Civilization* (New York: Norton, 1941), p. 889.

10. *Mein Leben* (Munich: List, 1963), p. 22.

11. Ernest Newman, *The Life of Richard Wagner* (New York: Knopf, 1933–46), I, 45f.

12. *Mein Leben*, p. 31.

13. *Ibid.*, p. 51.

14. *Ibid.*, p. 403.

15. See William Wallace, *Richard Wagner as He Lived* (London: Kegan Paul, Trench, Trubner, 1925), esp. pp. 14–16, 145–149, 283–297.

16. *Ibid.*, pp. 161, 145–149, 296.

17. Newman, *Life*, I, 57, note.

18. *Gesammelte Schriften und Dichtungen*[5] (Leipzig: Breitkopf and Haertel–Siegel, n.d.), III, 10. Hereafter cited in the text by volume and page only.

19. Kurt Hildebrandt, *Wagner und Nietzsche* (Breslau: Hirt, 1924), p. 47.

20. *Mein Leben*, p. 403; cf. Robert Petsch, "Der Ring des Nibelungen in seinen Beziehungen zur griechischen Tragödie und zur

zeitgenössischen Philosophie," *Wagner-Jahrbuch*, II (1907), 289–291.

21. Cf. Petsch, pp. 296f.

22. See Wagner's letter to Röckel, August 23, 1856, cited by Petsch, p. 325.

23. Wolfgang Schadewaldt, "Richard Wagner und die Griechen" in his *Hellas und Hesperien*² (Zurich and Stuttgart: Artemis, 1970), II, 342.

24. Cited by Schadewaldt, p. 341.

25. Cf. Schadewaldt, pp. 358f, and Wagner, "Mitteilung an meine Freunde."

26. Newman, *Life*, II, 21, quoting W. A. Ellis.

27. Schadewaldt, p. 351.

28. Robert Donington, *Wagner's Ring and Its Symbols* (New York: St. Martin's Press, 1969), p. 109.

29. Detroit: Wayne State University Press, 1960.

30. Cf. Leon Stein, *The Racial Thinking of Richard Wagner* (New York: Philosophical Library, 1950), pp. 85f.

31. *Mein Leben*, pp. 543f.

32. Newman, *Life*, IV, 635.

33. Stein, *Racial Thinking of Wagner*, p. 77.

34. Newman, *Life*, IV, 147.

35. Newman, I, 332.

36. Hildebrandt, *Wagner und Nietzsche*, p. 84.

37. See *Nachgelassene Schriften und Dichtungen* (Leipzig: Breitkopf und Härtel, 1895), pp. 72, 50.

38. See Walt Whitman, "Song of Myself," section 52.

39. Petsch, in *Wagner-Jahrbuch*, II, 297.

40. *Mein Leben*, p. 403.

41. Hildebrandt, *Wagner und Nietzsche*, p. 37.

42. Schadewaldt, *Hellas und Hesperien*, II, 341.

43. Wagner was apparently blind to the comic fact that *Wank* suggests "staggering."

44. *Nachgelassene Schriften und Dichtungen*, pp. 65f.

45. Lines 1720–21.

46. See *Mein Leben*, p. 451, and G. B. Shaw's famous *The Perfect Wagnerite*.

47. In "Das mythische Wahnbild Richard Wagners," *Deutsche*

Vierteljahrsschrift für Literaturwissenschaft und Geistesgeschichte, 29 (1955): 250.

48. Ernest Newman, *The Wagner Operas* (New York: Knopf, 1949), p. 634.

49. Nietzsche, *Werke,* II, 910f.

50. Mann, *Gesammelte Werke,* IX, 506.

Chapter V. Nietzsche and the Myth

1. Cf. Newman, *Life,* III, 359f.

2. Nietzsche, *Werke,* ed. Karl Schlechta (Munich: Hanser, 1956), II, 927. This edition cited in the text by volume and page only.

3. Newman, *Life,* III, 536.

4. Hesse, *Gesammelte Dichtungen* (n.p.: Suhrkamp Verlag, 1958), IV, 402.

5. Havelock Ellis, *Affirmations* (Boston and New York: Houghton Mifflin, 1915), p. 2.

6. Crane Brinton, *Nietzsche* (Cambridge: Harvard University Press, 1941), p. 45.

7. Walter Kaufmann, *Nietzsche* (New York: Vintage Books, 1968), p. 30.

8. Alfred Rosenberg, *Friedrich Nietzsche* (Munich: Eher, 1944), p. 3.

9. George Santayana, *Egotism in German Philosophy* (London and Toronto: Dent, n.d.), p. 140n.

10. Carl A. Bernoulli, *Franz Overbeck und Friedrich Nietzsche,* II (Jena: Diederichs, 1908), 219.

11. Carl A. Bernoulli, *Nietzsche und die Schweiz* (Leipzig: Haessel, 1922), p. 15.

12. Cf. R. J. Hollingdale, *Nietzsche* (London: Routledge and Kegan Paul, 1965), pp. 128f.

13. Karl Schlechta, *Der junge Nietzsche und das klassische Altertum* (Mainz: Kupferberg, 1948), p. 10.

14. Schlechta, p. 21, citing letter of 16.I, 1869.

15. Ernst Howald, *Friedrich Nietzsche und die klassische Philologie* (Gotha: Perthes, 1920), p. 11, citing a letter to Paul Deussen, mid-August 1868; *Gesammelte Briefe,* I, 122.

16. Cf. Kurt Hildebrandt, *Nietzsches Wettkampf mit Sokrates und Plato* (Dresden: Sybillen, 1922).

17. Karl Jaspers, *Nietzsche und das Christentum* (Hameln: Seifert, n.d.), pp. 69—73.

18. Bernoulli, *Overbeck und Nietzsche*, p. 230.

19. Ulrich von Wilamowitz-Moellendorf, *Erinnerungen, 1848—1914* (Leipzig: Koehler, c. 1928), pp. 129f.

20. Quoted in Martin Vogel, *Apollinisch und Dionysisch* (Regensburg: Bosse, 1966), p. 31.

21. Gerard F. Else, *The Origin and Early Form of Greek Tragedy* (Cambridge: Harvard University Press for Oberlin College, 1965), pp. 9, 30, 10.

22. Vogel, *Apollinisch und Dionysisch*, p. 62.

23. Actually, by the time he wrote *The Birth of Tragedy* he had moved quite far from Wagner's position, but he was "pressured" into including enthusiastic praise of the composer. See T. M. Campbell, "Nietzsche's *Die Geburt der Tragödie* and Richard Wagner," *Germanic Review*, 16 (1941): 185—200; further material in *PMLA*, 56 (1941): 544—577.

24. Karl Kerényi, *Apollon* (Vienna: Franz Leo, 1937), p. 47, cited by Vogel, *Apollinisch und Dionysisch*, p. 37, n. 1, and p. 341.

25. Walter Kaufmann, *Nietzsche*, pp. 391—411, and elsewhere, shows convincingly that Nietzsche greatly admired Socrates, but he drastically plays down Nietzsche's objections to and sarcasms about Socrates.

26. See Richard Chase, *Quest for Myth* (Baton Rouge: Louisiana State University Press, 1949), and Fritz Strich, *Die Mythologie in der deutschen Literatur von Klopstock bis Wagner* (Halle: Niemeyer, 1910). See also Nietzsche, *Werke*, I, 125.

27. Cf. T. M. Campbell, "Nietzsche—Wagner, to 1872," *PMLA*, 56 (1941): 544—577.

28. Goethe, *Gedenkausgabe* (Zurich: Artemis, 1948—1954), II, 50.

29. Cf. Kaufmann, *Nietzsche*, pp. 155f.

30. Cf. Kaufmann, p. 199.

31. Cf. Karl Jaspers, *Nietzsche und das Christentum* (Hameln: Seifert, n.d.), p. 70.

32. See Ludwig Klages, *Die psychologischen Errungenschaften Nietzsches* (Leipzig: Barth, 1926), p. 204.

33. On Heine as Nietzsche's predecessor in proclaiming the death of God, see E. M. Butler, *The Tyranny of Greece*, p. 308.

34. Santayana, *Egotism in German Philosophy*, p. 143.

35. In *Faust* I, l. 490, and in the poem "Zueignung."

36. Shelley, *Complete Poetical Works* (Boston and New York: Houghton, Mifflin, 1901), pp. 338f.

37. See Simmel, *Schopenhauer und Nietzsche* (Leipzig and Munich: Duncker and Humblot, 1923), p. 183n.

38. See Kaufmann, *Nietzsche*, p. 327.

39. Kaufmann, p. 324n.

40. *Die Leiden des jungen Werthers* in Goethe, *Werke*, IV (Zurich: Artemis, 1953), p. 316.

41. The phrase was coined by Leonard Forster.

42. Byron, *Don Juan*, canto lv.

43. Santayana, *Egotism in German Philosophy*, p. 115.

44. Edgar Salin, *Jacob Burckhardt und Nietzsche*, 2 Aufl. (Heidelberg: Schneider, 1948), pp. 74f and above, pp. 79f.

45. III, 881. On the misnomer, see Schlechta's excellent comments in his edition. As was to be expected, the ineffable Elisabeth Förster-Nietzsche was mainly to blame.

46. Jaspers, *Nietzsche und das Christentum*, p. 9.

47. *Gesammelte Werke* (Frankfurt a. M.: S. Fischer, 1960), X, 183.

48. Jaspers, pp. 69–73.

49. See Max Kesselring, *Nietzsches "Zarathustra" in psychiatrischer Beleuchtung* (Affoltern: Aehren Verlag, 1954), p. 149.

50. Similarly, Nietzsche claimed to prefer Bizet to Wagner; but this was more to bury the German musician than to praise the French. See Ernst Bertram, *Nietzsche: Versuch einer Mythologie*, 7 Aufl. (Berlin: Bondi, 1929), p. 167.

51. See Richard M. Lonsbach, *Nietzsche und die Juden* (Stockholm: Bermann-Fischer, 1939), pp. 43f.

52. *Gesammelte Werke* (Munich: Musarion, 1920–1929), XX, 129.

53. *Wagner und Nietzsche: Ihr Kampf gegen das neunzehnte Jahrhundert* (Breslau: Hirt, 1924), pp. 169f.

54. Lonsbach, *Nietzsche und die Juden*, p. 44.

55. See esp. Ingeborg Beithan, *Friedrich Nietzsche als Umwerter der deutschen Literatur* (Heidelberg: Carl Winters, 1933).

56. See Anni Carlsson in *Deutsche Vierteljahrsschrift für Literaturwissenschaft und Geistesgeschichte*, 29 (1955): 250.

57. Mann, *Gesammelte Werke*, IX, 683. See also Jaspers, *Nietzsche und das Christentum*, p. 70.

58. E. A. Robinson, *Collected Poems* (New York: Macmillan, 1928), p. 348.

59. Brinton, *Nietzsche*, p. 159. Mann, *Gesammelte Werke*, IX, 685, speaks of "super-journalism."

60. *Doctor Faustus*, sc. XIV, ll. 127–130.

Chapter VI. Greek and Germanic Myths in Stefan George

1. See the works of Theodor Däubler, Otto zur Linde, Ludwig Derleth, and so forth.

2. See Edgar Salin, *Um Stefan George*, 2 Aufl. (Munich and Düsseldorf: Küpper, 1954), p. 271.

3. See above, pp. 88–92.

4. Cf. Salin, p. 279, and Claude David, *Stefan George, Sein dichterisches Werk* (Munich: Hanser, 1967), p. 329. (Original French edition, 1952.)

5. See above, p. 82.

6. George, *Werke*, Ausgabe in zwei Bänden (Munich and Düsselfdorf: Küpper, 1958), I, 426. Citations of this edition are given henceforth by volume and page.

7. Robert Boehringer, *Mein Bild von Stefan George* (Munich and Düsseldorf: Küpper, 1951), illustration 86.

8. Quoted in Robert Boehringer, *Mein Bild von Stefan George*, p. 116.

9. See many of the illustrations in Boehringer.

10. Thus several volumes of reminiscence, especially Salin's.

11. Hubert J. Meessen, "Stefan Georges *Algabal* und die französische Décadence," *Monatshefte*, 39 (1947): 304–321.

12. Victor A. Oswald, Jr., "The Historical Content of Stefan George's *Algabal*," *Germanic Review*, 23 (1948): 205.

13. See Werner Richter in *Collier's Encyclopedia* (n.p.: Crowell-Collier, 1970), XV, 95.

14. Cf. the underground realm in J. K. Huysmans' *A Rebours,* which boasts among other things of mechanical fish.

15. See Albert Béguin, *L'Ame romantique et le rêve* (Paris: J. Conti, 1939).

16. See C. M. Bowra, *The Heritage of Symbolism* (London: Macmillan, 1943), p. 116.

17. Oswald, in *Germanic Review,* 23: 203f.

18. Oswald, pp. 198, 201, citing Dio Cassius.

19. Eric Bentley, *A Century of Hero-Worship* (Boston: Beacon Press [1957]), p. 200.

20. Bowra, *The Heritage of Symbolism,* p. 131.

21. Hofmannsthal, *Gesammelte Werke,* I (Stockholm: Bermann-Fischer, 1946), 165f.

22. Herbert Steiner, *Begegnung mit Stefan George* (Aurora, New York: Wells College Press, 1942), pp. 12, 15.

23. U. K. Goldsmith, *Stefan George: A Study of His Early Works* (Boulder: University of Colorado Press, 1959), p. 121, quoting Boehringer, p. 53.

24. Bowra, *The Heritage of Symbolism,* p. 142.

25. Friedrich Gundolf, in his *George* (Berlin: Bondi, 1930), p. 157, calls this cycle the last great poem of European weltschmerz.

26. See Claude David, *Stefan George,* p. 140.

27. See note 16 above.

28. Thus George broke with Friedrich Gundolf, his most gifted follower, when the disciple insisted on marrying a woman of whom the master did not approve. Cf. Elisabeth Gundolf, *Stefan George* (Amsterdam: Castrum Peregrini, 1965).

29. David, *Stefan George,* pp. 258–274.

30. David, p. 255.

31. Maximilian Kronberger, *Nachlass* (Zurich: privately printed, [1937], p. 49.

32. Albert Verwey, cited by David, p. 275.

33. David, pp. 258f.

34. See Ernst Morwitz, *Kommentar zu den Werken Stefan Georges* (Munich and Düsseldorf: Küpper, 1960), p. 272.

35. See the poem "Goethe's Last Night in Italy" (I, 401–403).

George described Shakespeare as "the dark prince of the spirits of the Cloud Islands" (I, 183), which is both anti-Shakespeare and anti-British.

36. See Morwitz, p. 345.

37. A somewhat arbitrary distinction is made between *Körper*, a body in the ordinary sense, and *Leib*, body linked to soul.

38. Morwitz, p. 360, takes the poem to be an attack on the Cosmic clique.

39. George excepts only the unpretentious old Hindenburg from his condemnation of German military and political figures.

40. See Morwitz, p. 422.

41. Morwitz, p. 432.

42. The poet seems to mean Goethe's last night in Rome; Goethe's second Italian journey—to Venice—left him disappointed and embittered.

43. Cf. David, *Stefan George*, p. 368.

44. Morwitz' commentary, p. 447, agrees that the swastika plays a part here.

45. "Faun" is an approximate translation of *Drud*, a mythological creature also resembling a centaur or satyr.

46. Alternate translation: "the Christian dancing."

47. See Hatfield, *Aesthetic Paganism*, pp. 91f.

48. See Morwitz, *Kommentar*, p. 483.

49. See Cyril Scott, *Die Tragödie Stefan Georges* (Eltville am Rhein: Hempe, 1952), pp. 91, 42.

50. Scott, p. 79.

51. David, *Stefan George*, p. 383.

52. Salin, *Um Stefan George*, pp. 109, 341, citing Max Weber, *Wirtschaft und Gesellschaft* (Tübingen: Mohr, 1952), p. 142.

53. Salin, pp. 48, 275, quoting *Blätter für die Kunst*, IX, 2.

Chapter VII. Rilke, Mythology, and Myth

1. Cf. E. M. Butler, *Rainer Maria Rilke* (New York: Macmillan, 1941), p. 4.

2. See Erich Simenauer, *Rainer Maria Rilke: Legende und Mythos* (Frankfurt a.M.: Schauinsland-Verlag, 1953), pp. 136f, quoting *Rilke, Briefe 1902–1906* (Leipzig: Insel, 1929), p. 243.

3. Rilke, *Sämtliche Werke*, ed. Ernst Zinn (Wiesbaden: Insel, 1955–1966), I, 522f. Hereafter, this edition is cited only by volume and page.

4. Simenauer, pp. 183, 188.

5. Quoted by Walther Rehm, *Orpheus: der Dichter und die Toten* (Düsseldorf: Schwann, 1950), p. 464, from Rilke, *Briefe aus den Jahren 1907–1914* (Leipzig: Insel-Verlag, 1939), p. 298.

6. See Marcel Kunz, *Narziss: Untersuchungen zum Werk Rainer Maria Rilkes* (Bonn: Bouvier, 1970), p. 93.

7. See Eudo C. Mason, *Rainer Maria Rilke* (Göttingen: Vandenhoeck and Ruprecht, 1964), p. 86.

8. Rilke, *Briefe an einen jungen Dichter* (Leipzig: Insel, 1929), p. 28.

9. In the German tradition, this tendency runs back to Heine and the Young Germans, ultimately to Goethe.

10. See I, 361, 365f.

11. Kunz, *Narziss*, p. 69.

12. See letter to Rudolf Bodländer, March 23, 1972, *Briefe aus Muzot 1921–1926* (Leipzig: Insel, 1935), pp. 126f.

13. I have not discussed Erika Mitterer's rather derivative verses.

14. See Nietzsche, II, 1032, 1157.

15. See Lou Andreas-Salomé, *Rainer Maria Rilke* (Leipzig: Insel, 1929), p. 52.

16. See especially K. R. Eissler, *Goethe: A Psychoanalytic Study, 1775–1786* (Detroit: Wayne State University Press, 1963), 2 vols.

17. Kunz, *Narziss*, p. 78.

18. Simenauer, *Rilke*, p. 42.

19. *Briefe aus Muzot, 1921–1926*, p. 135. Letter to his wife Clara, May 12, 1922. See also Simenauer, p. 421.

20. Simenauer, pp. 236, 242.

21. *Ibid.*, p. 288.

22. Butler, *Rilke*, p. 238, lists many of the relevant passages.

23. Kunz, *Narziss*, pp. 5f.

24. Kunz, pp. 10–19.

25. Kunz, *passim*.

26. Butler, *Rilke, passim;* Simenauer, *Rilke*, p. 44.

27. See Butler, p. 420.

28. Butler, p. 341.

29. See Else Buddeberg, *Rainer Maria Rilke: eine innere Biographie* (Stuttgart: Metzler, 1955), pp. 370, 380–385, who interestingly discusses the relations between "magical" and lyrical thinking.

30. Cf. Buddeberg, pp. 370, 375.

31. Butler, *Rilke*, p. 319.

32. Eudo C. Mason, *Lebenshaltung und Symbolik bei Rainer Maria Rilke,* 2nd printing (Oxford: Marston, 1964), p. 200.

33. Frank Wood, *Rainer Maria Rilke: The Ring of Forms* (Minneapolis: University of Minnesota Press, 1958), pp. 183f.

34. Erich Heller, *The Disinherited Mind* (Philadelphia: Dufour and Saifer, 1952), p. 111.

35. Cf. Goethe, *Gedenkausgabe* (Zurich: Artemis, 1948–1954), XIX, 85.

36. Mason, *Lebenshaltung,* p. 64.

37. Letter of December 17, 1912, to Marie von Thurn und Taxis; *Briefe aus den Jahren 1907–1914* (Leipzig: Insel-Verlag, 1939), pp. 269, 270.

38. Buddeberg, *Rilke,* p. 467, who also points out that the angels of the *Elegies* are not mediators.

39. George, *Werke,* I, 176.

40. Emerson as quoted by Oliver Wendell Holmes, Jr. See Max Lerner, *The Mind and Faith of Justice Holmes* (Boston: Little, Brown and Company, 1943), p. 197.

41. See Buddeberg, *Rilke,* p. 401.

42. Butler, *Rilke,* p. 130; cf. Mason, *Lebenshaltung,* p. 63.

43. See the poem "Gott im Mittelalter" (I, 502f).

44. See *The Disinherited Mind,* pp. 97–140.

45. Mason, *Rilke,* p. 36.

46. See Butler, *Rilke,* p. 173.

47. See Mason, *Lebenshaltung,* pp. 38f.

48. Angelus Silesius (Scheffler), *Cherubinischer Wandersmann,* ed. Georg Ellinger (Halle a. S.: Niemeyer, 1895), p. 15.

49. See Bernhard Blume, "Ding und Ich in Rilkes *Neuen Gedichten,*" *Modern Language Notes,* 67 (1952): 217–224.

50. This is the title of the translation by John Linton (New York: Norton, [c 1930]).

51. See Andreas-Salomé, *Rilke*, p. 102; Buddeberg, *Rilke*, p. 467.

52. See esp. Jacob Steiner, *Rilkes Duineser Elegien* (Bern and Munich: Francke, 1962), pp. 15f.

53. Rilke, *Briefe und Tagebücher aus der Frühzeit, 1899 bis 1902* (Leipzig: Insel, 1931), p. 390.

54. Mason, *Rilke*, p. 95.

55. J. G. von Herder, *Sämmtliche Werke*, ed. Suphan (Berlin, 1877–1913), III, 254.

56. See Steiner, *Rilkes Duineser Elegien*, p. 13.

57. See Hans Egon Holthusen, *Rainer Maria Rilke: A Study of His Later Poetry*, trans. J. P. Stern (New Haven: Yale University Press, 1952), p. 31.

58. Rilke, *Briefe aus Muzot, 1921–1926*, p. 337; letter of November 13, 1925.

59. C. M. Bowra, *The Heritage of Symbolism* (London: Macmillan, 1943), p. 85.

60. Cf. Simenauer, *Rilke*, pp. 389, 393, 413.

61. In any case, there is nothing wrong with with afterthoughts; on the contrary. See Ernst Zinn, afterword to Rilke, *Duineser Elegien/Die Sonette an Orpheus* (Zurich: Niehaus and Rokitansky, 1948), p. 122. See also J. M. Stein, in *Germanic Review*, 27 (1952): 278.

62. Cf. Steiner, *Rilkes Duineser Elegien*, pp. 289–291.

63. Quoted by Butler, *Rilke*, pp. 416f, from *Briefe 1921–1926*, pp. 312f.

64. Hermann Pongs, "Rilkes Umschlag," *Dichtung und Volkstum (recté Euphorion)*, 37 (1936): 75–97.

65. Butler, *Rilke*, p. 341.

66. Holthusen, *Rilke*, p. 34.

67. Butler, *Rilke*, p. 347.

68. T. S. Eliot, *Collected Poems* (New York: Harcourt Brace, [1945]), p. 61.

69. Butler, *Rilke*, p. 135.

70. Rehm, *Orpheus*, p. 617.

71. *Ibid.*, p. 625, noting that the notorious Alfred Schuler (above

p. 132), some of whose lectures much impressed Rilke, was also fascinated by death.

72. J. R. von Salis, *Rainer Maria Rilkes Schweizer Jahre* (Frauenfeld: Huber, 1952), p. 234.

73. See Hatfield, *Aesthetic Paganism,* pp. 17–20, and H. J. Weigand, "Rilke's 'Archaïscher Torso Apollos,'" *Monatshefte,* 51 (1959): 49–62.

74. Rilke borrowed this phrase from J. P. Jacobsen but used it very differently from the Danish writer, whose assumptions were atheistic and Darwinian. (See Buddeberg, *Rilke,* p. 136.)

75. Holthusen, *Rilke,* pp. 23, 30.

76. Mason, *Lebenshaltung,* p. 11.

77. Heller, *The Disinherited Mind,* pp. 99–101.

78. Eudo C. Mason, *Rilke's Apotheosis* (Oxford: Blackwell, 1938), p. 41, citing Friedrich Gundolf, *Rainer Maria Rilke* (Vienna: Johannes-Presse, 1937).

79. Mason, *Rilke,* p. 92.

Index